The Shan: Refugees Without a Camp
An English Teacher in Thailand and Burma

The Shan: Refugees Without a Camp
An English Teacher in Thailand and Burma

By

Bernice Koehler Johnson

TRINITY MATRIX

Paramus, New Jersey 07652

TRINITY:.MATRIX
Publish@TrinityMatrix.com

Trinity Matrix Publishing
www.TrinityMatrix.com

Copyright © 2009 by Bernice Koehler Johnson

The Shan: Refugees Without a Camp
An English Teacher in Thailand and Burma
by Bernice Koehler Johnson

Printed in the United States of America

ISBN 978-0-9817833-0-7

For refugees from Shan State, Burma,
and for those they left behind

Under the British, Burma boasted a total of fifteen infantry battalions, two in Shan State (then known as the Federated Shan States). These days the Burma Army is not fighting a declared war, but the number of its infantry battalions in Shan State has increased more than 35-fold to 555 at the last count.

This has been a great burden to its people and especially its youth. In the past, their rice culture was enough to feed, clothe and shelter the whole family after paying taxes. These days, with the Army living off the land, it is barely enough for four months.

The youth don't know what to do to bring back peace to their land. Their elders are unable to give much advice except telling them to go to Thailand. So they came to Thailand, the land of their cousins, to find the answer.

This is the story of these youth, as told to a sympathetic Western ear.

Khuensai Jaiyen
Editor
Shan Herald Agency for News

THE SHAN: REFUGEES WITHOUT A CAMP©
An English Teacher in Thailand and Burma

India

China

Bangladesh

Kachin

○
Myitkyina

Sagaing

○Lashio
○Hsipaw

○
Hakha

Maymyo
○
Sagaing ○○ Mandalay

Chin

Shan

○Keng Tong

Mandalay

Laos

○Taunggyi
○Yawnghwe
○Inle Lake

○Magwe

Sittwe

Magwe
□
Naypyidaw

Rakhaing

○Loikaw

Kayah

Thailand

Bago

Bay of
Bengal

Bago
○

Pathein
○

Yangon

Kayin

○Hpa-an

Ayeyarwady

Yangon
○○
Mawlamyine

Mon

Andaman Sea

Dawei
○

States and Divisions
of
Burma

The Shan: Refugees Without A Camp
by Bernice Koehler Johnson

Tanintharyi

Refugees Without a Camp

Original Shan language poem by Sai Leng Hsim
English language adaptation by Bernice Koehler Johnson

Burmese soldiers advance. They kill our animals, take our rice.
From our schools they take the learning and the light.
They burn our villages and steal our minds.
We hear the soldiers' voices, and we are filled with fear and hate.
And we must run, run, run, until our legs break,
Refugees without a home, refugees without a camp.

They dress our Buddhas in women's underwear.
We see our people floating bloated in the river,
We have land but cannot farm it, forced labor is our lot.
"Peace, peace, peace," they say. Burma says we are at peace.
But we are not. We hear gunshots night and day.
And we must run, run, run, until our legs break,
Refugees without a home, refugees without a camp.

Some Shan live in Thailand, work as servants or as slaves,
some live in relocation camps, without money, food, or hope.
Some live in the jungle and hear their dying child's cries,
mosquitoes on their limbs, and leeches in their eyes.
They dig a shallow grave and place the child inside.
And then they run, run, run until their legs break,
Refugees without a home, refugees without a camp.

PROLOGUE

A History of Shan State and Burma

People are trapped in history and history is trapped in them.
—James A. Baldwin

About three thousand years ago, a tribe known as the H'su or Shan existed in southwestern China, an area now known as Yunnan Province. For six hundred years, the Shan were the dominant race in southwestern China. They called themselves Tai, "free men," a name they still use, although they are no longer free.

First records of their existence coincide with the reign of the morally rigid Chou or Zhou Dynasty in northern China, where drinking alcohol, insubordination to royalty, and neglect of parental duties were all punishable by death. The Shan were allies of and protected by their Chinese neighbors, from whom they learned literature, art, and weaving. In time, the two groups became enemies and both races became subject to the Mongol warrior Kublai Khan.

A grandson of Genghis Khan, Kublai ruled a Mongol empire that included China, Shan territory, and the adjacent land to the east that present-day rulers call Myanmar. British colonists would call that land Burma, a name preferred by the country's present-day ethnic groups and referred to as such throughout these pages.

* * *

The Shan were allowed great freedom under Mongol rule. They expanded into Laos and conquered the territories of Burma and Siam (present day Thailand), annexing Chiang Mai Province in northern Thailand, and dividing their territory into eight Shan States.

At the end of Kublai Khan's eighty year reign, Shan princes governed most of today's Burma, perhaps triggering the resentment that impels today's Burmese warriors to inflict atrocities—burnings of homes and rice fields, murder, and rape—upon the Shan. But to accuse today's Burmese warriors of those crimes at this point in the book would plead their case too soon, before examining their early history.

The Burmese people are believed to have descended from Tibet about one thousand years before the Shan. They occupied territory west of where the Shan would settle, and the fate of the Burmese ethnic group and that of the Shan would become irrevocably entwined.

During the ensuing two thousand years, fortune changed sides several times, first with the Shan in control of both territories, and then the Burmese. By 1555, the Burmese were again in control of the land they had settled west of Shan State. An autonomous country, Shan State was bordered by Burma, China, the country now known as Laos, and Thailand, a configuration that exists today.

In a moated palace in Mandalay, King Thibaw was the absolute ruler of upper Burma, a reign he began by executing eighty relatives, including eight of his brothers. Possible threats to the throne, the relatives were stuffed into velvet bags and clubbed to death. Elephants trampled their remains.

Mighty with elephants and club-wielding assassins, Thibaw was helpless against British colonizers who marched into Mandalay in 1885, sent Thibaw into exile in India adjacent to eastern Burma, and incorporated the independent countries of Burma and Shan State into their British Indian Empire.

There are different historical versions of existing Shan government at the time of British occupation. In anthropologist Leslie Milne's book, *Shans at Home*, Rev. Wilbur Cochrane wrote that the Shan States were "in a condition of social and political confusion, little short of utter chaos."

Maurice Collis, a British subject who wrote about his travels among the Shan in the early 1900s, had a different opinion: "The administration of justice and the collection of revenue [in Shan State] were left in the hands of the chiefs . . . [but] in 1922 the states were made into a federation with a senior English as president." That was the year George Orwell began a five-year stint as a policeman for the British Empire in Burma.

Orwell's experiences there formed the basis of his famous novel *Burmese Days*, which illustrated the snobbery of occupying British officers, who tried to prove their superiority by excluding Indians, Burmese, and the ethnic tribes of Burma from their country clubs.

In the 1930s, reacting to British occupation, a group of thirty Rangoon University students started calling themselves Thakins, "Masters." They formed an alliance and plotted a silent and cunning rebellion. Thakin Aung San became a Burmese hero, studying the art of war in Japan, an art the Japanese demonstrated on December 7, 1941, by bombing Pearl Harbor.

Just two months later, in February 1942, the Japanese invaded Burma with Aung San and the Thakins fighting at their side. They soon conquered the country, forcing the British and their allies to flee through the Himalayan foothills into India, a temporary retreat from which they returned through mud, leeches, and malarial mosquitoes to rout the Japanese.

In 1944, Aung San pursued his heroic destiny by changing sides, allying himself and his troops with the British. In line to become Burma's first president, he traveled throughout the country, proposing that the Shan and other non-Burmese join in the struggle for independence from the British and subsequent reconstruction.

Shan princes negotiated with the Burmese, asking for full autonomy for Shan State, democracy, and the right to secede after ten years, terms that were written into the agreement. In 1947, the Shan joined the Burmese and other ethnic groups in signing what became known as the Panglong Agreement, the foundation for the Union of Burma. The agreement's terms were never honored.

A few months after the agreement was signed and the British had granted independence, Aung San and eight comrades met in Rangoon's city hall to plan Burma's future. Machine-gun-toting men burst into the meeting room. An explosion of bullets left Aung San, his eight comrades, and hopes for a unified country dead upon the floor.

There is speculation that Ne Win, Aung San's friend and one of the original Thakins, instigated the murder. Ne Win would later become head general of the Burmese Army and rule the country with bullets and brawn.

In 1948, with Aung San only a memory, his dream of independence from Great Britain became reality. Shan Prince Shwe Thaike became Burma's first president, with Thakin U Nu, Aung San's former friend, as prime minister. It was not a quiet reign. Without authorization, the military began harassing hill people, tribes like the Karen, the Karenni, the Kachins, the Rohingyas, and the Shan.

To complicate matters, after their defeat in China, former Kuomintang (KMT) soldiers from Chiang Kai Shek's Nationalist Chinese Army had moved into Shan State and began dealing in opium. In 1952, martial law was imposed in Shan State.

In his book *Burma in Revolt*, Bertil Lintner quotes a Shan student who wrote about conditions at the time: " . . . On one hand the KMT are killing, looting, and terrorizing while on the other hand a great many army bad heads are raping, menacing and creating racial prejudices . . . today beneath the boom of guns, the marching boots, rifle butts and harsh orders the Shan are reeling . . ."

By 1957, ten years had passed since the Shan princes signed the Pan-glong Agreement. They demanded the right to secede from the Union of Burma. Prime Minister U Nu stated the government's case, saying the United States had become the strongest nation in the world because Abraham Lincoln had prevented the southern states from seceding—Burma must follow their example. The Panglong Agreement would not be honored.

That was when General Ne Win, presumed architect of Aung San's death, took control of the government. He stepped down again in 1960, only to instigate a second coup in 1962. This time, Myee, the 17-year-old son of Burma's first president, Shwe Thaike, was shot dead outside the family home in Rangoon, and Shwe Thaike was hauled off to Insein Prison. At Insein he died of what the military called "natural causes."

That same year, hundreds of miles north of Rangoon, in the Shan capital of Taunggyi, Prince of Hsipaw Sao Kya Seng was kidnapped and executed by the military. In 1994, more than thirty years after his death, his former wife, Inge Sargent, immortalized the prince in her aptly titled book, *Twilight Over Burma*.

In that twilight, Prime Minister U Nu and many Karenni and Shan leaders were jailed. At Rangoon University, General Ne Win's soldiers fired upon protesting students. Hundreds were killed.

In 1963, Ne Win took over the distribution, import, and export of all commodities, including rubies, sapphires, jade, rice, and tea. To control the flow of information, he nationalized all private schools, wire services, and newspapers.

When university students protested, the government responded by closing all schools and colleges. Under British rule, Burma had been fa-mous for its fine educational system. The situation has changed so drasti-cally under military rule that, in 2006, Save the Children estimated that one million Burmese children were not getting an education.

* * *

At the onset of the countrywide repression of the 1960s, Sao Hearn Kham, wife of deceased Shan President Shwe Thaike, escaped by trekking through the jungle between Shan State and Thailand with three of her children. Her son, Tzang, active in an underground Shan insurrection, remained in Burma.

Soon after she arrived in Chiang Mai Province, Thailand, Sao Hearn

Kham formed the Shan State Army, a rebel group which opposed the Burmese military government and which has continued its clandestine maneuvers for more than forty years.

With the Burmese military in control of all imports, exports, schools, and newspapers, opium trade flourished in the Golden Triangle, where the borders of Thailand, Laos, and Burma meet. This process was set into motion during World War II when Chiang Kai-Shek's Kuomintang Army descended into Shan State and joined the allies in their fight against the Japanese. Skilled in the art of opium smuggling, the Kuomintang who remained in Shan State were valuable assets to General Ne Win, who planned to wipe out the Shan State insurgency by using newly formed guard units. These guards were called the KKY or *Ka Kwe Ye,* Burmese for "defense." Opium and heroin sales would finance the campaign.

First class opium smuggler and KKY commander Khun Sa, who had a Chinese father and a Shan mother, attacked Shan rebels, who were also using opium taxes to fund their insurgency. General Ne Win rewarded Khun Sa by granting him free trade in opium and heroin.

Khun Sa frequently switched sides, fighting first with the Burmese, and then with Shan rebels. In 1973, and again in 1975 and 1977, opium warlord Khun Sa bargained with the United States, trying to get US support in exchange for destroying opium fields in Shan State. The U.S. government declined the offers.

By 1974, the Mon, Kachin, Karenni, Karen, Rohingya, and Shan ethnic groups were all resisting Burmese control, and the government declared martial law throughout the country.

The people of Burma suffered another indignity in 1987 when superstitious General Ne Win, whose lucky number was 9, demonetized all 25, 35, and 75 *kyat* notes, replacing them with numbers divisible by 9. Seventy-five percent of the money in circulation became worthless. Currency holders received no compensation, increasing overall poverty.

Opposition to the government fomented among students at Rangoon University, who had a new hero for their cause: Aung San Suu Kyi (pronounced Jee). Daughter of the revered Aung San, Suu Kyi had returned to Burma from England to care for her ailing mother. Educated at Oxford, Suu Kyi joined her voice to those who protested military rule. News that Suu Kyi would speak at Shwedagon Pagoda circulated throughout Rangoon. Thousands trekked on foot, bus, and bicycle to hear her make a case for democratic rule, thereby becoming a threat to the military government.

In 1988, one year before the Tianamen Square massacre in China,

Rangoon University students organized peaceful demonstrations for democracy and were joined by thousands of ordinary citizens. Similar demonstrations took place throughout the country. The military turned their guns on demonstrators. Thousands were slaughtered—an event that got little international publicity. Many survivors fled across the border into Thailand. They did not find safe haven.

Historically hostile toward Burma, Thailand had made logging and fishing deals with the military regime. In exchange, they agreed to repatriate dissidents living near the border. In 1989, Amnesty International reported that Thailand was forcing Burmese students to return to Rangoon or be charged with illegal entry.

In June of 1989, government-owned Burmese newspapers attacked Aung San Suu Kyi and her political party, the National League of Democracy (NLD). Within a few months, she was under house arrest, a sentence that would be renewed for thirteen of the ensuing twenty years.

Despite her detention, Suu Kyi's political party won by a large margin in Burma's 1989 multi-party election. The military government refused to hand over power. A new constitution would have to be drafted first, they said, emphasizing that it would be a lengthy process. With Suu Kyi excluded from participation, the process has continued for nineteen years.

In 1991, Suu Kyi was awarded the Nobel Peace Prize, but was not allowed to accept it. Her eldest son Alexander, who had remained in London with his father and brother, accepted the prize on her behalf.

The following year, the United Nations condemned the Burmese government, which called itself the State Law and Order Restoration Council (SLORC), for human rights abuses.

That was when the government changed the name of the country. Burma became Myanmar, an attempt perhaps to distance the military regime from the detention of Aung San Suu Kyi and the slaughter of innocents. Opposition groups believed "Myanmar" designated only ethnic Burmans and reflected government-decreed domination over minorities. These groups do not accept the renaming, nor does the U.S. State Department.

In 1997, the State Law and Order Restoration Council (SLORC) would also change its name. The new name became the State Peace and Development Council (SPDC) but the group remained as warlike as before.

Conditions were growing worse in Shan State. In an ultimate betrayal of the Shan people, Khun Sa, who by this time had assumed control of the Shan State Army (southern faction) and renamed it the Mong Tai Army, surrendered in 1996 to the Burmese government, together with eight thousand of his men. Wanted for drug smuggling in the US, Khun Sa lived in luxury among the Burmese generals in Rangoon until October 2007 when, having suffered from diabetes, high blood pressure and other ailments, he died.

* * *

Between 1996 and 1998, the Burmese military relocated more than one thousand four hundred villages in central Shan State. Soldiers burned homes, seized rice fields, and raped Shan women. More than three hundred thousand Shan civilians were forced to leave their homes at gunpoint. According to the pamphlet *Dispossessed*, published by the Shan Human Rights Foundation, eighty thousand fled to Thailand.

Because of their common ethnic heritage with the Thai people, their common facial features and similar language, the Shan were seldom turned back. At the same time, they were not officially welcomed into the country. They have no refugee camps, but like illegal immigrants in the U.S. must work at the least desirable and most dangerous jobs in the country. In Thailand, many migrants are construction workers, balancing on flimsy bamboo scaffolds to reach the upper stories of buildings. And they work on farms, planting and picking vegetables, spraying insecticides on fruits, all for subsistence wages.

Yet the Shan exodus to Thailand continues, as do the human rights abuses in Burma. In early 2006, more Shan villages were relocated, more displaced people moved into improvised hovels in the jungle.

While the persecution of the Shan and other ethnic groups continued, Aung San Suu Kyi could not utter a word of protest—she was confined incommunicado to her home. When her latest term of house arrest was to end May 2006, a government official set the terms of her release: no political activity. She did not agree. Her detention was extended. On her 64th birthday, June 19, 2009, Suu Kyi was still confined to her home, but her concern for the people of Burma had not diminished.

In November 2006, after considerable pressure from the United Nations, UN envoy Ibrahim Gambari was allowed a one-hour visit with Suu Kyi. She told him of her sympathy for the persecuted ethnic groups, including the Shan.

The only Nobel laureate in the world who is under house arrest, Suu Kyi has had little chance to utter another word for public ears.

* * *

In 2001, with scant knowledge of the history of Burma and no knowledge at all about the Shan, I traveled to Thailand to teach English to Shan refugees. Their situation and that of their families became clear to me as I read books about Burma and Shan State and as I listened to the students' stories: stories of abandonment, hunger, poverty, and repression. The young people who told them dreamt of a better future for themselves and their families.

In 2004 and again in 2005, I traveled to Burma to see the reality of the stories my students had described to me. Despite obvious poverty, the threadbare clothing of residents, the oxen carts and the pickup trucks held together with wire, the cities had pleasant, peaceful facades. But large areas of the country were off limits and I knew from my students what was happening there: The homes of the poor were being burned, their possessions and rice fields confiscated; they were being shot or raped for the slightest infractions.

Fear of the military was paralyzing. When I mentioned the name of Aung San Suu Kyi, I heard the whispered caution: "Cannot say her name. Cannot say her name," or "Do not talk about her. Spies might be listening."

In some areas, the regime has been successful in repressing all knowledge of Suu Kyi. Most of my Shan students in Thailand did not know who she was. Their hope lay with the Shan leaders and their ability to lead them out of destitution and despair.

In 2005, ten of the most prominent Shan leaders were arrested. Their prison sentences varied from seventy-five years to one hundred six years. In 2006, one of them died in prison.

* * *

In the ensuing years, government reactions to peaceful protests and a devastating cyclone demonstrated the ineptitude of military rule. Continued oppression of ethnic groups, including the Shan, multiplied the number of displaced persons, hiding in the jungles of Burma.

These disasters are detailed in the epilogue. The ensuing pages revolve primarily around my time with refugees, who escaped from the pogrom in Shan State, and about my excursions into Burma.

The Burmans have not lost hope. Confined to her home for thirteen of the past twenty years, Aung San Suu Kyi remains their symbol of hope for free democratic rule.

Shan refugees have not lost hope. Their hope is that the United States and the world will intervene on their behalf.

PART ONE: EDUCATION

An Introduction to Refugees

Refugees are defined as persons who are outside their country and cannot return owing to a well-founded fear of persecution because of their race, religion, nationality, political opinion or membership of a particular social group.

—United Nations, 1951

FIRST IMPRESSIONS

January 2002

People's fates are simplified by their names. —Elias Canetti

"GOOD MORR-NING, TEE-CHER!" Twenty-five golden-skinned students stood next to hand-made tables with hands clasped prayerfully to their chests. Their greeting thrilled me, made my cheeks, pink with tropical heat, flush deeper. They stood at attention until I returned their greeting.

We were in fertile northern Thailand, where flowers sprout from cracks in the pavement, but if I looked through the open garage doorway behind the students, all I could see was a large asphalt expanse leading to another garage, a smaller version of the one in which I taught English. A former family home, the school was open to youth from all ethnic groups of Shan State, Burma, but although there are more than one hundred such groups scattered throughout the hills of Burma, the twenty-five students, aged fourteen to twenty-nine, were predominantly Shan. And their names confounded me.

I arrived at school early each day and stood staring at the list of names, trying to fix them in my head. Most of the eighteen men were Sai something. The seven women were all Nang something, the "ng" sound at the end half swallowed. Impossible to remember. For weeks I did not know which Nang or Sai I was talking with and marveled that most men had variations of the same name and the women had variations of another. Names I memorized in the morning eluded me in the afternoon when the converted garage became a sweat chamber.

By the time tiny translucent lizards appeared and clung to the walls and ceilings, waiting to feast on mosquitoes that descended with dusk, I reverted to the generic "you." Looking into a student's eyes, I would say, "What do *you* think?" "Do *you* know the answer?" "Have *you* finished your homework?" or I would point to this Nang or that Sai, a gesture, I later learned, they considered impolite.

I was excited to be in Thailand, where orchids, exotic in Minnesota, filled planters and hanging baskets, and where Minnesota pines were replaced by graceful palms. And I had been surprised and pleased by the refugee students, who treated me with loving respect. It should not have been so difficult to remember their names.

Perhaps it was the too-sudden change. In twenty-seven airborne hours, I had traveled from snow and cold to heavy, humid heat; from dismissive Minnesota youth, to courteous young people eager to meet an American. A minor change, really, when compared with the recent major change in my life.

* * *

My mother died in 2000, and with the massive stroke that felled her I lost a confidante and friend, as well as the farm that all my life I had called home. Never more could I idle away the summers, visiting the big slough to watch tadpoles sprout legs and turn into frogs, or sitting in the tall grass next to the depression that marked the place my immigrant grandparents built their first home. The summer of 2001 was long and lonely. I went through life by rote, trying to do what I had always done.

In July, I began searching the Internet for English-teaching jobs in warm countries, as I had done for the past ten years. It was a way of avoiding the icy highways and overheated apartments of Minnesota winters, a way of keeping two lives going at once. My Minneapolis life, where I biked, hiked, read, and went to movies, plays, and concerts, was enhanced by the anticipation of winters in new settings: Spain, Mexico, Indonesia, Ecuador, the Dominican Republic, Turkey, Guatemala. I had lived in all of these countries, and I liked adding new countries to the list.

Sitting in my sunny Minneapolis condominium, where the spreading branches of an elm tree filled my east patio window, I found the Internet site for Dave Serling's ESL Café and clicked on the Burma Volunteer Program. Founded by George Soros, an immigrant American millionaire, the program needed English teachers for Burmese refugees in Thailand.

Refugees: The word connoted deprivation, poverty, and need. I feared the emotional drain of becoming involved with displaced people and their problems. I almost skipped over the website.

Then I saw that one school was near the ancient city of Chiang Mai, in northern Thailand, next to Laos and the Shan State part of Burma. Thailand, Laos, Burma. I am drawn to names and the mind-pictures they convey: silk, elephants, golden-skinned people.

One of those people was Aung San Suu Kyi, whose photo I had seen when she won the 1991 Nobel Peace Prize for peaceful resistance against the Burmese military regime. The memory of her beautiful, calm face, convinced me to apply to teach English to refugees from Burma.

By September 11, 2001, I had been accepted to teach at the school in northern Thailand. That morning a friend alerted me to the terrorist attacks in New York City, and I watched horrifying television images of airliners crashing into the World Trade Center. The sight solidified my decision. I could either curl up and wait for the world to end, or book a flight to Thailand. I chose the latter.

* * *

Now here I was in a mini-version of Shan State, Burma, re-created in Thailand, a place with bright-eyed young people, most of whom were named Nang or Sai something, and who looked not at all like the ragged refugees I had imagined. The Nang/Sai part of the name puzzle was simple to resolve.

Charm Tong, the school director, said that in the Shan language, *nang* meant miss; *sai* meant mister. She said the Shan do not automatically take their fathers' surnames, and the two names that followed each *nang* and *sai* were used together to impart their full meaning. One boy's first name translated to "Love" in English; his second name meant "Country"; either name alone would have been misleading, and although I often use one name here, I never did at school.

Of the seven young women in the class, Ying Tzarm (Charm) was the easiest name to remember—perhaps because at fourteen Ying was the youngest student and one of the brightest. Nang May's name stayed with me, too. She was the shyest student, could not or would not say a word in English the first time we met.

Of the eighteen young men, the first name I remembered was Sai Shang Phun, who said his name meant "Green Fields" or "Green Forests" and reflected his dream of restoring Shan State to the beauty it had before Burmese troops harvested Shan teak forests, burned villages and rice fields, and sent Shan villagers to relocation camps to become fodder for forced labor crews. And I remembered Sai Soe (Everybody Loves Me) and Kham La (Beautiful Golden) because their names reflected personal qualities.

Others interpreted their names differently: According to a Shan elder, Shang Phun meant "Gem Seeds," Sai Soe meant "Persuasion or Invitation," and Kham La meant "Golden Latest," but I did not know about the different interpretations until much later, and I remember them by their own fitting definitions of their names. I had a harder time getting other names to stick in my head.

I had their faces firmly fixed in my mind: This one had bright eyes, a broad white smile, and shiny, glowing skin; that one had eyes dulled at times by malaria; another had acne-prone skin, and seldom smiled. The problem was remembering which name belonged to whom.

The first time I called roll, I pronounced Shang Phun's second name like "Fun." Yes, he said, and I thought it was fixed in my head forever. The next time I called roll, I said, "Like 'fun'?" and he said, "Yes, Teacher, you said that before," and I felt as though I had failed him. Years later, I realized the Shan pronunciation of Phun is actually "pun"—Shang Phun had been too polite to correct me.

After a week of name fumbling, I took photos of each student and with the help of staff members, wrote their full names on the photo backs. At night in my room, I showered and then spread the pictures across the corner desk. I sat at the desk staring at *nangs* and *sais* and others—male students from other ethnic groups in Shan State did not use the Sai appellation—trying to remember who was who. When I glanced up, I could see myself reflected in the window, a puzzled look of intense concentration on my face. Sometimes I switched my gaze to the columns of omnipresent miniscule ants, crawling in formation across the wall, and then looked quickly back at the photos, testing myself. After several weeks of staring, I thought I had mastered their names until I got a paper from a Sai I had never heard of, a man who used two different names, depending upon how he felt on a particular day.

Several years later I would read a book by Leslie Milne, a British anthropologist who lived among the Shan in the early 1900s and wrote about their naming practices. At birth, Shan babies are named based upon real or hoped-for physical characteristics or temperament. If a child is sickly, renaming might fool the evil spirits that plague it. A girl might keep her baby name, but most boys got another name when, at the age of eight or ten, they spent an obligatory two or three weeks in a Buddhist monastery and were re-named by monks. Afterwards, some kept their monastery names; others reverted to their baby names. If they were unlucky, they might change their names again to fool the evil spirits and find a good life.

Most students had taken entirely new names when they escaped to Thailand, and they were not sure how to spell them in English, one way one day and another way the next day. They grew more consistent with

time, and remembering them became easier, but it was several weeks before I could call each student by name

* * *

Frightened, loving, and respectful. The reality of the students was far
different from what I had imagined in conjuring up the ragged, needy
people I had expected refugees to be. They washed their clothes and bodies every day, sloshing shirts and skirts in buckets of cold water. Then, in
three small bathrooms with drains in the middle of the floor, they poured
more water over their bodies and emerged gleaming with cleanliness and
smelling of soap. Their self-discipline amazed me.

Then I found out that three of the men had probably learned discipline
in the Shan State Army (SSA), where they had fought against the Burmese military. I might have guessed two of them were soldiers: Sai Myat
could fall asleep with his head resting on the marble fireplace hearth; Sai
Hseng, even seated, had a soldier's erect posture.

The third soldier, Sai Tong, was a gentle man who was unfailingly polite. He loved children, carried the son of a school administrator in his
arms, kissing his hair and crooning to him, though he himself looked like
a child. At 5'1" and one hundred ten pounds, I am small. Sai Tong was
so tiny I might have picked him up and cradled him the way he cradled
the worker's son.

On a day when we talked about feeling safe, Sai Tong said he felt safe
at night. When I asked why, he said, "Because we have a security guard
then." Another time he said, "I cannot go back to Burma, Teacher. They
will kill me."

* * *

For six months the students were confined to the fenced school yard and
to the large home, where they lived and studied computers and English.

At day's end, they tee-peed their hands below their chins and said,
"GOOD AFTER-NOON, TEE-CHER. THANK YOU, TEE-CHER."
And, although I try not to practice magical thinking, each time they did
that, twice a day five days a week, I wondered if these young people had
come into my life for a reason.

CHARM TONG AND THE GIRLS

Beauty is not in the face; beauty is a light in the heart. —Kahlil Gibran

The day I arrived at the School for Youth from Shan State, a girl dressed in blue jeans and a tee-shirt greeted me with a hug. It was the founder and director, Charm Tong, a girl with an amazing history.

Charm Tong was six years old when the civil war raging in Shan State persuaded her parents to send her to safety in Thailand. They placed her in a hand-woven basket attached to a horse's back and brought her to an orphanage inside the Thai border, within earshot of gunfire that erupted from clashes between the Burmese military and the Shan ethnic group. The orphanage would be her home for the next eleven years.

At night, Charm Tong lay in a bed of rough-hewn lumber and cried herself to sleep with fear and loneliness. During the day, she studied the Thai and Shan languages and became proficient in Chinese and English, so proficient that at the age of seventeen, she was sent to the United Nations to testify about human rights abuses against the Shan. "I was very nervous," she said. "But I have to do it."

Shortly after that first UN experience, she co-founded a women's group, the Shan Women's Action Network (SWAN), and at the age of twenty, started the School for Youth from Shan State north of Chiang Mai, Thailand. No ordinary girl, Charm Tong.

* * *

Of the school's twenty-five students, seven were young women between the ages of fourteen and twenty-eight, and from my sixty-nine-year-old point of view, they were all girls. In the beginning, I tried to relate to them in a professional way both in and out of the classroom, but I soon gave up.

They followed me as my children had when they were little— only later did I learn that in their culture it was the polite thing to do. They were keeping me company. When I escaped to the veranda to catch the breeze between classes, eighteen-year-old, sweet-faced Kyi (pronounced Jee) would appear and sit at my feet. Sometimes she reached up and with her tiny fingers caressed the time-enlarged veins on my hands. Other days, she caressed my feet.

One of the boys had flattered me by saying I looked like her, but the only similarity I saw between us was our rosy cheeks, mine a heat-induced red, hers a rosy, golden flush, the color of ripe mangoes. No, she did not really look like me, but she might have been my granddaughter or the daughter I never had.

Smiling so that her dark eyes crinkled shut and her round cheeks rose high on her face, she would talk about her home in Shan State, about how her parents grew red tea, and how she and her father ate a lot of fruit. One day I leaned over as she spoke and kissed the top of her round head. Her glossy black hair smelled like baby shampoo. Only afterward did I remember the Thai prohibition against touching anyone's head, a sacred part of the human body, and hoped it was not a Shan prohibition as well. Kyi did not pull away. Far from home and family, the students missed their mothers. I became a willing surrogate.

I still hear Nang Lwin, Kyi's best friend, singing *You Are My Sunshine* in a clear alto voice, as we stood in a circle outside the classroom. She would dance up to me, bow, and dance away, her long braid swishing back and forth.

One of the most extroverted students, Nang Lwin would speak first when I urged the girls to participate. Clustered together at one long table in that concrete classroom, with heat waves shimmering off the pavement outside and surrounded by eighteen boys, the girls were silent unless the boys or I insisted they join in.

Yet on a day when students gave two-minute speeches, Nang Lwin stood calmly in front of the class and, in a deep, musical voice, talked about her father, a former medic with the Shan State Army, who died at the age of forty. Nang Lwin's father died young; Kyi's uncle, also a Shan soldier, died in battle with the Burmese military. Other girls were not so forthcoming with their stories, but most had risked being locked up in Burmese or Thai jail-like detention facilities just for entering the country. These were no ordinary girls.

These same girls, all seven of them, might have met a very different fate if they had not been accepted at the School for Shan, for neither the dangers of contracting AIDS, which is rampaging through Thailand and Burma, nor the degradation of the profession deters some poor families from selling their daughters into prostitution.

In Shan State, young women who did not live under the threat of being sold as prostitutes lived with the threat of rape, a Burmese military tool to induce fear and encourage Shan farmers to relocate without a struggle, leaving their rice fields, their ruby and diamond mines, their teak forests, and their poppy fields to the Burmese.

Migrating with Hope, a compilation of statistics and anecdotes about Burmese refugees in Thailand, quotes a woman who said Burmese soldiers would come to their village at night and rape the women.

> Many women . . . [were] caught and given to senior officers.
> After the officers raped the women, they would be given to the other men . . .
> Those women who are too ashamed [will] move to another area or
> flee to Thailand to be sex workers.

A few years after *Migrating with Hope* was published, Charm Tong's women's group, SWAN, published *Licence to Rape*, which detailed sexual violations of Shan women by the Burmese military, including the 2001 rape of a girl whose arms and legs had been tied spread-eagled to a bed. Her parents came home from the rice fields and found her there, bloody and weeping. She was five years old.

* * *

In their Thai haven, the Shan school girls were relatively carefree, and they were the most elegant looking students I had ever seen in their long, sarong-style skirts. A tubular piece of fabric with the ends tied together at the waist, the skirts came loose at the slightest movement and had to be retied. No-nonsense, fourteen-year-old Ying Tzarm, usually wore slacks. Between classes, boys hovered around Ying, competing for her attention, but she ignored them. She was there to learn and paid no attention to their antics.

Amazingly disciplined, Ying Tzarm had a daily practice of writing English-language sentences at home and bringing them to me for correction. When I complimented her study habits, she said her parents had been teachers in Shan State. They left, she said, because inflation had eroded their salaries so much they could no longer feed themselves and their two daughters.

In Thailand, her parents worked as janitors at an apartment building. There was no space for Ying in the small room where they lived, so she lived with her aunt. "I love my aunt, Teacher," Ying said, wrinkling her small nose. "But I can do nothing to help her. Just a little housework."

Normally cheerful, Ying looked dejected the day she said, "I did not graduate, Teacher. I could not finish tenth standard because we had to leave." In Burma, tenth standard is the equivalent of our twelfth grade.

Most of the girls had graduated from tenth standard; Nang Yot, the oldest, most serious girl, had a university degree. The military government had closed most universities in 1988, when students throughout the country demonstrated for democracy. Nang Yot, who had known nothing else, did not resent having been relegated to correspondence school classes.

The university degree had not helped her find a job. She had fled to Bangkok after graduation and worked as a maid until she heard about the School for Shan. Once there she had nurtured the younger women.

Nang May suffered from severe head and stomach pains and was regularly confined to her mat on the floor in the room she shared with five others. A doctor diagnosed the pains as anxiety-related and hospitalized her for ten days. When she returned to school, a thin, shaky fifteen-year-old, Nang Yot wrapped an arm around her waist and escorted her back to classes.

The other two female students were beauties. Crecy, a tiny girl with a perfectly formed, long limbed body and oval face, was the first girl to drift away from the all-girl student table and sit with the boys. She vied for the boys' attention and got it until Nang Myo happened by.

Taller and fairer than most students, Nang Myo had a dancer's posture. "Our queen," said one of the boys. I detest beauty contests, but I supposed he was right. If there had been a class beauty contest, Nang Myo might have won.

As their teacher and surrogate mother, the girls' beauty was not as important to me as their sweetness and good cheer, qualities of this culture that have entranced others for generations.

During World War II, American medical missionary Dr. Gordon Seagrave trained young women of Burma to work as nurses. In his books *Burma Surgeon* and *Burma Surgeon Returns,* Seagrave raved about his wonderful nurses, about their dedication to duty and their bravery. Many of the nurses were Shan.

The English and American soldiers they worked with grew to love them, Seagrave wrote, and quoted a song soldiers sang, "There's not a sweeter bunch of ladies in the whole universe." Some of those nurses may have been the grandmothers of the Shan girls in my class.

No ordinary girls—not the grandmothers, not the girls in my class.

LESSONS IN LOVE

We are all born for love. It is the principle of existence, and its only end.
—Benjamin Disraeli

At the end of each school day, I wrote a song on the whiteboard, sang it through once and the entire class was singing with me before I finished the first verse. Students' favorites were *Imagine*, by John Lennon, which they finger-drummed against their desktops, imagining a better world, and *You Are My Sunshine*, popular after I said a person who made you very happy, perhaps your girlfriend or boyfriend, was your sunshine. Most were students on the cusp of adulthood, and they liked to think about love.

On February 13, I told them my parents' love story and drew pictures on the whiteboard to illustrate it: a cornfield with a stick man walking through it toward a stick woman who stood on the other side. I told them how my German father had sneaked through the fields against his mother's wishes to visit my Finnish mother on the neighboring farm, told them how angry his mother was when she found out, and about how they had married anyway. They were mesmerized by the story, their attention riveted to the whiteboard as they murmured their appreciation. I asked them to tell their parents' love stories, but they could not; telling love stories is not part of the Shan culture.

So I taught them my parents' favorite song, *Let Me Call You Sweetheart*, and we sang and danced to it in a circle, as I remembered my mother and father swinging around country dance floors, their steps perfectly matched. They had taught many young people to dance in their day. I was not so adept.

The students' waltz steps were stiff and awkward; the tune was difficult to sing, so on Valentine's Day I taught other songs, including one I remembered as "Oh Baby, How You Can Love," a zippier sort of tune from the '50s. For those with poor English skills, group singing was less daunting than individual pronunciation practice. Giddy with the idea of love, they sang so loudly that the class monitor, Sai Khin, and I had to hush them.

Afterwards, small groups of students came to the front of the classroom. With solemn faces, they sang their ethnic songs, their voices sad with longing for their families and their homeland.

In the beginning, I knew little about the Shan except that the Burmese government persecuted the ethnic group. Persecution was just a word—it had no meaning. I had been at the school a month or two before Charm Tong gave me the Shan Human Rights Report, *Dispossessed*, which exposed the brutality of the Burmese military regime: the rapes, the torture, the murders. On Valentine's Day, I was free of that knowledge and concentrated only on ensuring that everyone had fun, talking and singing about love.

Singing their ethnic songs had sobered them. They lightened up as soon as I suggested the Hokey-Pokey, and I marveled at their ability to live in the present when we gathered into a circle and sang and danced the Hokey-Pokey and then *You Are My Sunshine*.

Sai Leng danced into the middle of the circle and held out his hands to the girls. No one accepted, so he got stuck with me, and we swayed back and forth while others sang. I did not count as a girl, of course, and although he did not say so, he probably felt defeated. Later in the day, he had a victory. He won the Valentine's Day story contest by writing a story that turned on the scent of Jasmine, indigenous to Thailand and Burma and his Shan girlfriend's favorite flower.

Sai Leng seemed a carefree sort of fellow. One day he asked me to play a cassette tape of *Old Timer Rock and Roll*, and to the admiration of his fellow students, he gyrated through a wild version of `60s style rock and a Charleston. He had lived a different sort of life in Shan State.

There he had worked for a charitable organization that served children. Since the Burmese government is suspicious of all foreign groups, he was suspected of being disloyal. Police and the military followed him wherever he went. "In Burma, we must be afraid all the time, Teacher," he had said, pounding his fist against his legs. "We must run, run, run until our legs break." Sai Leng was a poet. He turned his plaint into a poem, a poem where each stanza ended with the drumming of his fists against his legs: *run, run, run until our legs break*.

The truth of his poem was borne out in *Dispossessed*, which listed statistics about relocations, the seizure of villagers' land and homes by the Burmese military and the removal of residents to government encampments. The government's stated purpose is to cut off support to Shan rebel groups. In reality, they acquire valuable land, and the relocation camps become a ready source of unpaid forced labor. Some villagers sneak back to former homes to salvage hidden stashes of food, but penalties for trying to retrieve a sack of rice or the family water buffalo are horrendous.

In 1997, Shan Human Rights Foundation documented six hundred sixty-four killings of Shan in relocation areas by beatings, gunshot, and burnings. Among the Shan women who were raped to death were one ten-year-old and one twelve-year-old girl. Shan who died at military bases suffered electric shock before being beaten to death; some died of stab wounds; others were beheaded.

The report included photos of thin, broken bodies, dressed in rags, lying crumpled on the ground, and I was grateful the students in my class had run, run, run to the school in which I taught. Shan State shared a border with northern Thailand. For some it had been a two-hundred-mile trek; others had traveled farther—five hundred miles perhaps. No one told me how the border crossing was accomplished. All were grateful they had made it.

* * *

Sai Leng, who talked about the omnipresent fear of his country people in Shan State, was confident and relaxed in the classroom, where music and girls were his special interests. Among the girls he pursued was Nang Myo, the tallest girl with the fairest skin, considered most beautiful by her classmates; but in Shan State as elsewhere, beauty does not ensure a lover's loyalty.

Nang Myo won the girls' Valentine's Day contest by writing about the man who had loved her and left her in Shan State. In "My Sweetheart," she described her first love as handsome, honest and simple, a hard worker, who did not smoke or drink. They had loved each other since childhood, she said, and he had never done anything she did not like, but Nang Myo's parents did not approve of the match because the young man's "mother was very selfish" with rice and tea.

Nang Myo and her boyfriend had separated. She went away to school but continued to write to her sweetheart. When she returned home, Nang Myo wrote, "A friend told me my sweetheart had got married to some lady. I felt heart broken. I thought no boy will ever keep his promise."

On a day that the students visited temple Phra That, on Doi Suthep Mountain, Nang Myo and the fairest-skinned male student walked the grounds together. They bought ice cream cones and ate them leaning over the platform railing, looking into the smoggy distance where Chiang Mai lay blanketed by exhaust fumes from motorbikes and pickups that swarmed its streets. Tall and slim, they looked like an advertisement in a young person's magazine.

He was a gentle boy, movie star handsome, and I wondered if he might become her special friend, a more constant sort of friend than her former sweetheart, but it was not long before he came to me broken-hearted, saying he had discovered the woman student he had fallen in love with had only wanted him for a "love slave." A love slave. I wondered what the term meant to him, but he was a shy boy and I did not want to embarrass him by asking. Although he did not mention her name, I was sure the girl was Nang Myo.

Several years later, another student told me Nang Myo had been a source of trouble in the school: too many boys, too many long hours away from the girls' dormitory. Although I suspected she was simply proving herself over and over again after her first lover's rejection, the implications of her behavior worried me.

In 2000, Amnesty International director William Schulz wrote *In Our Own Best Interest.* There are at least two hundred thousand sex workers in Thailand, he said. Fifty percent have HIV/AIDS. Many of these women are refugees. In the winter of 2002, neither the students nor I were aware of those statistics. When school ended, Nang Myo served an internship with an NGO that worked with prostitutes, an exposure that I hoped would keep her chaste.

* * *

Class monitor, Sai Khin, was one of the few who did not court Nang Myo. The first time he introduced himself to me, other young men chimed in and said he had never had a girlfriend. Sai Khin laughed and said, "That's right, Teacher. I never had," and I wondered how girls could resist him.

On Valentine's Day, Sai Khin gave a card to fourteen-year-old Ying Tzarm. Turning to smile at me, he said, "We have the same name." I did not ask which name was the same, and Ying Tzarm did not care. Maybe it was because Sai Khin was twenty-seven, too old for her. She returned his card and made a valentine for the bulletin board: "I hope everyone finds their true love on Valentine's Day."

Ying Tzarm's rebuttal did not dampen Sai Khin's spirits. Except during recurring bouts of malaria, when he became cloudy-eyed and listless, Sai Khin was one of the most animated students in class.

He spoke Shan, Burmese, and Thai, and, although English was difficult for him, he joined in every exercise and joyfully threw himself into singing songs, adding gusto to *She'll Be Coming Around the Mountain, Are you Sleeping, Row Your Boat,* and, most especially, *You Are My Sunshine.* We belted out the words as we stood in a circle on the back patio, next to the kitchen and the classroom with an ant-infested tree in the background, but we soon had to restrain ourselves. The neighbors had reported the noise to the police.

Sai Khin became more subdued and tried to hush others when they forgot their circumstances. This was serious business. The students were in constant danger of imprisonment and deportation.

Thailand has internationally supported refugee camps for other ethnic groups from Burma. Not for the Shan. Ethnically related to the Thai people, early Shan emigrants were accepted without question. Prices and inflation soared in Burma simultaneously with increased military purging of the Shan. As more villages went up in flames and more rice fields were confiscated, droves of Shan refugees fled across the border to Thailand. They were no longer looked upon kindly by the Thai government.

Sai Khin quieted boisterous students, reminding them of their precarious situation in the country, and he was adept at monitoring fairness. When I brought bananas or rice cakes to school, some students grabbed more than their share, until Sai Khin took over. He would divide the remaining treats equally and parcel them out to those who hadn't gotten any.

When I asked students to write essays about someone special, Sai Khin wrote about me. He had copied most of it from a writing text we were using, standard practice when he had studied in Burma. I might not have recognized the toe-tapping, frenetic drama teacher he wrote about except that the title of the essay was "My Teacher Miss Bernice." Above the title he had written, "Teacher Bernice has a mind good for everyone," an unmistakable Sai Khin invention.

Copying aside, Sai Khin's essays were better than some. Sai Nok, a broad-shouldered young man with smooth brown skin who looked like actor Yun Fat Chow in the film *Anna and the King,* could write only short sentences that he assigned himself.

The first time I met him, Sai Nok stood staring at me from behind another student's back. "Doesn't she look like our old teacher?" the other student asked. Sai Nok didn't say a word. He had learned some English when he was a monk at a Buddhist monastery, but he was dumbstruck when asked to speak. And he was worried about it, so worried that he could not understand assignments.

When other students worked in class, Sai Nok bent his head over his notebook and wrote over and over:

I must study hard. I must study hard.

I must try hard. I must learn English.
I must learn English.

I might have asked myself *why* he must learn English, why any of them must, why I was there forcing our language on them, but the students had given me a reason. They had lost homes, possessions, and family members to the Burmese military regime. They were outnumbered and outpowered. They wanted to learn English so they could tell the world their stories, the same reasoning George Soros had used in setting up the Burma Volunteer Program, but I wondered if that strategy had ever worked. Aung San Suu Kyi was educated at Oxford, she spoke and wrote English eloquently—and she had been under house arrest most of the time since 1989. I hoped Soros and the students were right, hoped they would benefit from the language, but what a struggle it was for Sai Nok.

Watching him write and rewrite "I must learn English. I must study hard," I would say, "You don't have to try harder, Sai Nok. You're trying hard enough. You will get better." He would smile and keep writing.

I never found out how old Sai Nok was—he appeared to be in his twenties—and I do not know why he was so frightened. I *do* know he lived in a monastery from the age of ten. He did not have the words to tell me why, but I supposed the reason was poverty. When he fell asleep in class, other students would say, "He gets up very early," and that was all I ever knew about Sai Nok. Although he did not seem to learn anything in class, he slowly began to speak.

One day after school, he used his newfound English to ask, "Which is the strongest country in the world?" I said I supposed it was the United States. He smiled triumphantly. I was not sure what that smile meant, but the knowledge seemed to add to his personal pride.

During World War II, the U.S. helped chase the Japanese out of Burma. The students' parents and grandparents might have had some exposure to Americans, but I was the first one Sai Nok and others had met. They liked knowing I was from a country the world considered wealthy and strong; maybe we would intervene to help them. It was a belief I did not encourage, for I did not think it would happen.

* * *

My fondness for the students must have been obvious. Several wrote in their journals, "Teacher Bernice loves us very much." Love is a strong word. I was not sure it fit. But I did have a great deal of admiration for those courageous young people.

One of the students I admired most was twenty-seven-year-old Shang Phun, who had escaped from Burma to avoid forced labor as a porter, carrying heavy loads of ammunition and supplies and marching ahead of the Burmese military into rebel encampments.

In 2000, Amnesty International issued the report, "Myanmar: Exodus from Shan State to escape forced labour." It quotes a Shan refugee who had been a forced laborer before escaping to Thailand. "They didn't give us anything and we were treated just like dogs or pigs," he said.

Shang Phun went to Bangkok to escape a similar fate. There he worked eleven-hour days, six days a week, in a garment factory to earn money for his parents in Burma. Later he got medical training at a clinic sympathetic to Shan refugees, filled a backpack with medical supplies and food and trekked into the Burmese jungle to help displaced persons hiding from the military. He got malaria, but stayed until his money ran out, walking from family to family, dispensing supplies. His dream was to get more medical training and return to help those still hiding. He had been back at the garment factory for one year when he heard about the School for Shan.

Shang Phun was fine-boned and slim, with thick black hair, a full mouth, and eyes that seemed filled with love and sadness, a compassionate young man.

One evening I stayed late at school and sat at a table in the garage, correcting papers. Shang Phun appeared, turned the fan toward me to blow away mosquitoes, brought me a small cup of hot, sweet coffee and sat across from me. The high-pitched hum of cicadas lessened as dusk fell and I imagined them tenting their wings over their bodies to rest. As stars began to flicker, tiny gecko lizards called their names, the timbre of their calls belying their size, and Shang Phun told me about the time he had been working late when the factory was raided. "This, Teacher," he said, pinching his gray knit shirt between thumb and forefinger. "I was making this. I didn't see the police come, so I could not run."

They sent him to a crowded detention center where there was no room to lie down to sleep. He held his right hand up, pressed it back with the left so they were at forty-five degree angles, and said, "Like this, Teacher. That is how we slept." He pulled out a photo of himself before imprisonment, and I could hardly believe it was the same person. In the photo, he was almost husky. He must have lost one-third of his body weight in the detention center. He did not lose interest in helping others.

In the latter part of February, I asked the students to think about a special person in their lives, make notes, and then tell the class about him or her. To demonstrate, I told them about my sixteen-year-old nephew, Neil, told them that from the time he was old enough to hold cards in his hands and read, the two of us would play card games and Scrabble in our secret places, clearings in the woods of my mother's farm. I told them about the e-mail I had gotten from Neil in which he sent me a poem about our camp-out with his cousins. He wrote about playing basketball, about playing the saxophone in the school band, and about acting in school plays.

Shang Phun thought a few moments. Then he walked to the front of the class to talk about *his* special niece and nephew. They had contacted him recently, asking for money for a Buddhist celebration. Shang Phun had no money. But he sent them twenty-five dollars he borrowed from a friend. Twenty-five dollars was nearly one-quarter of his monthly wages at the garment factory. I was humbled by Shang Phun's generosity and by his devotion to those he loved, a devotion so deep he readily borrowed money to help them.

Another young man who captivated me was intelligent, dreamy-eyed Sai Soe, who wrote about climbing trees to pick orchids in the jungle. After reading *Romeo and Juliet*, he wrote an essay imagining himself at a fancy dress ball, mingling with the guests and looking for his personal Juliet. Like so many of the students, Sai Soe was in love with love. It was a love that extended to me.

After he learned to use the Internet, he sent me an e-mail message: "When you are here, you look like our mother. Sometimes I wish I could stay with you forever, but we cannot."

I printed the message at the Internet shop and brought it back to my room. That evening I read it again. The words traveled from my brain to my body, making me feel warm clear through. I remembered other students writing in their journals, "Teacher Bernice loves us very much." Love is a scary word, with its connotations of undying loyalty and devotion—too strong for what I felt. At least that is what I had thought when I read their journals.

Holding Sai Soe's message in my hand, I saw twenty-five Shan students, standing to attention when I came into the classroom and when I left, a scene that would be repeated the following day, and I wondered about what I felt. Maybe it was ego gratification, the knowledge that the students thought I was special. Maybe it was love.

ALONE IN CHIANG MAI

Winter 2002

One travels more usefully when alone, because he reflects more.
—Thomas Jefferson

Between classes, I tried to prepare lesson plans and correct papers. Impossible. Students brought me coffee, tea, or fruit and stayed for lengthy chats, and I longed for time alone.

In the evenings, a male staff member rode his motorbike to the school entrance while students gathered my books, my handbag, hat, and the sunglasses they had taken from me when I arrived and carried them to the bike. I slipped onto the skimpy leather seat behind the driver, settled my feet onto the footrests, and hoped for few cars and careful drivers on the narrow, twisty road to my apartment building.

In Thailand, fearless, bareheaded bikers zoom in and out of traffic and around corners, creating zigzagged high-speed lanes. Riders have little protection from collisions with the cars and pickups that compete for space. *The Bangkok Post* reported forty thousand motorbike accidents during the weeklong 2002 water festival.

In my mind, my broken, bloody traffic-side leg dangled at my side, as we careened through the streets on the way home from school. I relaxed only when we arrived at my apartment building. Far from busy roads and public transportation, my room represented temporary freedom from fear of motorcycle maiming and breathing space away from the loving but omnipresent students.

Those first few weeks at the school I rotated between the busy school atmosphere and the isolated neighborhood where I lived. I was the only English-speaking person in the building, and my Thai was limited to a few phrases. When a drunk tried to get into my room at 3 a.m., I called management and got a sleepy young woman who repeated *sawadee-kha*, "Hello," to every phrase I uttered until I thanked her, hung up, and waited out the drunken knocking at my door.

Outside, the gravel streets of the village were lined with the thatched shacks of vendors selling animal intestines and vegetable and rice dishes so highly spiced with chilies that my eyes burned during their preparation. When I pointed timidly to bunches of small, sweet bananas, vendors smiled and held up their fingers: five fingers, five baht, twelve and one half U.S. cents, for a bunch.

* * *

One Sunday morning I decided to travel to the nearby city of Chiang Mai. The apartment manager went outside with me and pointed a finger down its length. The street led to a main highway where I might catch one of the red pickups called *songthaews*, canopied pickups which provided transportation to the city.

Armed against thirst with a bottle of water, I trudged the road with eyes to the ground, trying to avoid the rats and giant frogs that looked like cookie cutter cutouts from a horror movie after being flattened against the asphalt by passing cars and motorbikes.

At the highway, I saw a red *songthaew* in the distance and edged into the street to flag it down. The small red truck had padded seats that extended the length of the pickup box. The only other occupant that morning was an old woman with a white plastic market basket on her arm, so I was able to find a seat away from the sun for the one and one-half hour ride to Chiang Mai. We drove through mountain valleys heavy with smoke from the slash-and-burn farming practiced by hill tribes.

Near the city, the *songthaew* merged with throngs of exhaust-spewing cars, other *songthaews*, motorbikes, and a few three-wheeled canopied bicycles ridden by intrepid pedicab cyclists, old men, their legs hard and thickly veined from years of cycling.

The contrast between the city and the school environment was disorienting. In the eleventh century, the Shan had occupied much of Chiang Mai Province. In time, they retreated to the adjacent Shan State, where their descendants are now being forced off their land by the Burmese military. Many flee to Thailand. A few lucky ones attend the school for youth from Shan State, where they were afraid to sing loudly for fear of triggering Thai neighbors' wrath.

That atmosphere changed after my half-hour's walk to the *songthaews* and another hour and one-half ride in the truck. Thailand has dubbed itself "The Land of Smiles," and its people pride themselves on the quality of *sanuk*, creating fun out of any situation. Compared with my refugee students, Thais had a lot to smile about: The country had a decent economy, and citizens did not have to fear being imprisoned for lack of proper identity papers.

Chiang Mai did not look much different from a Western city, except for its brilliant gold pagodas and saffron-robed monks and the store we passed that had darkened glass windows imprinted with a scale, the store where I was later told opium was weighed.

In Thailand, as in the U.S., opium derivatives such as morphine and codeine are legal with a prescription. Perhaps that is why the store was tolerated, for a while, on the well-traveled city street, although I suspected the opium had arrived there illegally, trafficked from Shan State, where poppy fields flourished.

The Burmese military regime, which called itself the State Peace and Development Council (SPDC), was making a show of eradicating poppy fields and opium production in Shan State, but it was simply that: a show. According to an investigative report published by the *Shan Herald Agency for News,* pressure from China to stop drugs from flowing across the northern Shan State border had influenced the regime to create a poppy-and-opium-free zone, so the military destroyed poppy fields near main roads. Invisibility, not eradication, was the real policy.

Vacated fields under the control of the Burmese police and military were exempt from restrictions on poppy growing and opium production. Some former rice fields blossomed with poppies. After contracting to buy the finished opium, the militia in charge of the land imposed a tax on each field before the growing season and another tax on the harvest. It was a lucrative business.

On a future trip to Chiang Mai, I noticed that the sign in the window of the Opium Store was gone, and I regretted lost opportunity. I would always wonder whether someone could buy a few grams of opium over the counter.

The Opium Store was next to a market, my first stop on the trip into town. I got off the truck and held up a handful of change to the driver. He picked out twenty baht, fifty U.S. cents. The old woman got off behind me with her shopping basket. I followed her into the market, where she disappeared among the rows of fruits, vegetables, and meat.

At home in Minneapolis, I visited the Farmer's Market every summer, selecting fresh fruit and vegetables and imbibing the mix of nationalities that congregated there: Asians, African Americans, and Latinos mingled with Caucasian farmers, with their cap bills pulled down low over white foreheads. I expected this market to be not like ours but like the markets of Latin America, delightful places with a wide array of fruits, vegetables, and artifacts. I had visited markets in Mexico, Guatemala, the Dominican Republic, Ecuador and Peru but had often cut short shopping trips because of sewer odors and the stench of rotting meat. This market, presided over by smiling vendors, practicing *sanuk,* smelled spicy and clean—even the artistic displays of pigs' heads and entrails and the crickets and giant cockroaches with pinioned legs ready to be stir-fried into the evening's meal.

The fish stalls were another matter. Fish guts smell like fish guts the world over, and some vendors had left them piled next to their stalls. Buckets of eels writhed below the clouds of flies, hovering over the fish. I averted my eyes, held my breath, and walked past, my belly shuddering with disgust. But I liked the foreignness of the place: bugs, eels, exotic fresh fruits and vegetables. Leaving the market, I detoured around the squirming eels, and bought small ears of multi-colored corn, still warm from cooking, and tucked them into a plastic bag for supper. Then I walked to the street to catch another *songthaew.*

I had read about Chiang Mai in my *Lonely Planet* guidebook. The city has been settled for more than seven hundred years and was once occupied by the Shan. At its center is a restored moat surrounding remnants of a thick wall built to defend the city from raiding tribes. It did not work. In a series of wars, the city fell to Burmese troops and was part of Burma from 1558 to 1774. As a final desecration, the Burmese burned the city, and the few remaining occupants abandoned the ruins.

Eventually, Thailand reclaimed Chiang Mai, and, in 1891, King Chulalongkorn restored it as a pleasant resting place for foreigners logging teak from Northern Thailand's forests. Now, though the forests are decimated, foreigners still drive the economy. Thousands of tourists use Chiang Mai as a starting point for jungle treks or as a place to study massage or yoga and buy inexpensive mementoes of Thailand.

As we neared the city center, pale-skinned tourists hailed the *songthaew,* and we rode the rest of the way together. We chatted a while, but I had secrets to keep, could not tell them what I was doing in Thailand for fear of revealing too much about the students.

Tight-lipped as I was, I found nothing in common with the Westerners who joined me in the pickup. I got the impression that most were there for cheap food and drink and to loll on the beaches. Others came for sex. I actively disliked the men who patronized young sex workers, many of whom were refugees forced into prostitution by poverty.

When an old man left the passenger seat next to the *songthaew* driver, I got out of the pickup box and moved into his vacated seat. The driver seemed delighted to see me. In broken English, he asked me if I liked songs, and at a nod of my head, he boomed out Thai songs in an operatic voice. He laughed and sang all the way to Tha Phae Gate, the eastern entrance to the city, where I got out feeling primed for my next exploration.

I set off to eat lunch at Daret's, an open-air, dirt-floored restaurant across from the city gate. As I sat eating a dish of fresh vegetables on a bed of rice, topped with fried cashews, a muscular, athletic Austrian man sitting at the table next to mine, leaned over and introduced himself.

He talked about the beaches and about the Thai people with their polite, gentle manner. Only when he said goodbye and rose to leave did I realize he was wearing a roller blade: one roller blade, for he had only one leg. The other leg ended in a stub below the knee. I watched with amazement as he gracefully rolled out of the restaurant, over the roots projecting from the dirt floor and onto the cracked and uneven sidewalk. I told myself to remember him whenever I found life difficult.

On my way out of the restaurant, a blond man reached out his hand and asked me to join him. He seemed a harmless sort of fellow, so I perched on the edge of the bench, and he told me he was from Sweden.

He was a skinny, wrinkled fellow with several teeth missing, and he talked a lot. I think he wanted absolution, for he talked about his Thai girlfriend, who was a prostitute. He tried to give her enough money so she did not have to see other men, he said. "I am good to her." He paused a while, then he said. "In Sweden, no one will have me." I felt sorry for him and wondered if I should be less negative about men who used prostitutes, but it is a bias I cannot easily surrender.

I left the Swedish man, as he was sucking on a bottle of Singha beer. A few feet beyond Daret's, I walked through the entrance gate to Tha Phae Road, a busy place on Sunday afternoons and evenings. At these times, it is closed to traffic and artisans spread their wares on the pavement.

Throngs of people coursed through the streets: pink-skinned tourists, who had visited the beaches to get a head start on tans; old Thai men and women, tottering along, hand-in-hand with their grandchildren; slim, long-limbed young men and women talking to each other in Thai, the high, low, just-so incomprehensible tonal tongue through which only a few words emerged with meaning to my uneducated ear: *sawadee kha/*

khap, the Thai greeting (kha for women, khap for men); *Khap Kuhn kha/ khap,* thank you. I wandered through the crowds, clutching my bag of cooked corn and jockeying for position to see the artists' wares.

There were hand-painted umbrellas, lengths of slubby Thai raw silk in the autumn colors that look so good on Thais: golds, rusty oranges, and avocado greens; imitation silk, smoother and slicker to the touch, in delicate shades of pink, blue, and green; cotton blouses and slacks; wide-brimmed straw hats; stationery of handmade paper; and elephants, the Thai royal symbol, carved in wood, painted on canvas, and tapped into tin ware. The exotic crafts excited my greed, and I might have bought more if I had not had a nagging sense of guilt about my impoverished students and a strong memory of how tiring it is to lug overloaded suitcases through crowded airports.

I veered away from the artisans early in the afternoon, for I feared meeting roaming dogs on the poorly lit road after dark, and returned to Daret's. There I had a fruit drink of papaya, bananas and mangoes mixed together with icy-cold canned milk, and well before sunset, I hailed a *songthaew* to take me home.

Back in my room, I reflected upon the day, upon my encounters with the amazing one-legged Austrian athlete and the Swedish man who was good to his prostitute, and I reflected upon the superficial conversations I had had with other tourists, Europeans who were astounded that I was an American: not big enough, not loud enough, it seemed. Maybe some were teachers; maybe some worked with refugees, as I did. I would never know for I had not broached the subject.

I had been as alone in the crowds of people as I was at my apartment, as isolated by my sworn secrecy as by the location of my apartment building. I tuned my shortwave radio to BBC and was comforted by hearing the English language. Sitting at my desk with the voices of BBC and my reflection in the window as company, I prepared the next day's lesson plan.

A CURIOUS YELLOW

Life is a quarry, out of which we are to mold and chisel and complete a character. —Samuel Butler

<u>January 2002:</u> When the school day ended and the sun went down, lack of public transportation, poorly lit streets, and vicious dogs confined me to my room. Occasionally, BBC News reported the U.S. war in Afghanistan, but short wave reception was erratic, and left me with a lot of time to concoct lesson plans, think about the future, and ruminate about the past. When I got tired of my thoughts, I played solitary Scrabble.

One night, sitting cross-legged on my bed, leaning over the Scrabble board, I looked at the o-w I had made from a letter board that had no other options, and added the letters y-e-l-l. Y-e-l-l-o-w. It stopped me.

Watching a column of tiny ants follow their usual route across the corner of my bedroom wall, I remembered 1974, when I worked as a clerical supervisor for Hennepin County. We were at war with Vietnam; men were burning their draft cards; women were throwing away their bras; Betty Friedan's *Feminine Mystique* had triggered women's awareness of their subjugation to men's definitions of them. Friedan, Rosa Parks, Gloria Steinem, and Jane Fonda were my heroes.

Hennepin County was offering awareness seminars for women. I went to a one-day course called Women in Management. To get there, we walked several blocks northeast of the Government Center to the Normandy Hotel, where a nondescript room was set up schoolroom-style with tables and chairs. Coffee and sweet rolls were arrayed on a table covered with a white cloth. Time off work and free coffee and rolls: It was a new experience. It seemed exotic.

A strong-voiced, forceful woman, dressed in a severe business suit directed our activities, most of which have been erased from memory by the intervening thirty years—all except another woman's assessment of me, as I sat in the "hot seat."

The "hot seat" was placed in the middle of the room, and one-by-one we took turns sitting in it. The rest of the women stared at us, asked questions, and commented. I wish I could remember what questions were asked, but I cannot; nervousness wiped them away. It seemed that all my imperfections were on display in the hot seat. I recalled my husband's appraisal: Too big in the butt, too short in the legs. And I had a tendency to smile meaninglessly when I could think of nothing to say.

When I was allowed to stand, it seemed as if I had spent a week in the hot seat, but I could remember only one thing that had been said. A woman had stared at me a long time and decided on my color: I was a "Curious Yellow."

She said something else, but I was not sure what—her words had given me an emotional concussion, dulling my brain to them and everything that happened before and after they were uttered.

The coordinator of the session talked with us individually afterwards. I told her I could not remember anything. "The most important thing," she said, "was the woman who said you were a "Curious Yellow."

"That I remember, but what did she mean?"

"She said you were Doris Day on the outside and Jane Fonda on the inside."

It was a confusing assessment. Doris Day was not a person I would have chosen to emulate, but I liked the way Jane Fonda spoke out for what she believed; she lived by her principles. I knew, though, that I was as far from being a Jane Fonda as was fluffy Doris Day. I wanted to change, to live by my conscience rather than by whim.

But did I really? In my small room, thousands of miles from Minnesota, I remembered a poem I wrote the year I turned fifty-six, almost thirty years after I had been declared a "curious yellow." The first verse of the poem read:

> I long to be an integrated person,
> To live by my values and beliefs;
> Celibacy, simplicity, economy,
> Are values to which I would lay claim.

Succeeding verses poked fun at my failures to live up to those values:

> I fear I won't become an integrated person
> For I'm buffeted about by every whim,
> I know that I should work for world peace,
> But I'm too busy waging the war within.

So long as I laughed at and accepted myself as I was, I did not have to change. But time was growing short—I was sixty-nine years old—and

now I really did want to change. I set my Scrabble game aside, remembering Mary Oliver's poem, "The Summer Day," and its zinger of a final line:
"Tell me, what is it you plan to do with your one wild and precious life?"

For the past eight years I had escaped Minnesota winters by teaching
English as a Foreign Language in warm-weather countries. During the
spring and fall, I attended the University of Minnesota, a routine that
gave definition but not meaning to my life. At the University, I was an
anomaly. Young people, who looked through me on the streets of Minneapolis, marveled that I was in their classes, working toward a degree.

* * *

Deciding upon an answer to Mary Oliver's "...what is it you plan to do
with your one wild and precious life?" was made urgent by the knowledge
that I had precious little life left to live. Teaching English in foreign countries and piling up university degrees was no longer enough.

Watching the ants crawling across my bedroom wall that night in my
apartment, I marveled at how they seemed to have an ingrained plan, a
way of life programmed into them, not happenstance like mine.

The refugees, who had fewer choices than I, were more focused, their
goals were to stay beyond the reach of the Burmese and Thai military,
earn enough money for food and shared housing, and with great good
luck enough money to help their parents in Burma, and though it often
seemed an impossibility, to educate themselves for the future. I wanted to
give them another option, the chance to tell the stories they had not been
allowed to tell in Burma and to know that they were heard.

I picked apart the word "yellow," put the Scrabble letters in a bag,
closed the board, and moved to a small corner desk, next to the purpose-
ful ants. With notebook and pen in hand, I stared out the window. Reflected against the evening's darkness, my skin was iridescent pink from
the tropical sun, which permeated even my three-sided classroom. I was
not a curious yellow, nor was I Jane Fonda or Doris Day—just me, still
wondering how to live my life.

I bent my head to preparing the next day's lesson plan. It would revolve
about the Mary Oliver poem.

GRASSHOPPERS AND PRECIOUS LIVES

Your days are short here; this is the last of your springs. And now in the serenity and quiet of this lovely place, touch the depths of truth, feel the hem of Heaven. —Adlai E. Stevenson

<u>February 2002:</u> "Tell me, what is it you plan to do with your one wild and precious life?" I wrote the concluding line of Mary Oliver's poem, "The Summer Day," on the whiteboard, read it aloud, and looked at the students expectantly. The wooden tables had been placed in a "u" formation, and the twelve Shan refugees in my first morning class stared expressionlessly at the whiteboard, as unmoved by the question as the lizards lazing on the walls and ceilings. Fans whipped my skirt against my body and cooled the sweat running down my back. Papers flew off the desks and onto the tiled floor.

I pointed to the line. "Precious," I said. "Who knows what precious means?" No one. "Precious means very, very special. Rubies and diamonds are precious. *You* are precious." Half smiles. Nods. They knew about rubies and diamonds. Shan State was wealthy in precious gems. The more serious students wrote in notebooks.

"Wild," I said. "Does anyone know what wild means?"

Ying raised her hand. "Wild, like an animal?" she asked.

"Yes. Like an animal that lives in the jungle, an animal that can decide what it wants to do."

It was a foolish thing to say. Separated, perhaps forever, from their families, their homes, and their few possessions, many would spend their lives avoiding Thai policemen who could imprison them at whim or send them back to Burma where only the lucky would escape the military regime's systematic administration of beatings, torture, and imprisonment of ethnic minorities. The fortunate might escape into the jungle to be plagued by malaria-bearing mosquitoes and rifle-bearing Burmese soldiers, hunting Shan.

I erased the "precious life" line, held up copies of the typewritten poem, and asked for volunteers to write it on the board. The first student to come forward was Sai Ya Ya, a soft-spoken young man, who said the name he had given himself meant, "Great Warrior." Halfway through the poem, he handed the marker to Ying who had followed him to the board. The tallest and most studious of the seven women in the class, Ying pursed her cupid's bow lips, tucked the openings of her sarong tightly between her legs to keep the fans from blowing them apart, and wrote.

Together, she and Sai Ya Ya wrote out the poem line by line, wrote about the grasshopper that had "flung herself out of the grass," and then lifted her "pale forearms" to wash her face, that had snapped her wings open and floated away. They wrote about Mary Oliver's poetic persona, who questioned herself for wandering in the fields all day, wondering what she should have done, because "everything dies at last and too soon." Finally they wrote the last lines, the ones I wanted to impress on the students:

> Tell me, what is it you plan to do
> with your one wild and precious life?

Back at the whiteboard, I read the poem one line at a time, asking the students to repeat it after me. They chanted the words loudly and in unison. "Who" and "made" came out fine, but no matter how definite I made the "d" in world, it remained "worl." "Black bear" became "plack pe-ah." They improved with practice, but in speaking reverted to pronouncing "b's" as "p's," a pronunciation their teachers in Shan State had drilled into them; final consonants continued to be dropped, and "r's" remained "ahs," the pronunciation used by New Englanders and Brits, and not to be corrected.

As I grew hotter and more uncomfortable, they grew more enthusiastic, calling out the words they did not understand: amazing, grasshopper, complicated, flung, jaws, gazing, pale, forearms, thoroughly, snaps, floats. Most definitions I gave them included body language. Amazing: "Wonderful, great" I said, opening my eyes wide and trying to look awe-stricken.

Grasshopper: I drew a stick-line insect with popped eyes and long antennae on the whiteboard, said they were brown or green, and showed with my fingers how long they were and how they would flutter their wings, fly through the air, and light upon your body.

Speaking from a place where summer days had etched themselves upon my mind, I told the students about my childhood love of grasshoppers, and as I spoke I saw myself taking jars of cold water to my father in the field, where he rode behind a team of horses hitched to a binder, its wooden paddle arms sweeping oat stalks into the cutting blades, saw myself waiting at the edge of the field, extending my arms to make grasshopper landing fields.

I realized the extent of our cultural differences when they said they knew all about grasshoppers—about how delicious they were fried.

Slowly we proceeded through the list of words. Their assignment for the evening would be to look them up in their dictionaries. I would not easily move beyond the Mary Oliver poem.

* * *

The next day, I asked the students to make sentences using words I had written on the whiteboard: amazing (adj.), complicated (adj.), fling (verb present tense), flung (verb past tense), oppressed (verb).

A chorus of students called out, "Shan people are oppressed by Burmese soldiers." I should not have been surprised, having read about the Burmese military persecution of the Shan, but the effect of the group answer sent a shock through me.

Later I would learn the Burmese military had burned one student's family home; another student's home and rice field had been confiscated. The women had lived in fear of rape. Yes, the Shan people were oppressed.

We moved on to the word complicated, and someone called out, "I have complicated eyes." I nodded, "Yes." It was a natural response, since Oliver had called the grasshopper's eyes complicated, and so they are, all five of them, two of which are compound eyes with thousands of single lenses. Too difficult to explain I thought, like the word complicated itself. Besides, everyone has complicated eyes. Mine are complicated by two dark, vertical stripes running through the right iris, a phenomenon that fascinated men when I was younger.

All of the students used fling and flung correctly, for I had demonstrated the verbs by flinging a pencil across a desktop, then saying I had flung it. But there was more to be done with Mary Oliver's poem.

* * *

The following day, I wrote the entire list of words on the whiteboard, asked the students to look at them carefully and then leave the room. The twelve students raced onto a tiled area between the main house and the garage-classroom, and I lined up eleven chairs on the left side of the room. Putting the school's old cassette-recorder on a table near the door, I started playing John Lennon's *Imagine*, a tape I had brought with me. Curious faces looked toward me as I walked onto the tiled area and said, "When the music stops, come in and take a chair on the left side of the room."

I stopped the recorder abruptly, and they filed into the room. All of the chairs had been taken when Kyi walked in. She started to pull an extra one into the circle. "No," I said, pointing to the word 'amazing.' "You must make a sentence using this word." Not easily intimidated, Kyi, pulled the right side of her blue sarong away from her body to tighten it around her waist, and contemplated the word. "I am amazing," she said. The boys chorused "Yes," and she stood aside.

The next time I started the music the students rushed in excitedly and jockeyed for position near the doorway. Walking toward them as they backed up, I stopped six feet away from the door and told them to stand behind that imaginary line. When the music stopped, they ran, struggling to get through the doorway three or four abreast.

Khun Ohn, a shy fellow who could not speak in public without being overcome with giggles, was left without a chair. He stood in front of the whiteboard, shifting from side to side and looking apprehensive. I pointed to "fling." "You fling the pencil," he said and looked relieved when I nodded.

As the game continued, they grew wilder, tipping over chairs in their rush to claim a seat, until I called an end to the class. For homework, I told them to think about what they wanted to do with the rest of their lives.

* * *

I like to believe that by imagining something vividly and often we can bring it into being. Years earlier I had been intrigued by Victor Frankl's memoir, *Mans Search for Meaning*, about how he survived a Nazi prison camp by imagining a different future. Later, Shakti Gawain called this process *Creative Visualization* and devised a formula for making our dreams come true. Maybe it worked. My dream of Teaching English as a Foreign Language had come true; my dreams of Thailand had come true. I wanted the students to visualize and verbalize their dreams and make them come true.

The following day, I asked for volunteers to talk about what they hoped to do after the six-month training period ended. Khun Ohn would begin.

"I want to be a politician," he said. I was dismayed; something had been missing in my instructions. I should have said think about something you *could* do in the future, something you would be good at.

The rest of the students seemed to have chosen more appropriately. Kyi said she was interested in human rights, as were several others, a foreign concept before they came to the School for Shan, for they had had no rights under the Burmese government; three wanted to be health workers; a former soldier said he was going to work for the Shan organization that had sponsored his training.

The balance of the class might have answered in chorus, the way they learned pronunciation exercises and songs: They all wanted to be teachers. Two had already worked as teachers in Shan State after they had completed their public school training and graduated from tenth grade. But they were hungry for more knowledge because, as Sai Leng put it in his poem "Refugees Without a Home," the Burmese had taken "the learning and the light" from their schools: Only teachers had books; they taught memorization, not thinking. All of the students said they wanted to help the Shan people.

* * *

I write this three years after the Mary Oliver poem triggered the class exercises and the question about what we wanted to do with our lives. When I returned to Thailand in 2003, Ying took me to a Thai school where Khun Ohn, the boy who had wanted to be a politician, was working as a janitor.

Ying and I were sitting on a schoolyard bench when Khun Ohn approached. Barefooted, his gray work pants rolled to his knees, he tee-peed his hands in *wai* position below his chin, and upon my urging, joined us on the bench. He said he took care of the grounds and cleaned the toilets. "I like it," he said. "They let me sleep and eat here." That was the last time I saw him.

Thinking about Khun Ohn, I feel something akin to despair about his place in life, about the semi-colon in time one lifetime represents, and about the brief opportunity we are given to make the most of our precious lives.

DREAMING OF A MINNESOTA FARM

I've gone very far, far away, but my character keeps me close to home.
—Fran Drescher

January 1, 2002: My travel alarm emits high-pitched bleeps warning me it is 8 a.m., a work day at the school for Shan refugees, but I am lost in the past. Last night I woke thinking I was at the farm with my mother, Taimi. Looking for the stairway to the first floor, I saw a door at my right dimly lit by a window that did not belong there. Then I remembered I was in Thailand, that I had not been at the farm since my mother died a year ago. I lay awake a long time. The joys of yesterday vanished with the night. Today I wish I were more like the rest of my family, wish I had not ended up so far from the farm.

The alarm beeps again. I drag myself out of bed, fill the electric hot pot with water, plug it in, get a paper carton of pomelo juice from the small refrigerator across the room and pour myself a glass. When steam rises from the hotpot, I make a cup of instant coffee and settle back into bed, pillows propped behind my back, the juice and coffee at my side. I do not have to be at school until 10:00. I have time for reverie.

Outside my window, a bird with a high-crested plume sings a strange song in a tree I do not recognize, and I remember winter days when chickadees chirped their names over and over again in snowy evergreen branches outside the kitchen window of the third house my German grandparents built on our Minnesota farm, the house where their twelfth and last child, my father, Rudy, was born, where my older brother, Norman, and I were born.

The new year has not yet dawned at the farm. In Minnesota, it is 8:05 p.m., December 31, 2001, and I remember sitting with Taimi on the last day of the year, gazing at a spruce tree adorned with tiny white lights and hand-crocheted snowflakes, inhaling the scent of dropping pine needles as they pattered to the floor. After Rudy died, she said the days between

Christmas and New Year's were the hardest, and I had tried to fill that empty space. Impossible, of course, for they had been sweethearts from the day Rudy first saw her at a neighborhood house party in 1926, "a fifteen-year-old girl in a red dress," was the way he told it.

He lived in Pine Lake Township with his mother Emma, when Taimi's mother, also named Emma, rented the farm next to them. Two Emmas on neighboring farms, Rudy's little German mother and Taimi's big Finnish mother. They were Little Emma and Big Emma to the neighbors; they became Little Grandma and Big Grandma to me.

Big Emma's husband, Frank, had died and left her with six children. Taimi was the oldest and had to work hard on the farm, but she was not a drudge. She was lively and animated in her red dress the night they met, Rudy said. He could not take his eyes off her.

Like most people who met her for the first time, he probably called her Tiny—not appropriate, for she had big bones. "No, Taimi, Taimi," she would have said. "Just remember, tie me to your apron strings." Her mother named her after a girl she knew in Finland before emigrating to the United States, a girl who "took good care of her dolls," she said, but Rudy did not know that then.

He was twenty-six years old, eleven years older than she, and he made up his mind right then: He would marry her when she turned eighteen. And so the courtship began.

Big Emma gave Rudy coffee and Finnish flat bread slathered with butter when he walked the quarter-mile of gravel road between their homes to talk with Taimi. His mother, Little Emma, glowered when he left home, for she could not understand what he saw in a Finn when there were so many nice German girls around.

Despite Little Emma's objections, Rudy married Taimi three years after they met, an event I have tried to recreate in imagination and make it mine. Taimi's youngest sister told me that after the wedding, there was a house party in New York Mills, the town nearest the farm. I imagine fiddles playing and German and Finnish voices joining together to cheer as Taimi and Rudy were given special chairs and lifted high above their guests. They were lifted high above their guests—that is all I really know about the wedding party.

The next day they left for Itasca State Park where Rudy bought Taimi a photo of Douglas Lodge inscribed, "Sweetheart," and succeeded by a romantic verse assuring her "That life is richer, sweeter far, for such a sweetheart as you are." But they could not return to the farm—Little Emma would not have it. After a few days at Itasca, they moved into a small home on Big Pine Lake, where Rudy's brother, Adolph, had a resort, and Rudy traveled back and forth on horseback to the farm where he worked long days tilling the fields and milking the cows.

Taimi was soon pregnant with my older brother, Norman. Maybe that softened Little Emma's ire, for Rudy and Taimi returned to the farm in time for Norman's birth, with both Emmas in attendance. Two years later, I was born, and Taimi was busier than she had ever been.

I see her running between the kitchen, the fields, and the outbuildings, bending her body to whatever task needed doing: throwing oats to the chickens, collecting eggs. Back to the house to feed us and then to pickle cucumbers, can tomatoes, peas, green beans, and corn. She hurried from task to task, moving at the same steady pace from sunup till dusk, stopping only to prepare meals: roast beef or pork with potatoes and carrots browned in the fat that oozed out in cooking and filled the house with tantalizing aromas. She sliced thick chunks of homemade bread, warmed a jar of canned corn or beans from the cellar shelves, and put a jar of dill pickles on the table. If she forgot them, Rudy looked confused. "No pickles?" for he was a man of regular habits and pronounced tastes.

In September, his favorite vegetables, rutabagas and cabbage matured, and whenever we had them he pronounced one of his absolutes: "Rutabagas and cabbage are the best vegetables." I cook them now, frying cabbage, the way Rudy liked it, and baking mashed rutabagas with a bit of cinnamon, the way Taimi and Big Emma did. Their pungent odors permeate my small apartment, and I wonder if I inherited Rudy's tastes or if I like them because they trigger the memory of his conviction that they were "the best."

Rudy was a little guy. "Weighed one-twenty-eight when I married your mother. Still do," he would say. He moved slower than Taimi, and so do I. He had arthritis in his knees, and so do I. His fingers were knobby and gnarled, and so are mine. I look like him, too, have the same lean frame, longish nose, and high forehead, the same small mouth. Taimi didn't like it much when he said, "The daughter she takes after me—she'll never get fat."

Taimi was not fat; she was sturdy. And she was a beauty. If the truth were told, I would have preferred to look like her. Her skin glowed pink when she was excited; she had big hazel-colored eyes, and thick black hair. After suffering a massive stroke at the age of eighty-nine, she spent her last difficult months in a nursing home, where people still called her beautiful.

As a teenager, I thought it was her even features that made her so pretty that even my high school boyfriends talked about her. Moments after death, her face was ordinary. Only then did I realize her beauty had come from within, from the generous heart that propelled her uncomplaining from job to job and joy to joy. For to Taimi, life was a joyous event. Her enthusiasm vitalized sleigh rides, whist games, wedding dances, visits to family and friends, quilting bees.

Together with neighborhood women, Taimi would piece together scraps of fabric into colorful patchwork mosaics, line the finished work with thick wool bats, and tie front and back fast with scraps of yarn. In later years, Taimi made quilts with new fabrics—enough so each child and grandchild got one when she died. But money was tight in the early days. From that time, I remember only one quilt with store-bought fabrics: yellow water lilies appliquéd onto a white background and edged with green. That was 1937, and I was five years old.

The appliquéd quilt was stretched on a wooden frame in the living room, while Sadie Israelson and Mrs. Dertinger sat on the red plush couch at one end of the quilt and Taimi and her best friend, Lila, Cousin Jake's wife, sat in straight-backed chairs at either side, making precise tiny stitches through two layers of fabric and a third layer of batting. I sat underneath and created a world where yellow water lilies were my stars and women's legs encased in warm brown stockings were my trees.

I remember a cold winter day when someone grumbled "It's not good for kids to be inside so much," and Taimi shooed me out from under the quilt, helped me into my heavy wool snowsuit, and sent me outdoors. Brother Norman walked up from the barnyard, grabbed a shovel, and pointed to a snow bank at the far side of the driveway. "Good place for a cave," he said, and carved out an opening big enough for the two of us. He soon returned to Rudy and the barnyard, for Norman was a born farmer, and at seven years old he tackled men's jobs. Surrounded by snow sparkles I continued my quilt-home reverie: about the future, for I did not yet have a past.

In that future, I stitched quilts with friends and cooked coffee for them, stirring Folgers into a bit of raw egg for better flavor, the way Taimi did, and talked with my own Rudy, a Rudy who loved and adored me, who whirled me around the dance floor on nimble legs the way he whirled Taimi so they became one person with four legs and four arms, pumping perfect time to German waltzes or hopping like kids to the Beer Barrel Polka.

When I was six years old, Taimi became pregnant with my younger brother, Duane, whom we would call Buzzer after the way he buzzed toy cars around the kitchen floor. I thought Buzzer was my baby, too, mimicked Taimi as she cooed and cuddled his chubby little body. He came along at the right time, because that was when Norman got fed up with me.

In early childhood photos, Norman stands with his arm protectively across my shoulders. It is hard to believe we were once good friends, for he spent the rest of our childhood and adolescence taunting and teasing me, making me march ahead of him while he pelted my snowsuit-padded bottom with bee-bees or making me carry his heavy lunch bucket as well as my own when we walked the Crooked Road two miles to the one-room hilltop school.

School. Maybe that was it. He was smart—probably Miss Brunko's clear favorite till I showed up. I was smart, too, and I loved Miss Brunko, loved her pretty moon-shaped face and sweet manner. Maybe I stole some of her attention away from Norman, grabbed a piece of his glory.

Then Buzzer came along and stole more attention at home—he was too little for Norman to torment, so he took out his frustrations on me, ending each torment with words of warning: "If you tell Mom and Daddy, you'll really get it." But he made a mistake when he socked me in the nose for refusing to carry his lunch pail to school: I bled all over the snow. A neighbor reported it, and Rudy took the razor strop to his bottom. Maybe that was when he learned some limits, for he never did any of the really reprehensible things that make best selling memoirs these days. I do not have enough material for a *Liars' Club* or *Story of Ruth* sort of book.

No, I cannot blame my difficulties with men on Norman, although when I was separating from my husband, a counselor, seeming to talk to himself, said something like, "Hmm, a kind father, a younger brother you felt motherly toward, and an older brother who was mean to you." He never drew a conclusion from that information and neither have I. I moved on to another counselor, who probably hit it right. "I think a man paying a lot of attention to you was more important than what kind of person that man was."

In childhood, my man was Tarzan. Sneaking away to avoid chores, a Tarzan book tucked under my arm, I would climb into the branches of the elm tree in the front yard, while Norman worked in the fields. One unforgettable summer day, he mounted the tractor, lowered the long blade of the attached mower, and swept through the alfalfa field east of my treetop hideaway, cutting swathes of hay. Our dog, Rex, cavorted along beside the tractor. The musky smell of cut alfalfa permeated my fantasy as I swung with Tarzan on vines that stretched over our land, beyond Cousin Jake's farm, and into the distant horizon—until a whimpering, whining sound entered my consciousness.

Looking down, I saw Rex, his left front leg nearly severed and covered with blood, the right leg deeply gashed. With a pathetic three-legged limp, he hobbled to the elm and lay in its shade. I climbed down with my Tarzan book under my arm and stood helplessly patting his head, as he looked up at me with glazed eyes. Rudy and Norman were soon next to us and I heard Norman say, "Didn't see him. Ran over him with the mower."

Rudy looked at the dog sympathetically for a few moments, then said, "He's not gonna make it. Take him out to the gravel pit." A few minutes later, he drove his old green Chevy next to the elm tree, got out, turned to Norman, and said, "Put him in back."

Norman lifted the whimpering dog into his arms and drove the Chevy across the road to the gravel pit while Rudy went into the house. I was crossing the yard behind him when I heard a gunshot from the direction of the gravel pit and knew that was the end of Rex.

A part of me felt responsible for the dog's brutal ending. I had stood there speechless while Rudy and Norman decided its fate. What should I have said? What should I have done? Men had all the power—but not over me, I vowed.

* * *

I was ten years old when I got a copy of *Gone With the Wind*, and Rhett replaced Tarzan in my fantasies about men, only I was sure my Rhett would never say he didn't "give a damn." Two years later I graduated from eighth grade and the little schoolhouse on the hill. That fall I was ready for town school.

The bus stopped one-quarter mile from the farm, and I would run to meet it, books in hand. But it was friends, not learning, I was running toward. New York Mills had little interest for me before I started ninth grade. When Taimi and Rudy had gone to town to buy groceries and farm supplies, I stayed home with a book. Suddenly the place was peopled with friendly faces, girls to giggle and play pretend-sisters with, to drink coffee with in Karjala's Café, boys who wanted to play Tarzan to my Jane or Rhett to my Scarlet, and school became the stage where love fantasies that began in the elm tree played out their adolescent ways.

I skimmed the surface of my classes, thoughtless, giddy, and caught up in the attentions of boys, glorying more in a note from an unidentified boy that said I was "A Lonely Little Petunia in an Onion Patch," than I might have in getting a decent grade. Shortly before graduation, reality broke through the giddiness, and life suddenly seemed sad: My closest friends were going away to college. With a mediocre high school transcript and no money, college was not an option for me. I would work at Cousin Clarence's Resort.

* * *

The bird with the high-crested plume flits onto another branch of the tree outside my window. I sip my cold coffee and see myself across the years, a sixteen-year-old girl in the summer of 1949, working as a waitress at Cousin Clarence's resort on Big Pine Lake, looking out the window at the rolling lake and the white pines that covered Sioux Point across the way, where Indians lay buried in mysterious mounds.

I dream myself back into the mind of that girl and feel her pleasure at knowing what her adult self is doing with her precious life.

PART TWO: EDUCATION

We cannot hold a torch to light another's path without brightening our own.
—Ben Sweetland

SAI SOE AND KHAM LA, FUTURE ENGLISH TEACHERS

2002 - 2003

Be as a bird perched on a frail branch that she feels bending beneath her, still she sings away all the same, knowing she has wings.
—Victor Hugo

Sai Soe and Kham La were respectful, serious young men, who were always in my line of vision at the School for Shan. If I stood directly in front of the classroom whiteboard, where I used blue markers to demonstrate spelling, I could look toward the back of the room and see the two young men sitting side by side in the far center of the "u" formation.

Gleaming with cleanliness, they tracked my movements and my words with eyes that shone with enthusiasm and intelligence, whispering to each other and nodding their heads when I presented new material, laughing out loud at my feeble jokes. With big grins, they joined the class, chanting "Peter Piper picked a peck of pickled peppers," working hard on the difficult "p" sound, trying not to slip into what a Burmese English teacher might have taught as "Beder Biber bicked a beck of bickled bebbers."

In Burma's Shan State, both Sai Soe and Kham La had completed tenth grade, the highest schooling available before college. They wore blue jeans, and outside of class they wore baseball caps, looking more Americanized than the young men who wore loose-fitting traditional Shan trousers that wrapped around their waists and tied in front.

During class breaks, Sai Soe and Kham La played cane ball with other students. I would watch as Kham La flipped his slim body into astonishing contortions to kick or head bunt the hard cane ball over a net. If he spotted me watching them, he would pause long enough to turn a handspring. Sai Soe's sturdy body was not so agile, but he was one of the strongest, most determined, and most popular players.

The young men were physically different. At eighteen, Kham La was one of the taller students. He looked perfectly coordinated and at ease in his body until we spoke one to one. Then he grew quiet and shy.

Sai Soe was three years older than Kham La and much shorter. We stood eye-to-eye when we spoke, so he was probably five feet tall. He was strong and well-muscled and reminded me of my nephew Loren, who had the same solid farmer's body. It may have been that likeness that drew me to Sai Soe. I wanted to take him home and meld him into my family, number him among my sons or my nephews.

When I was getting to know the students, I set aside time to meet with each of them individually. Some, like Kham La, were intimidated by the one-to-one setting. They chose to meet in small groups so each of them might speak less. Sai Soe was excited about the meeting and eager to talk.

We sat on the verandah ledge where a slight breeze rustled the leaves on nearby trees and cooled the air. Sai Soe told me that he had a different name in Shan State, that in Thailand he had chosen the name Sai Soe Khur because it meant "Everybody loves me." It would be impossible not to love him, I thought. Then Sai Soe told me about his past.

He had lived on a rice farm near Hsipaw, the Shan town infamous for the manner in which the Prince of Hsipaw was abducted, held captive, and then killed by the Burmese military. Sai Soe's mother left his father and him when he was one and one-half years old. "My father worked hard in the fields and couldn't take care of me," he said. "So he took me to a widow lady, but she only took care of me one week." Sai Soe looked into my eyes, as if to reassure me. "My father loves me, Teacher," he said. Next, his father gave him to a couple. Sai Soe is troubled because he can't remember them or the woman who took care of him earlier. Finally, the father took him to his maternal grandparents, who were also poor rice farmers and were not particularly happy to get him.

"When they traveled, they left me home alone. Once they went to China, but I could not go." Whether or not his grandparents loved him, they raised him and sent him to school, not an easy task in Burma where public schools charge tuition and government-imposed quotas force farmers to give rice to the military before taking the rest of their crop to market.

Sai Soe wanted to attend university after he graduated from tenth grade, but his grandparents could not afford to send him. He escaped to Thailand, went to Bangkok, and found a job spray-painting furniture, working from 7 a.m. to 9 p.m. six days each week, exposing himself to noxious fumes ten hours a day. He had worn a facemask, he said, but his nostrils looked distended and I wondered if it was from struggling to breathe through paint-clogged masks.

He earned one hundred fifty baht per day painting furniture, the equivalent of $3.50 U.S., and he had to spend $2.50 U.S. for food and bus fare. That left the equivalent of one dollar a day for housing and other expenses. It took ingenuity to live on such wages. He pooled his money with other illegal immigrants, and together they rented a room where they slept side by side on woven bamboo mats spread on the floor.

In 2002, Sai Soe heard about the School for Shan at a village in northern Thailand. He took an entrance exam while still in Bangkok, passed it, and boarded a bus to the northern Thai village, afraid at every stop that someone might ask for his papers and that he would be sent to a detention center or back to Burma. Sai Soe suffered needlessly through the five-hour trip. He looked like other passengers and had learned enough Thai to pass as one of them. Checkpoint authorities did not question him.

"Don't go back to the factory, Sai Soe," I said. "Don't work there again."

"I won't, Teacher," he said. "I will work hard to get more training."

After we talked, I took a photo of him sitting on the verandah ledge in front of a cluster of leafy green trees. He is wearing blue jeans and a blue-green shirt that emphasizes his bronze skin and deep brown eyes. Later, I gave him a copy of the photo together with a group photo. Sai Soe laughed, pointed to himself standing among the other students and wearing his blue-green shirt. "I have on the same shirt every time, Teacher," he said. "It's the only one I have."

Every day after school Sai Soe filled a bucket with cold water, scrubbed his clothes with bar soap and hung them outside. They dried quickly in the blistering heat, and he was always clean.

In the beginning, he was not one of the top students, but he learned quickly and was one of the better writers. His handwriting, like that of most students, was small. He crammed so much into each line that it was difficult to read, a habit he had developed in Shan State where writing paper was a luxury and had to be conserved.

Before I returned to Minnesota, Sai Soe wrote an essay about me saying, "She always smiles at me." It was impossible not to smile, looking at Sai Soe. But the first e-mail I received from him after returning to Minnesota induced tears, not smiles. He reminded me that I looked like his mother and that he had wanted to stay with me forever, and I knew then that I would return to Thailand and the school for refugees from Shan State the following winter.

* * *

<u>December 25, 2002:</u> Nine months after I had said goodbye to the Shan refugees, I returned to Thailand for the second time. I called the school in the morning and by late that afternoon they had arranged a welcome-back party for me in a restaurant owned by legal Shan immigrants, a place where they felt safe. By pre-arrangement with the owners, the students brought their own soft drinks and chips and ordered several rice dishes to be shared among the group.

Sixteen of the original twenty-five students were at the party. Among them were Kham La and Sai Soe on their first outing since they had started teachers' training seven months earlier. The students chattered happily among themselves. Many had not seen each other since they had completed their training in the School for Shan Youth. I had little time with Kham La and Sai Soe, but before leaving the party both young men asked me to visit them at their teachers' training site. Later, Sai Soe would send me their address by e-mail.

They were studying at a nongovernmental organization (NGO) founded by legal Thai immigrants from a different Burmese ethnic group. It was the last house on an out-of-the-way street that the taxi driver could not find. He dropped me six blocks away and I wandered most of the way on foot, showing Sai Soe's directions to every friendly looking face I saw along the way.

For a while each person I asked pointed me in a different direction, until, with hot and tired feet and wet with perspiration, I stopped beside an old woman weeding a flower garden, picking carefully among the roots of graceful white spider lilies and sturdy bright yellow cannas. She looked at me curiously and called her daughter. The younger woman examined my directions carefully. "Is it an NGO?" she asked. What should I say? It was an NGO, an NGO that trained illegal immigrants. And the Thai government could shut it down.

The woman leaned closer to me, smiled, and repeated, "Is it an NGO?"

"I . . . I don't know," I said. "My friends live there. If you can show me where this street is, I'll find them." She smiled slightly and I suspected I had happened upon one of the many Thais who are kindly disposed to immigrants from Burma. Opening the door to a van parked in the drive-way, she said she would take me, and, although I protested that I only needed to find the right street, she drove directly to the last house on a dead-end street. "This is it," she said, and as soon as I got out of the van, she drove away.

A chain link fence and wrought iron gate separated an unassuming house and a small yard from the street. I stepped through the gate, and on the doorstep of the house was greeted by a man with a pronounced limp, a refugee who introduced himself as an English teacher. He said I had spoken with him on the phone to get permission to visit Kham La and Sai Soe. As we stood there, Sai Soe burst out of a side door and rushed toward me, taking my hands in his. Kham La was a few steps behind. They did not show me the house but led me to a patio near the quiet street, where we sat on a low wall that ran along the east side.

They loved their training they said, but it was almost over. They had served teaching internships in refugee camps near the Thai-Burma border and would soon receive their assignments. A tenth-grade education and nine months of teachers' training would qualify them to teach English and Math to child refugees.

They were enthusiastic about everything, about studying Burmese and English, about the English-language songs they had learned, about the opportunity to teach others. "But first, Teacher," Sai Soe said, "We must have more knowledge. We want to be *good* teachers." I asked if they knew how they could study. "At the camps," said Sai Soe. "They have good foreign teachers there and we can learn many things."

In the days of British rule and for some years afterward, Burma had an excellent school system. Under the military regime that took power in 1962, the cost of living had gone up drastically and wages had been severely cut, inducing teachers to cover less material than necessary in the classroom so they could extort money from parents to tutor their children outside of class. When Sai Soe said the camps had good foreign teachers, he referred not only to their broad knowledge but also to the fact that they did not demand money to teach what students needed to know. I told him to find out how much it would cost for them to study at the camps.

Sai Soe brought me a glass of cold water, and I taught them the alphabet game where players find words for each letter of the alphabet and each consecutive player has to remember what the others have said. We played in a circle, "A, ax," "B, banana," "C, cat," laughing and struggling to remember each of the previous words until we got to "Z, zebra." Kham La, who had sailed through the entire exercise without a slip, said, "Is a good game, Teacher. We can teach to the children."

I asked them what they thought were the most important qualities in a teacher. "To know a lot of things," said Kham La.

"Is it important to like your students?" I asked. Words tumbled out of Sai Soe's mouth. "I love the little children very much, Teacher. At the camps, they swept our floor every day and I played with them."

Before trying to find a taxi for the return trip, I asked them to tell me how to get back. They looked at each other in embarrassment and said nothing. Then Sai Soe said, "We don't know where we are, Teacher." School administration was worried they might be discovered and closed down. Except for coming to my party and serving teaching internships at refugee camps, Sai Soe and Kham La had not been allowed to leave the house and small yard for seven months. They would have had as much trouble as I getting to my hotel.

As they walked me to the gate, I said, "Can you play cane ball here?" Nodding their heads in unison, they said, "Yes." Sai Soe pointed to the only clear space in the small yard, an area about eight by ten feet near a cluster of bamboo trees. "Right there, Teacher," he said. "That's where we play." They were as proud of their small play area as American students might have been of an entire football field.

* * *

The next time I visited Sai Soe and Kham La, they took me inside the home into the room used for classes. They slept with other students in another part of the house, they said. We sat in white plastic chairs next to a long wooden table. This time they knew what it would cost for them to study. "Our English teacher says we must each have four thousand baht to study at the camps," said Sai Soe. Kham La murmured to him in Shan. Sai Soe said, "Maybe five thousand baht, Teacher." Five thousand baht is the equivalent of about one hundred twenty-five U.S. dollars. "For a whole year?" I asked. They assured me that because the camps get international aid they would furnish food, bedding, medical supplies, and mosquito nets.

After visiting several camps near the Thai city of Mae Hong Song, I had been filled with sympathy for the refugees who lived in bamboo huts, roofed with woven thatches of leaves. To Sai Soe and Kham La, the camps were luxurious. All they needed, said Sai Soe, running his left hand down his right arm as though he were washing it, was money to buy soap, toothpaste, and other personal supplies. I almost laughed—it was doable!

For Christmas, my brother and his family had given me fifty dollars to use for the refugees. His friend gave me another fifty dollars, and the

Lions' Club he belonged to donated one hundred dollars. If I added fifty dollars, they would have all the money they needed to study for an entire year.

* * *

Sai Soe and Kham La asked me to attend their graduation from Teachers' Training at the end of February. The classroom they had introduced me to earlier was arranged differently. This time, there was a long table in front, facing rows of white plastic chairs. I had been ushered to the front row and sat near the twelve students, as they took turns standing in front of the assembly, addressing their teachers, their fellow students, and their guests.

They spoke Burmese, and I did not know what they were saying, but Sai Soe and Kham La stood erect and spoke with unhesitating poise. I was impressed with their fluency, for Shan was their native tongue. And they both received awards. Later I asked them what the awards were for. Kham La said he got an award for excellence in environmental studies and Sai Soe had gotten an award for excellence in all subjects. I felt as proud of them as if I were their mother. They said nothing then about the complications to their plans.

The next day I taught English to new refugees at the School for Shan. After class, I wandered into the yard to watch a student chess game. Sai Soe came running to meet me from the house where he had spent the night with school staff members. He got a chair from the classroom, motioned me to sit, and sat facing me on a low retaining wall. Taking both of my hands in his, he said, "Teacher, we cannot study."

The last time Sai Soe had asked his English teacher about studying, he was told they must first teach young children at the refugee camps. Only after they had worked one or two years, long enough to pay back the cost of their training, would they be allowed to study. Looking into my eyes, Sai Soe said, "Don't feel bad, Teacher. I don't. We can study later." But I did feel bad. And so did they.

* * *

Sai Soe and Kham La started attending the weekend English classes I taught at an ancient Shan monastery, where we studied in a garage-like building. The tables we used for desks were longer, older, and rougher than those at the school. Some had linoleum tops. Others had surfaces streaked with lumpy adhesive that had been used to secure linoleum long since peeled away. Between concrete columns that supported the roof, students lined up tables one behind the other, placing four or five white plastic chairs at each table. Most of my former students were working in menial jobs or taking further training, so three tables were enough for the twelve to fifteen students who attended classes.

At the end of the rows of tables stood a large blackboard; students improvised a desk for me next to it. My tools were a half-full box of chalk stubs that spewed dust when I wrote on the board and the corner of old gray towel for an eraser—until one day someone replaced the towel with a small handmade cotton pillow. I remembered standing outside the one-room country school I attended sixty years ago and slapping two felt erasers together to clean them. Here we had only one pillow and it soon spewed as much dust as the chalk.

Sometimes a truck was parked to the left of our tables. Beyond the truck, boards, buckets, and tools were stored. An area at the far right held additional equipment. Near the right side of the blackboard, a Shan woman, her husband and two little children, lived in a space where they had placed bamboo mats on the floor. Several tent-like structures made from blankets served as their bedrooms. A television set sat on a wooden box in the middle of the bamboo-matted area. The mother, a young, dark-haired woman, washed clothes and cleaned for the monks. She would bow, smile, and greet us at the door no matter which one of the five overhead doors we used to enter the building and her home.

The students were delighted with their surroundings. In 2002, we had used a pre-intermediate English text, and they were pleased to have graduated to the *Lifelines Intermediate English* textbook I bought at Chiang Mai's S&D Bookstore. As latecomers to the class, Sai Soe and Kham La shared books with those who had organized the group, peering over their shoulders and writing on small, lined tablets.

In addition to academic studies, we had discussion groups. They could not discuss drugs or political issues in Burma where education was restricted to what the government wanted students to learn. At the monastery, we talked about opium and its derivatives, codeine, heroin, and morphine, about how the rubbery, raw opium was harvested from fields of poppies, many of them in Shan State, about how Khun Sa, the former leader of the Shan State Army had been convicted of opium smuggling and was now living in harmony among the Burmese military elite in Rangoon.

I thought about how these young people, none of them more than twenty-five years old, had been betrayed not only by the Burmese government but by Shan leaders like Khun Sa, and I thought about the miracle of their surviving to become ethical people, eager to learn, and hopeful that one day they might be able to return to Shan State and serve their people.

To relieve the intensity of two hours of study, I would teach an English-language song at the end of class. When Sai Soe and Kham La joined the group, I let them teach the songs. They would take turns, writing the words on the blackboard, singing them through once, and then encouraging everyone to join in.

On the last day of class, I tried to forget I was leaving, tried to pretend it was a day like any other. I wanted to avoid crying, and I was successful until twenty minutes before class ended when Kham La said he would like to teach a song "for Teacher Bernice." Using a broken stub of chalk on the rickety blackboard, he wrote one verse of the John Denver song about "leaving on a jet plane." He sat in front of the class, strumming the school guitar and singing in a sweet, plaintive voice that melted my self-composure.

In 2003 as in 2002, the students' last memory of me would be with tears streaming down my cheeks as, in a tear-soaked voice, I told them to stay the way they were. Because they were perfect.

Before leaving Chiang Mai, I put two hundred fifty dollars in a checking account controlled by the school, with instructions that it be used for Sai Soe and Kham La when they were able to study. When that time grows near, I will add money for their transportation, which can be costly and dangerous for illegal refugees.

* * *

Afterword: I left Thailand six months ago. Sai Soe wrote to say he and Kham La have not been summoned to their teaching positions. They live in an old house in the country, which serves as an office for a student group that calls itself Shan Youth Power and was organized to publish a newsletter in the Burmese, Shan, and English languages. There they sleep on the floor with former classmates. No one has a salary, but one young man attends some sort of training and gets a stipend of one hundred twenty-five dollars per month. He shares that money with the others. They get money for rice from the school. Occasionally they send e-mail messages, telling me not to worry. Responding to a message from Sai Soe, I attached the complete words to the John Denver song and asked him to give them to Kham La. Kham La wrote:

May, 2003:

Dear teacher, Sai Soe gave me the song. You know I love that song so much. Thank you so much teacher. You know we all are remember you so much. If we can we want to meet you again. I hope one day we will meet again. Now we all are trying hard. Don't worry for us. Let me stop my letter here. May God Bless you always.

Your love student, Kham La

MURNG ZUEN LOOKS FOR LOVE

2002 and 2003

Love is a smoke made with a fume of sighs. —William Shakespeare

In 2002, Murng Zuen was a skinny, pimpled eighteen-year-old. When I asked students if I might take their photos, he said he wanted a photo with me. Before the shutter clicked, he said, "I am not handsome, Teacher."

Murng Zuen had lived near the Chinese border in northern Shan State. More than the other students, he resembled the Chinese ancestors from whom the people of northern Thailand and the Shan are descended. He had a small, round face, and his straight black hair was parted in the middle and fell to either side. In the photo, I look like a boiled russet potato with heat-induced red cheeks. Murng Zuen is grinning so broadly his eyes are almost shut.

He endeared himself to me with his diligence. He rose at five, studied English for up to an hour, and then washed his clothes before the school day started. But he lacked one important quality. He had no empathy for female students whose love and affection he did not crave.

I had bought an easy-read version of *Romeo and Juliet,* which I had introduced by saying it was "the most famous love story in the world," impelling Murng Zuen to read it in one sitting. "The ending is too sad, Teacher," he said.

Sad or not, the students were enthusiastic about the story, so I let them practice their pronunciation by reading the scenes between Romeo and Juliet in pairs. One shy girl had no partner. I asked Murng Zuen to read with her. "No, Teacher," he said, and rushed to the side of Ying Tzarm, the most sought after girl in the class. Another boy got there first, and I was not sorry to see Murng Zuen lose the competition, for I was disappointed in him.

Afterwards I realized I might have done the same thing at his age. Murng Zuen loved the idea of being in love and so had I. With me it had lasted a long time—the idea, that is. I, too, had been the youngest girl in my high school class and boys hovered around me. I loved all of them except the dull and awkward ones.

Among those I most favored were Bo Hepola, the curly-haired blonde football hero with a roguish glint in his blue eyes, who joined the navy before we graduated and who won my father's affection by milking cows when he came to visit me; Jack Stinar, from neighboring Wadena, who scared my parents with his rough-looking motorcycle-riding friends and with his fast driving; and Roger Lee, tall and handsome, with long-lashed green eyes and fine manners, who won my mother's heart and mine.

I was about twelve years old when love struck for the first time and I yearned after Leroy Breitenfeldt, a curly-haired, blue-eyed German, and my brother Norman's friend. When our parents visited his parents, Norman and Leroy would tear around the yard laughing and yelling, while I stayed indoors with the women and imagined Leroy looking into my eyes and saying, "I love you." Twelve years old. That is when my obsession with love and men began. Or maybe even earlier when I sat in the branches of the elm tree, reading *Tarzan* and imagined myself swinging through the jungle in his arms.

Valentines covered several pages in scrapbooks from those days. The most sentimental, with a stuffed satin heart in the middle, was from Bo: "Sweetheart, today and every day I give you my heart." The showiest was from Roger, a big, bold declaration of love. The simplest was from Jack, a child's valentine, showing a heart pierced by an arrow. And I forgot to mention Don Hall, from Parkers Prairie, who was eighteen years old and in the navy when we met. I loved the fit of his tight, bell-bottomed trousers and the way he looked at me out of the corner of his blue eyes. He, too, sent me a mushy, love-you-forever kind of valentine. I loved them all: the valentines and the boys. What I really loved was the idea of love.

That was what Murng Zuen loved, the idea of being in love. He asked me to teach the students a special love song for Valentine's Day. The evening of February 13, I sat in my isolated room, watching the ants that kept me company and the occasional small lizards that slithered across the walls, and thought about Roger and Bo, about Don Hall and Jack, and about our youth, and I wrote this little ditty:

> I love you baby,
> Say you love me, too.
> I want to do
> The Boogy with you.
>
> Oh, sweetheart,
> You're my guy!
> I love you so much,
> I could die!

I chanted it aloud several times. I liked the rhythm, saw myself swinging across the wooden dance floor at Mosquito Heights, my skirt swishing around my knees, long dark hair brushing my shoulders. I threw my head back and smiled with joy, as my saddle shoes took on an independent life and followed my partner in perfect Lindy rhythm. Yes. It sounded good—the boys could chant the first part and the girls the second part. I would call it a Rap Boogie and it would be our Valentine's dance.

With the tables in a large "u" formation, I stood at the center and wrote the words on the whiteboard. We chanted it together several times, the boys laughingly chanting the first part, and the girls giggling through the second part. Then I did a solitary version of a Lindy-style Rap Boogie. Holding out my arms I asked for a volunteer partner. Murng Zuen came forward.

"I love you, Baby, say you love me, too," he chanted as he swung me under his arm. Pulling me back, he repeated, "Say you love me, too." And so it went, until the young woman I purported to be capitulated, crooning, "Oh sweetheart, you're my guy! I love you so much I could die!"

Of course I did love him, and so had the other teacher, who left one month after I arrived. We loved him the way teachers love all students who are eager to learn, but Murng Zuen was sure we loved him more than other students. A confident fellow, Murng Zuen had said of his grandfather, "He loved me more than the others," meaning more than his other grandchildren, and, shortly before I left Thailand, Murng Zuen said, "I know you love me a little bit more than you love the others, so I will miss you more."

* * *

As a final class activity, the school arranged an outing where legal Shan immigrants loaded us into two pickup trucks that they drove up a nausea-inducing, windy road to the Buddhist temple, Wat Prathat. At the crown of the four-thousand five-hundred-foot Doi Suthep Mountain, the temple overlooked Chiang Mai. The pickups stopped near a three-hundred-step staircase leading to the temple.

A tram had recently been installed for the convenience of tourists, but I climbed the stairs with the students. Three young men hovered near me on the way up, carrying my shoulder bag, holding my arms, and cautioning, "Slowly, Teacher. Slowly." Murng Zuen was not one of them.

He was far ahead, sticking close to a cluster of girls. He stayed next to the girls as we toured the gold-leaf encrusted buildings, when we knelt in front of the Buddha images and the priests, when we formed a line and bonged the bells lining the back wall of the main temple, and when we gazed over the courtyard walls, trying to make out landmarks through the pall of pollution that obscured Chiang Mai.

On our way back to school, the students stopped to shop at souvenir stands that lined the bottom of the hill, and Murng Zuen spent part of his meager school allowance to buy a ring of simulated stone. He handed the shiny red ring to me with downcast eyes. "I'm sorry, Teacher. It is just plastic." Plastic or not, it was precious to me.

In April, when my first teaching assignment with Shan refugees had ended and the spring heat was at its worst, I left Chiang Mai. The school had hired a man who would work long hours and replace both the former teacher and me. In Minneapolis, one of the first e-mail messages I received was from Murng Zuen. "Teacher David does not like to talk to us after class, Teacher," he said, and I felt sorry for Murng Zuen who had thrived on after-class conversations.

Murng Zuen also said he had been selected to serve an internship with a human rights organization after graduation. Almost as an afterthought, he said he had "cried every night for two months" after I had left.

I wrote to Murng Zuen telling him that I, too, cried because I missed them. I would sit at the computer with tears running down my cheeks as I read their messages. The messages drew me back to Thailand, where at the urging of former students, I devised a class to teach English in a monastery.

* * *

2003: At the beginning of the new year, I saw Murng Zuen at a school reunion. He was no longer skinny—his shoulders were broad, and his body had filled out. In a short, black leather jacket and with a blue bandana tied around his forehead, he looked as if he had been reincarnated as a '60s era Minnesota teenager. A big smile crinkled his slanted eyes as he handed me a blue and gold-checkered scarf. "For you, Teacher." He watched me wind it around my neck and noticing my hand, said, "You still have your ring, Teacher."

At the party, he sat next to me and told me he loved his internship and that they would keep him on when it expired so he could be better prepared for a job—but that would change.

That winter and spring Murng Zuen could not attend the English classes I taught at the monastery because he was busy with his internship. He took one day off to join us, and when we chatted after class he talked about his girlfriend and how much he liked his internship at the human rights office. I asked him how long he could stay there, and he said, "I must leave, Teacher. They want me to stay, but I must work. My father had to sell his car to send my brother to school. He called me and said I must get a job to help my family."

Sensing my sadness, he said, "Don't worry, Teacher. A man has a job for me." He did not say what the job was—and in the crush of students who wanted to chat after class, I neglected to ask him. That was the last time I saw Murng Zuen that year.

In March 2003, we ended our English classes at the monastery, and I returned to Minneapolis.

* * *

During 2003, I got several messages from Murng Zuen. In the first, he said the job he had been offered had not materialized. He had left his internship and was working for a youth media group, he said, sleeping on the office floor with four of his former classmates.

In the next message he said, *"My heart is broken, Teacher. I have no work, and we have no salaries at the media office. Now I am broken heart, please send a satisfy letter for me. Please don't be angry with me that I am just priority for myself."*

I sat at my computer, twisting the red plastic ring on my finger, aware that it was splitting apart, and likened it to Murng Zuen's life splitting apart. My shoulders shook with sobs, and tears rolled down my cheeks: Murng Zuen's father had sold his car; Murng Zuen had no job and no salary. And what was going on with his girlfriend? He had not mentioned her. I hit the reply button on his message, and wrote. "My dear young friend. I hope things are better for you soon. Friends have been giving me money to help you. I am sending you and the students you live with a check for $200."

Two hundred dollars goes a long way in Thailand. It would be enough to keep the five students in food and motorbike gas for a few months.

Within a few days I got another message from Murng Zuen and wondered if I had been mistaken about the cause of his broken heart. This time he wrote:

Dear Mother, Teacher, or Friend,

Thank you for sending money to us. I feel better. My girlfriend isn't angry anymore.

With best wishes, Murng Zuen

SAI SAM SEARCHES FOR WORK

2002 - 2003

I was given away. If your mother gives you away, you think everybody who comes into your life is going to give you away. —Eartha Kitt

Sai Sam had a sly grin, and he was a giggler. I guessed him to be no older than eighteen, but he was twenty-five. He was small, about five feet tall and slight, and when a friend bought a knitted stocking cap in Bangkok and brought it to Sai Sam at the School for Shan, he wore it over his close shorn hair even on eighty-degree days. It was probably the only gift he had ever received. Sai Sam was the poorest of the poor and was always hungry.

The Shan School had little money for food. The students ate rice, supplemented in the evening and at noon with boiled squash or greens and a little meat. Sai Sam took a normal helping of food as the meal began. When other students had finished eating and were carrying dishes to the kitchen, wiping clean the desk-tables, and sweeping the floor, Sai Sam ate another helping of rice. For a small fellow, he had a prodigious appetite, and since I ate slowly and he ate a lot, we ended our meals together.

One day Sai Sam talked about his parents, rice farmers in Burma's Shan State, who had been too poor to feed him. The military government had demanded a portion of their rice crop, as it did with all farmers. After it took its share, there was not enough left to feed the family. Sai Sam was six years old when his parents sent him to live with an aunt. He hated it.

He had been speaking so quickly his words were garbled, and I had to slow him down many times to figure out what he was saying. After three or four attempts, "Theywerenotkindteacher," became "They were not kind, Teacher."

* * *

This is the rest of Sai Sam's story as he told and retold it, struggling for clarity. His parents visited him at his aunt's house when he was eight years old. He begged them to let him live in a Buddhist monastery, and they agreed. He liked the monks, he said, and going into the streets with them, a begging bowl in his hands, was preferable to life in a loveless home.

At the age of eighteen, Sai Sam left the monastery to help his parents. They and other villagers had been forced off their land by the Burmese military, which confiscated their rice fields and burned their homes. They were sent to relocation centers, small clusters of homes placed on open land. "My parents had no work and no food," he said. "I told them I would go to Thailand and find a job so I could send them money."

Watching Sai Sam devour his second helping of rice, I supposed he was making up for all those times he had been hungry. He was still talking after he finished the last grain of rice.

Sai Sam said he had worked on a farm near the Thai-Burma border where they gave him meager meals and a place on the floor for his sleeping mat. The owner had promised to pay him after he had worked three months, but when the time arrived he said he got no money. Sai Sam got a job in a brick factory and earned enough money for a bus ticket to Bangkok where he would look for his two sisters, who had preceded him to Thailand. He told me about finding his sisters and getting a job in Bangkok, where again he agreed to work for room and board, deferring his salary for three months. His employer reneged on their agreement. Again, he was not paid, and because he was an illegal immigrant, he could not complain.

Sai Sam gave up on Bangkok, accepted bus fare from his elder sister and boarded a bus to Chiang Mai. His illegal status was discovered at a military checkpoint. He was arrested, imprisoned, and then sent back to Burma. A foreign woman had seen him crying in the Burmese border town of Tachilek and gave him $2.50 U.S., enough to sneak back into Thailand, where he made his way to Chiang Mai and found a monastery that would take him in. That was where he was living when he heard about the free School for Shan in a nearby village.

* * *

After hearing Sai Sam's story, I changed my opinion. What I had thought was a rascally smile reflected simple joy. He was happy to be among his peers, to have three meals a day without going into the streets to beg, to be learning English. Perhaps more than any of the other students, Sai Sam wanted the world to hear his story. If people only knew what was happening in Burma, he thought, they would help the Shan.

Sai Sam was a faithful student, paying close attention to the lessons, never missing class, but although he spoke quickly and a lot, his syntax, grammar, and pronunciation were hard to untangle, and writing was difficult for him. They were not his strong points; he was an artist.

On one of our last class days, I asked the students to teach me about the Shan. Sai Sam went to the whiteboard and said he wanted to talk about a Shan house. He drew a bamboo house, so detailed I could almost see each slender bamboo log in the walls and each individual leaf in the thatched roof. Beside it, he drew the floor plan of a room with a table in the middle, explaining where a visiting monk would sit, where the father and mother would sit, where the children would sit. A separate structure behind the house held "paddy," he said, the word students used for rice. After class he brought me an architectural quality sketch of a Shan house labeled, "For my Teacher. From Sai Sam."

* * *

Back in Minnesota, I got an e-mail message from Sai Sam, He thanked me for teaching English and said he hoped I would return.

Sai Sam, with his sad childhood and hopes of a better future was one of the reasons I returned to Thailand the following winter. The night I arrived, I called the school to tell them I was at the Top North Guest House.

The next morning, the desk clerk called and said there was someone to see me. I walked down the stairs, and when I was halfway across a covered walkway to the lobby desk, I saw Sai Sam walking toward me, his arms outstretched, a broad grin on his face. Taking both of my hands in his and laughing with joy, he said, "Hello, my teacher." Sai Leng was waiting at a motorbike and said they were taking me to the school. Across town and into the countryside on motorbike. The thought made me nervous, but I did not want to dim the radiant smiles on their faces. I agreed to ride with Sai Leng.

Beside Sai Leng's bike stood an old and battered smaller bike—Sai Sam's. We set off into throngs of exhaust-spewing vehicles, Sai Sam riding escort at our side, sticking so close to us we might have been the only vehicles on the road.

Many of the refugees indulged in magical thinking. Sai Sam, for instance, had told me he did not need to wear a helmet: Nothing bad would happen to him because he was "a good person." I hoped his magic covered me, because Sai Leng was the only one with a helmet. Visions of bandaged heads and limbs subsided whenever I glanced at Sai Sam's small, serious face, intent on getting us safely to the school. The traffic thinned as we traveled. One and one-half tense hours later we arrived at the school.

The trip was almost accident free. At the school, Sai Leng tipped his bike to park. I tipped with it and landed on the asphalt driveway, skirt around my waist. Sai Sam ran over, lifted me to my feet, and I made an unceremonious entrance.

Only a few students had stayed at the school after the six-month English and computer training had ended. They were the unfortunates, those who had received no further training and had no work. With no money, nothing to do, and nowhere to go, they had lingered at the school. Sai Sam had been one of them, but he was now living in the country with another former student. The only student left at school was a 16-year-old boy, Sai Fha, who had lost training opportunities because he was too young. Sai Leng, Sai Sam, Sai Fha, the assistant school administrator, and I sat at a round concrete table in the yard, drinking tea, and I felt as though I had returned home.

Shortly after sunset Sai Sam and Sai Leng revved up their bikes. The roads were still crowded with motorbikes, trucks, and cars, and were probably even more dangerous in the dusk than they had been earlier, but I adopted Sai Sam's magical thinking as we neared Chiang Mai and lights came on in restaurants and then along the wall that surrounded the old city. Streetlights reflected in the waters of the moat. Chiang Mai became a fairy-tale city that absorbed me in its ancient beauty.

* * *

Sai Sam was working for a Shan organization, collecting signatures from other refugees for a petition that protested the practices of the military regime in Burma. The organization paid him a small stipend, and he rode his bike through the countryside, trying to convince people to add their names to a list of protestors. It was not an easy job—many feared they would be punished if they disclosed their names to those in power. But the stipend allowed Sai Sam a degree of independence. The friend he lived with also had a training stipend, and whenever any of their former classmates needed a place to sleep or a bowl of rice, Sai Sam and his friend shared what they had.

When several former students asked me to teach an intermediate level English class on weekends, Sai Sam made arrangements for us to meet in a Buddhist monastery. The group of twelve young people, ranging from fifteen to twenty-five years old, met for two hours each Saturday and Sunday.

Sai Sam always arrived early, carrying someone on the back of his old motorbike and often going out again to get another student.

In the beginning, as we were deciding on books, class content, and rules of conduct, I asked the students if they wanted to pay a fine if they spoke anything other than English during the two-hour class, adding that they could use the money to buy treats before I left. A laughing Sai Sam was the first student to say, "Is a good idea, Teacher." In 2003, as in 2002, Sai Sam was one of the most diligent and enthusiastic students in the class, but English was still difficult for him.

We had been meeting for one month when Sai Sam said his job getting signatures had ended, and he had to find work so he could buy rice, for to Sai Sam, as to most of the refugees, to eat was to eat rice.

The next week Sai Sam seemed happier than usual. He had gotten a job, working in the Chiang Mai Night Bazaar where vendors sell merchandise to tourists. The only requirement was the ability to speak English.

The Night Bazaar was open from 4 p.m. till 12 a.m. and covered many blocks north of the Mae Ping River and west of Tha Phae Road. It was an area of luxury hotels interspersed with custom tailoring shops, banks, and restaurants and was peopled by tourists speaking English, French, German, Arabic, and other languages I could not decipher.

It would be hard for anyone to walk through the blocks and blocks of Night Bazaar merchandise without being enticed to buy: The stalls were filled with lightweight cotton slacks, glossy silk pajamas, robes, and underwear, raw silk scarves, small gourds intricately painted in brilliant reds, yellows, greens and blues and covered with lacquer, teak boxes with hammered tinware decorating their covers, handmade stationery, picture frames, photo albums, women's suits and coats of elegantly tailored silk or hemp, intricately embroidered and beaded handbags, and commercial products, such as music CDs and cassettes.

There was little order to the arrangement of the wares. Workers like Sai Sam spent time making their individual stalls attractive, creating narrow product-packed aisles of merchandise. They worked eight hours a day, every day, and the salary was equal to about eighty U.S. dollars, enough to pay rent for a small room and buy rice and motorbike gas. Sai Sam considered himself lucky.

After he started working at the Night Bazaar, Sai Sam could only join the English class for an hour on Saturday and an hour on Sunday, and he was too tired to do homework when he returned to his room after work.

During his hour-long stay in the classroom, his head often nodded and his eyes drooped shut. He would shake himself awake and try to pick up the thread of the lesson, but I realized he was learning little.

One day an unsmiling Sai Sam stayed for the entire class. Afterwards I asked him if something was wrong. "I have no job, Teacher. I cannot work more because I do not have identity papers." Someone had reported him, or the police had made a random check of workers. Somehow he had avoided being sent to a detention center or deported, but he was down-hearted. "What should I do, Teacher?" he asked. "I must make money to buy rice." I told him we would think about it and asked him to have dinner with me later.

I had moved nearer the monastery and lived in a cheap hotel with several restaurants nearby. Early that evening, Sai Sam putt-putted into the hotel driveway on his motorbike. I was waiting on the hotel verandah. As always, he greeted me with bowed head, his hands teepeed below his chin. I asked him what he wanted to eat, and he said, "I don't know, Teacher. I never ate in a nice place." The restaurant I had in mind was about as ritzy as a Minnesota truck stop and featured inexpensive rice dishes. I started to tell Sai Sam we were not going to a nice place, but I realized he had probably never eaten in a restaurant at all. He and his roommates cooked rice, and when they had enough money, they went to the market and bought what they called "curry." The only difference between curry and boiled vegetables or soup being that occasionally curry was flavored with curry powder.

Walking down the street, Sai Sam said, "Sometimes I have to laugh, Teacher. Seven years ago I told my parents I would make a lot of money for them in Thailand. But I have no money even for myself." He laughed then, and I thought of the saying, "If I didn't laugh, I might cry." Remembering his small face and brave laughter, I no longer think of him as a giggly rascal, but as a determined struggler—Sisyphus on a beat-up motorbike.

We crossed the street, Sai Sam with my shoulder bag slung over his narrow shoulder, and entered the air-conditioned restaurant. Sai Sam was awed by the sparkling clean chrome tables and chairs and by the extensive menu. "Is very nice, Teacher," he said. He selected fried rice with chicken, and I asked for two orders. He devoured the rice, frequently looking up to say, "Is very delicious, Teacher."

When we finished eating, I asked Sai Sam what he would like to study if he had the opportunity. Without hesitation he said, "Computers, Teacher. Now we have no computers in Burma. When we get them, they will need workers. I want to be a computer worker." I told him he should find out how much it would cost to study at a computer school.

That night I fought with myself. With the former and new students at the School for Shan, I now knew more than fifty refugees. I could not help all of them, and it was not fair to help Sai Sam and not the others. Besides, at bottom I am a penurious person—I have to think long and hard before I part with money.

The next day Sai Sam returned with a folio written in the Thai language and with pictures of people sitting at computers. I asked him what the literature said, and he told me it was a three-month program for basic computer software and hardware training.

We chugged to the school on his motorbike, and the English-speaking Thai owner said if Sai Sam did not learn the material in the allotted time, he would work with him until he had mastered it. The cost was surprisingly low: one hundred twenty-five U.S. dollars. Still, I went through my usual mental gyrations.

If I spent that much on each refugee it would come to more than six thousand dollars, a totally unaffordable figure. I had one month left in Thailand, and I did not want to run out of money. Friends had given me money for the students, but I had already given them that and more. Yet it seemed too cruel to say he could not study after encouraging him to check the school.

In bed, during the time between waking and sleeping, I would see the students' faces floating before me. Sai Sam was among them, a smile on his face as he sat at a computer, mastering a skill that might one day enable him to keep his promise to help his parents. I chastised myself for my miserly indecisiveness: I did not have to worry about getting money to buy rice. All I had to do was slip an ATM card into the proper slot and the money would be propelled into my hand. I did that before I left Thailand, and with a combination of guilt and pleasure, I gave one hundred twenty-five dollars to the school director for Sai Sam's computer course.

After returning to Minneapolis, I had several e-mails from Sai Sam. He wrote to say he was learning a lot at computer school and that he planned to teach his former classmates everything he had learned—if they could get a computer. When a friend said he would donate a Macintosh laptop, I wrote to Sai Sam. He answered, saying he did not think it would work in Thailand, that it must be Intel-based, and with the language of those who are accustomed to defeat, he wrote, "Thank you very much, Teacher. You tried for us."

NANG MAY BATTLES MALARIA AND FEAR

2002 - 2003

Anxiety is the rust of life, destroying its brightness and weakening its power.
—Unknown

Nang May was the only student in my 2002 English class who wore a jacket even on the hottest days, and although she rose to her feet with other students when class began and ended, she said little. Not during the greetings and farewells they regularly observed, not during class, not when class was over.

She was fifteen years old, a dark-skinned girl troubled by recurring acne, who tried to camouflage her curves by wearing loose slacks, over-blouses, and jackets—the response of the shy to puberty's onset.

The first week I was at the school, I invited the students to visit with me one-by-one in the living room. The unfurnished room was a pleasant place that opened onto a verandah shaded by leafy trees. I sat on a woven bamboo mat near the verandah door and waited for the students to present themselves. Most of them chatted eagerly for a few minutes before giving their place to the next student. May was the last to appear.

She sat cross-legged, facing me on the bamboo mat. I told her my name was Bernice, said I was happy to be there, and asked her easy questions, enunciating carefully. "What is your name?" "How old are you?" "What part of Shan State are you from?" May stared at me in uncomprehending fear and said not a word. When I spoke, she pressed her upper body away from me. Another student walked by and said, "She's been sick, Teacher."

As though the words were a signal for her departure, Nang May rose from the mat without saying a word and rushed into her room. A half hour later she emerged, carrying a sketchpad and crayons.

When I left school that day, I saw May sitting on the verandah ledge, holding a sketchpad and shaping a world of blue sky and green trees. She still would not speak but smiled when I peered over her shoulder and complimented her artwork.

May suffered from recurring malaria. When the fever and sweats started, she would go to the room she shared with five other young women, lie
on a bamboo mat on the floor, and cover herself with layers of blankets,
even when the temperature was more than 100 degrees Fahrenheit. The
day we met, May had been recovering from such a bout of malaria.

She also frequently huddled under blankets on the floor of her dormitory room, nursing a headache or stomachache. During a prolonged
bout of illness, a staff member used the school motorbike to take her to
the hospital, where she was examined, pronounced well, and put to bed.
Three days later, she was diagnosed as suffering from anxiety, an under-
standable condition to anyone who knew about the persecution of the
Shan by the Burmese military regime, and about the ever-present threat
of rape Shan women faced.

When May was released from the hospital and returned to school,
there was an uncertain smile on her face. She looked as though she were
walking through a dream, as though nothing seemed real. I saw her descending the stairs from the living room into the garage-classroom, alone
among a group of girls. I met her at the bottom of the stairs, put my arms
around her, and she melted into me, like the child she was. All save three
of the students shunned her, as though anxiety were contagious. Two girls
and two men befriended May, and with their help she reentered classroom activities.

We were reading *Romeo and Juliet,* and the students were eager to practice reading the love scenes together. Because there were only seven female students and eighteen males, the men vied for opportunities to read
with the girls instead of with each other. Shang Phun read with May.
She beamed with happiness, reading Juliet's part aloud as though she had
never hesitated to speak. During the rest of the term, May occasionally
raised a tentative hand and volunteered answers.

At the farewell party the school arranged for me, the students lined up
for a group photo. Most men wore shirts with Mandarin collars and handmade loops that encircled fabric buttons. Just six of the seven women, all
of them wearing long skirts, were at the photo shoot. May was missing.
Her friend Ying said May did not have a long skirt, and they could not
convince her to be in the photo.

* * *

If the lack of a long skirt had been traumatic for May, it was short-lived.

She sent me e-mail messages in Minnesota. Once she attached a love story she had written about a boy and a girl who picnicked at a waterfall where the boy proclaimed his love. Another time she attached a story about her previous school, a one-room building that had housed eighteen students near the Thai-Burma border until it had to be closed because of cross-border fighting between the Shan who had escaped to Thailand and the Burmese military. It was then that I realized the source of her anxiety: She had been forced out of school by bullets.

I was impressed by May's writing ability, by her initiative, and by the loving messages addressed to "Dear My Teacher" and signed, "Your lovely student Nang May."

* * *

January 2003: I called the school immediately after I returned to Chiang Mai and told them I was at the Top North Guest House. Soon afterward Nang May knocked at my door. As before, she wore loose slacks and a gray jacket. The same uncertain smile flickered on her mouth as had been there when she returned from the hospital. Once again she had difficulty speaking. In time, she managed to say she wanted to show me something at Chiang Mai University.

May and I walked to the main street and found a *songthaew* taxi, one of the red pickups outfitted with benches. We drove on, and the snarls of vehicles thinned as we drove out of the city center onto a wide, blacktopped highway leading to the university. May did not speak during the ride. I followed her lead when she pressed an overhead button that triggered a buzzer in the pickup cab, and we jumped out of the *songthaew* near the university.

She stopped on the pathway leading to the campus buildings and pointed to a brown, domelike structure. Now she could speak: "There, Teacher. That's it!" She was pointing at a mud home with unscreened openings for doors and windows, standing like a sculpture on the campus lawn. I had read about the house in *The Bangkok Post,* in an article about housing for the poor. Mud and straw were the only ingredients necessary, the article said. It could be built for four hundred U.S. dollars.

Inside the structure, May grew ever more vocal. "I love this house, Teacher. I dreamt about it one night. She caressed the mud surfaces, marveled at the little kitchen that had built-in fireplaces and woodbins. "Sometime I want to have a home like this for my mother," she said. Her enthusiasm brought tears to my eyes. The mud house was aesthetically pleasing, and to May it was luxurious.

The thrill of seeing her dream house made it easier for May to speak English, and she chattered enthusiastically as she led me into the campus art department where we looked at paintings. Art was her love, she said, but she had no time for it.

After May had finished the six-month computer and English course where I met her, she got an internship with a nongovernmental organization (NGO) in Chiang Mai. Her family had lived on the Thai side of the Thai-Burma border a long time; she had a hill tribe identity card and could legitimately hold a job in Thailand. At the NGO she translated Shan and Burmese radio broadcasts into English.

May turned sober and worried-looking when she told me about her job. "It is very difficult for me, Teacher. Sometimes I must work very long to get the words right. Seven days a week, Teacher." But what a victory over herself, over her shyness and anxiety, I thought. "You should be proud of yourself, May," I said. "That sounds like a very difficult job."

She continued to look worried, not proud, until I said, "I couldn't do it, May. I'm proud of you." A small smile crossed her face, but thinking about the job had put her into worry mode, and she was silent during most of the ride back to the guesthouse.

As we neared the Top North, she seemed to recollect how much fun she had had. She straightened her back and said, "For me this is a special day, Teacher. *Really* special. I never forget." I was touched and thought about my granddaughters who are near May's age but have a hard time fitting me into their social schedules. May would be my granddaughter until I left Chiang Mai. I invited her to accompany me to Chinatown the following weekend.

* * *

May called the guesthouse Saturday morning. "We will go to Chinatown, Teacher?" Within twenty minutes she was knocking at my door.

We found a *songthaew*, and May gave the driver instructions. The *songthaew* followed Loi Kroh Road, parallel to one-way Tha Phae Road that led to the heart of the city, passing souvenir shops and tourist restaurants packed with sun-reddened travelers, and delivered us to the arched entrance of the Chinese enclave.

The smell of incense and fried noodles permeated the air of the narrow, winding streets, as we walked from shop to shop, looking at silk and cotton fabrics, stopping to finger hand-dyed Thai silk scarves that sparkled like jewels in shades of pink, red, purple, and orange; blues that ranged from blue-green teals and aquas to navy blue with magenta borders; golds, greens, and iridescent browns. May, dressed plainly in her loose dark blue slacks and gray jacket, caressed the scarves, marveling at their beauty.

Nestled among the shops was a red and gold Buddhist temple. "Let's go in, Teacher," May said. We slipped off our shoes at the doorway, adding them to the heap of rubber thongs piled there, and walked barefooted to the altar. There we knelt before a gold statue of the Buddha. I copied May, folded my hands prayerfully below my chin, and bowed my head. In a few minutes, she popped up and said, "Let's get our fortune, Teacher."

On a table near the altar, May found a cylindrical wooden container with a small slot at one end and shook it until a thin, numbered bamboo stick fell out. She handed the container to me, and I, too, managed to dislodge a stick. May took both sticks to a chest placed against the south wall of the temple, thumbed through pieces of paper inscribed in Thai, found the numbers that corresponded to our respective sticks, and hurried back to me. Both of our fortunes were very good, she said, clapping her hands. "Let's do it again, Teacher." The second try was even better. "Ooo," she said. "Is so good, Teacher. You will be invited to a very important tea party with many people. Is very good for me, too."

I like to think I am not superstitious, do not believe in fortune telling, but when someone or something predicts good luck for me, I believe it. If a paper or a person predicts bad fortune, I tend to forget it.

Buoyed by the paper predictions, we took a *songthaew* to an open-air restaurant near Tha Phae gate and the old city. May was unsure of herself in the restaurant, until I asked her what we should eat, when she took obvious pride in suggesting Pad Thai and telling the waitress to bring us two orders of the popular noodle dish prepared with small chunks of tofu, scallions, crushed peanuts, and lime juice. We sat side-by-side, looking across Tha Phae Road. We saw people walking into the alley where a blind masseuse had pummeled and twisted my limbs and back so hard I had yelled with pain, evoking only the sweet-voiced question, "Do you like?" and I was glad I was eating instead of lying on a massage bed.

We slurped our noodles and watched big, pink tourists lumber clumsily along the streets, sidestepping occasionally to avoid crushing the small, delicate Thais who earned meager wages serving them in restaurants and hotels and in legitimate and not-so-legitimate massage parlors. When we finished our noodles, May hailed a *songthaew*.

She accompanied me to my hotel, exclaiming all the way about what a wonderful day it had been. "Special, Teacher. Really special," she said. She had not lapsed into sadness during the entire day. I kissed her on the cheek when we parted.

I would see May once more that year, at a farewell party the school gave for me in March when the air was heavy and hot. We had a dinner of rice, meat soup, and vegetables, served with hot, black Shan tea, and I remembered the tea party prediction at the temple, concluding that the good luck prophecy had come true. Young people with numerous problems, little money, low-paying jobs, and problems with authorities in Burma and in Thailand, had used scant resources to have a tea party for me.

Sitting at my side, May held her hand to her cheek and said, "Teacher, when you kiss me on the cheek that day, it is so special." Before leaving the party, I kissed her cheek a last time.

* * *

In Minneapolis, I have gotten several e-mail messages from May. In one of them she wrote about going to the zoo with other students and said she was "very tired and very happy." Remembering the fearful fifteen-year-old girl who had suffered from anxiety, I was delighted to read about the zoo trip:

> *I'd love to have you go with us so much. At the time I miss you so much. I love gibbons so much. Love to listen to their scream that is a very nice sound. I also scream with them and they look at me. The last thing I want to say with you . . . wherever you are whatever you do, I always miss you. I think you miss us so much now and thinking about us.*

She was right.

THE EDUCATION OF YING TZARM

April 2003

Injustice in the end produces independence. —Voltaire

At fourteen, Ying Tzarm (Charm) was bigger than most of the women, over five feet tall and well rounded. The young men stumbled over each other trying to get a seat next to Ying at the wooden tables that served as desks. They liked her looks and they liked her intelligence, but Ying was an assertive young woman. She told boys not to bother her when she was busy, corrected them if they made mistakes during class.

In the beginning, when the students' names were a confused jumble in my mind, I identified them by appearance and mannerisms. Among that register in my head, Ying Tzarm stood out for her serious manner. I never would have guessed she was the youngest student—until she told me.

Ying created extra homework for herself. Every day after class she looked up new words in the dictionary and wrote them in her vocabulary notebook, where she noted the part of speech and the definition and wrote a sentence using the word. When I asked her where she had learned her study habits, she said her parents had been teachers in Shan State. They had immigrated to Thailand because in Burma they could not make enough money to feed their family.

Burmese schools were seized by the military in 1965, three years after the military takeover. Foreigners were asked to leave the country, and the missionary schools went with them. The literacy rate had been almost eighty percent before the dictatorship took power. In 1987, Burma appealed to the United Nations for "least developed country" status and reported a literacy rate of less than nineteen percent. It was no wonder the Shan students considered learning a privilege.

* * *

When I returned to Thailand in 2003, Ying Tzarm was living in Chiang Mai and was one of the first students to find her way to the Top North

Guesthouse where I stayed. She wanted me to meet her parents, she said, and led me to a *songthaew.*

We joined throngs of piston-pounding pickups and roaring motorbikes that circled past the southern city wall and noodle shops, past shops that sold real and imitation silk and cotton handbags and clothing to tourists, past the store where opium was weighed, past the outdoor market where eels writhed in buckets that held just enough water to keep them alive until dinnertime, to the southern edge of the city, where the streets were lined with office and apartment buildings. Ying Tzarm said, "Here, Teacher." She pushed the button that signaled the *songthaew* driver to stop and we jumped down.

"Back there," said Ying Tzarm, pointing to a large building that loomed above and behind the others. "Now you will see how refugees live."

"Did you tell your parents we were coming?" I asked. She had not— they had no phone. "It will be all right," she said.

Large glass doors opened into a huge marble-floored foyer. We crossed the foyer to the back of the building. A small woman, shorter than my five feet, who wore a gold-colored ethnic Shan jacket with a mandarin collar, stood washing dishes in a latticework open-air cubbyhole. It was a tiny space, large enough for the sink and a few dishes sitting on a small table. Several dirty rags lay on the wet floor. The surprised woman turned and smiled at Ying. The smile grew strained when she saw me. "My mother," said Ying.

Drying her hands on a white cloth, the woman walked toward us, staring in my direction. Ying spoke to her in Shan. She ushered us around the corner and into a concrete-block room about twelve feet wide by fourteen feet long. Near the ceiling, it looked as though the drying concrete blocks had been punched into flower designs with a giant cookie cutter. The openings provided ventilation for the windowless room. At the end of the room nearest the door, boards formed a platform bed on which lay a few tangled blankets. An overhead wire held curtains that could be pulled shut for a semblance of privacy.

At the opposite end of the room, a young man lay stretched out on a cot, his eyes glued to a television on a wall shelf. He did not rise from the couch, did not glance in our direction, said nothing. Ying's brother, I thought, but so antisocial, so different from his sister.

Ying's mother led us to a plank table in the middle of the room, where a man sat watching us. She motioned for us to sit, asked Ying in Shan if I wanted coffee or tea. When I declined both, she disappeared, leaving us with the man, who was unmistakably Ying's father. He had the same Cupid's bow mouth and oval face as his daughter. Ying told him in Shan that I was her teacher. In English, he said, "Hello, Teacher." Then, in Shan, he told Ying to tell me that he could understand some English, but only poor English, the kind they speak in Burma. "If someone speaks good English," she said, "he cannot understand." Ying became our interpreter.

He said he had been a primary school headmaster in Shan State and his wife had taught kindergarten. Their combined salaries had been the equivalent of ten U.S. dollars per month. Recently, inflation and the cost of living had soared. Ten U.S. dollars per month was not enough to buy rice for the family.

Recent books about Burma, *Living Silence,* by Christine Fink, and *From the Land of Green Ghosts,* by Pascal Khoo Thwe, have talked about the corruption of Burmese school teachers, about how in the classroom they would not teach children everything they needed to know so they could get extra money from students for after-school tutoring, a practice brought about by low salaries and the high cost of living. Ying Tzarm's parents had chosen to escape to Thailand rather than ask their students for money. In Chiang Mai, he and his wife worked as janitors. This concrete block room attached to the rear of the building they cleaned was living space furnished by the apartment owners.

The father smiled while he told his story, smiled at the expressions on my face as Ying Tzarm retold it in English. I wondered at his seeming acceptance of their fate, at his good humor about their misfortune; then I remembered Pascal Khoo Thwe's comment in his book, *From the Land of Green Ghosts.* He said the Asian smile does not necessarily express goodwill but is a mask to cover embarrassment and humiliation.

Ying Tzarm's mother returned from a nearby store with three containers of juice and a plastic roll of Ritz crackers. She put them in front of us. "She got juice for you, Teacher," said Ying. I said something about its not being necessary, and Ying said, "It is our custom, Teacher. Drink."

While Ying and I ate Ritz crackers and drank juice, her parents stared at us, and the boy on the couch stared at colorful scenes flickering across the television screen, accompanied by fake laughter and by dialogue in the Thai language. Ying's mother said little.

I was uncomfortable in this humble room, troubled by the unspeaking boy on the bed, troubled because I wanted to tell Ying Tzarm's parents that I knew they were intelligent, honorable people and that it was not fair for them to spend their lives cleaning an apartment building. Afraid I might offend them, I said little. The conversation consisted mostly of Ying's ever-smiling father telling her what to ask and what to tell me.

Had I been to Burma? *Yes, but just across the border to renew my visa.* Did teachers get a lot of money in America? *A lot more than in Burma.* How long would I stay in Thailand? *Two more months.*

When we finished our juice, I told Ying I had to leave. Her parents walked across the marble foyer with us and stood looking after us as Ying flagged down a *songthaew* for my return trip. She would stay behind; she lived with her mother's sister and had to take a different *songthaew* to get there.

Walking toward the street to flag a *songthaew*, I asked Ying if the boy on the bed was her brother. "No, Teacher," she said. "He is another worker in the building." In Minnesota, I had gotten several e-mail messages from Ying saying she had to live with her aunt, that she loved her but worried because all she could do to repay her generosity was a little housework, and I had wondered why she did not live with her parents. Now I knew. Modesty would not allow her to share housing with a strange young man.

As the *songthaew* carried me down Tha Phae Road toward the Old City, I reflected on Ying's situation. She had not been able to get further training after finishing the six-month computer and English training at the school where we met. "Everyone says I am too young, Teacher," she said.

* * *

I remembered my feeling of being too young when I graduated from high school at sixteen. I had another handicap, too, one Ying did not have. I was immature; saw no future for myself but office work, the only thing high school had readied me for, and then marriage. My parents were too poor and I was too ill-prepared to even consider college.

What I foresaw for myself came to pass.

After high school and a month or two working at my Cousin Clarence's resort on Big Pine Lake, I got a job as a secretary to Mr. Buerkle, the benevolent New York Mills banker, who treated me more like a daughter than an employee, never criticizing my work, accepting with a smile whatever I produced.

Wanting to see more of the world than New York Mills, I left that job before a year had passed and moved to Moose Lake, where my mother's sister, Violet, lived. There I worked at the State Hospital for the Insane, smiling sweetly at visitors while playing away my time at the reception desk where I was supposed to be recording information in inmate's files, such as the dates and times of the shock treatments that sent them wandering dazedly through the halls.

During the evening shift, after patients were put to bed and most employees went home, there was only a guard to keep me company. I ignored the files and immersed myself in books. My deception was soon discovered, and a supervisor chastised me with a well deserved "shape up or leave" sort of speech.

It took me a long time to grow up—a college student I met while working at the hospital helped the process. A blonde of Norwegian descent, who looked a bit like popular movie star Van Johnson, he was studying Psychology at the University of Minnesota in nearby Duluth. One of his class assignments was to observe patients at the mental hospital. He and a friend arrived early to attend the patients' Saturday night dance: real college boys attending the dance. I thought they were big stuff and so did they.

They stood at the reception desk, the blond Norwegian and his dark-haired friend. The Norwegian—actually he was part Irish on his mother's side, but he ignored that part of his heritage—looked me over, and, turning to his friend, said, "I think we should put her on the stage." On the stage! I was impressed.

The following week one of the nurses said her boyfriend knew someone who wanted us to double date on my next night off. Only when they arrived did I realize my date was the Norwegian who wanted to put me on the stage. I soon left the state hospital and moved to Duluth, where the Norwegian lived, and where I got at job as a secretary in the Chun King processing plant. I liked my female boss, who was both demanding and appreciative, and I produced better work than I had at the mental hospital, but it did not last long.

The Norwegian was bursting with testosterone, and while my mind might have resisted my body did not. I was eighteen years old when we committed to marry. The thought was frightening. But there was something I really liked about the Norwegian, his sense of adventure: he liked to swim and camp and sail, and he wanted to travel. Too timid and inexperienced to create my own adventures, I hoped to piggyback on his. Not much of a foundation for marriage. Actually, nothing could have saved that marriage—we had nothing in common apart from a love of adventure.

My primary interest was books, but when I brought up a book or an author in company, the Norwegian would turn to me and say, "No one wants to talk about books." He was a controller, a pseudo-psychological term that was bandied about those days and that fit him perfectly. He successfully controlled me for a few years before I started living my life in my head, the way I had as a child on the farm.

It was toward the end of our marriage that I finally started college. I was thirty-eight years old and working part-time, compiling figures for real estate closings at a mortgage bank. Our two sons were in school, and I got home from work by the time they got home. The Norwegian gave permission for me to attend Osseo Community College part time. That was the beginning of many years of study. It was also the beginning of the end of our marriage.

Aware of my growing disenchantment with the marriage, both my husband's sister and mother warned him that once I finished college I would leave. They were wrong; that was not my plan. The fascination and diversion of learning were the only things that might have kept me with him—especially if he had blessed my interests, rather than trying to impose his. I wanted to pursue a degree in English, but when I got an "A" in astronomy, he thought I should become an astronomer, an "A" in geology meant I should become a geologist, and so it went, except for English. He had nothing but disparagement for those who pursued English degrees, nothing but derision for teachers.

When he started talking about moving to the country, where I would have no friends to buffer his presence, no classes to escape into, I could not endure the thought. That was what triggered the six-year divorce process that ensued, a process that included appeals to the Supreme Court on the part of the Norwegian and that physically and emotionally exhausted me. It tires me to think of it now as the *songthaew* carries me back to my room.

I relegate the marriage and divorce to the past and inhale the scents of incense and jasmine wreaths and sewage as I watch the city pass: the opium shop, the golden temples, the orange-robed monks.

* * *

That winter of 2003, I taught English to Shan refugees in a monastery garage. Ying joined the class, and I saw her every week. She paid fewer social calls at my hotel after that, but toward the end of February she called me. "Maybe I can get training, Teacher," she said. "There is a new school for journalism. How old I am is not important. Will you write letter for me?" Of course I would. It would be easy to praise Ying Tzarm.

By March, Chiang Mai temperatures soared to over one hundred degrees Fahrenheit. The monastery garage sizzled under the sun, and teaching became a chore. I returned to Minneapolis. Shortly afterward, I got a phone call from a woman who identified herself as an instructor at the Chiang Mai Journalism School. She was calling to get a reference for Ying Tzarm, she said, and asked me to tell her more about the girl.

I started repeating what I had said in the recommendation letter: Ying was one of the best students in the English class I had taught; she had created extra homework for herself by selecting English words from the dictionary and writing sentences using each word. I told her Ying was prompt and dependable. She interrupted. "I'll get right to the point," she said. "She is one of the best candidates we've interviewed, but does she have a bit of an attitude?"

I had to think about what she meant. From her tone of voice, I guessed "an attitude" meant a bad attitude. "No!" I said. "She is the last person I would say has an attitude. She was always helping other students and me. Everyone loved her."

"Well," she said, "when I interviewed her, she sat there tapping her foot like she didn't care if she got the training or not. I thought she was either nervous or she had an attitude."

"Nervous," I said. "She had to be nervous. She *wants* the training."

On April 9, I got an e-mail message from Ying Tzarm. In capital letters and bold print, she wrote: **"I AM ACCEPTED FOR THE JOURNALISM SCHOOL."**

SAI SAI MASTERS DISCIPLINE AND PERSEVERANCE

As a child our dreams got scattered all about and all our future prospects got scattered to so many places, and we spend our lives trying to find the little pieces that make up our lives and make up the dreams that we had as a child that got blown away in the windstorm. —Terence Howard

In 2002, eighteen-year-old Sai Sai was beset by emotions that colored his dreams by night and set his legs tapping by day. He was shy and nervous, excited by girls and future possibilities, but so disturbed by a difficult past and uncertain present that he got headaches and insomnia, neither of which affected his performance in the School for Shan in northern Thailand. He got good grades with little study, as he had in schools he attended in Shan State, Burma.

The first time I took Sai Sai's photo, he turned his head and giggled; in subsequent group photos, he was one of the most serious students.

Sai Sai wrote a lot, filling his journals with interesting and imaginative stories, one of which was triggered by a class discussion of self-discipline and perseverance, qualities I had suggested as two of the most important in attaining success. After class, while most students were dutifully writing one or two pages in their weekly journals, Sai Sai wrote a seven-page essay that began, "Discipline and perseverance are the most important in the world." By the time I got to the second page, I thought he had missed part of the explanation. I had talked about the importance of *self*-discipline, the quality that makes us start and complete projects when no one is watching or telling us what to do. Sai Sai wrote: "My parents taught me to sit on discipline and perseverance."

Then he wrote about other-induced discipline, leading to self-discipline, and the essay became a love story. "I loved one girl whose name is Phang . . .I told her 'Phang, I love you very much, more than I can say. I think you know it. Can you answer me?' Phang replied, 'If you really love me you should try hard. If you would like to get my answer and stay together can you obey discipline and perseverance?'" And he wrote about his reaction, "I think at that moment I fell into hell. Discipline and perseverance, I don't want to hear it again. And I said, 'If I love you and you love me, we can stay together. Love can make anything in the world.' She said, 'No, Sai Sai, listen to me. You must try hard. If you don't try hard when we have children we will be in trouble. If you really love me and want to stay together, please try hard. Let's go, I don't have much time.'"

He went back home, Sai Sai wrote, and told his mother he was going to get a job. "I want to become a man who has a job and can follow discipline and perseverance." After working five years, he wrote, "I have much experience and I understand how discipline and perseverance are important. And I also have got an answer from Phang that she loves me."

Sai Sai concluded his essay by writing, "Phang is very beautiful. She said, 'Sai Sai do you know, it is the result of you obey discipline and perseverance.' Yes, now I know discipline and perseverance are important. I will remember it forever."

I was touched and amused by Sai Sai's essay, impressed by his creative writing ability. He was creative in other ways, too.

One day I divided the students into two groups to play a listening game on the order of Simon Says. The garage where we studied English was full of tables and chairs, so we crossed the heat-reflecting asphalt driveway to an open-air storage shed across the way. Earlier in the year we had used the shed as a second classroom but had abandoned it to the spring heat, which the students seemed oblivious to as they lined up in rows on the concrete floor. Wet with perspiration, I stood between the two rows and read a list of activities I had prepared earlier. No army commander could have had the troops more complete attention as each group tried to comprehend and complete instructions before the other group.

Sai Sai was one of the first to understand and instruct the rest of his group how to proceed. When I asked them to line up according to height, Sai Sai pulled and pushed students into place, then put himself at the tall end of the row. When lining up according to age, Sai Sai talked with others and placed them where they belonged, taking his place with the younger students. And when I asked them to shake hands with as many classmates as possible within a set time, Sai Sai crossed his arms and shook hands with students on either side of him; then he walked around with crossed arms, shaking hands with everyone. Others followed suit and the group became a circle where everyone shook hands with two people. Because the students took every game seriously, at the end I said the two groups had tied, but Sai Sai had clearly outshone most students when it came to understanding and performance.

He understood how to get women's attention, too. While most young men tried to win a woman's favor with compliments, Sai Sai would shyly stand next to the woman, saying nothing but with a longing look on his face. And at the inception of class sessions he rushed to sit next to Ying, the most popular girl in the class, wangling his way into whatever group she happened to be in for listening games. His shyness was an asset: Girls were not threatened by him. But, although he was successful romantically and academically, he suffered from headaches and bad dreams.

In a story he titled *Incubus or Bad Dream*, he wrote about being three years old and holding his father's hand as they ran away from a burning house and the Burmese military. His mother ran in the other direction with Sai Sai's baby brother strapped to her back. After class, I asked him if the story was true. He nodded his head. "Is true, Teacher."

He said they had lived in a village near Kengtung. Afterwards, his father had taken him to his grandparents in another village. They raised him. He never saw either of his parents again, but every month his mother had sent money for Sai Sai's education. After a long pause, he said, "She is here, Teacher." When I asked him where, he said she was in Thailand but he did not know where. He looked at the floor and shifted uneasily. "I want to find her, Teacher, but my grandparents don't know where she is."

I thought about the pain of losing your mother at the age of three, then trying to track her down in a foreign country fifteen years later, about the loneliness and loss Sai Sai lived with. And I thought about being a mother and about what a joy it would be to find a son like Sai Sai. "She would be very proud of you," I said.

On a day when the two of us retreated to the school verandah to catch the evening breeze, Sai Sai said that before he left Burma for Thailand he found out his father had died after leaving him with his grandparents. His father was dead; his mother had disappeared. And Sai Sai could not sleep at night.

Sai Sai asked me to correct his "Bad Dream" story. After doing so, I told him he should rewrite it and send it to me in Minneapolis. In April 2002, I received an e-mail from Sai Sai. The school term was over and he was worried: "We have no relatives, place, work and money," he wrote. "It is terrible for me. I have some headache for it."

A few days later he sent me his revised story attached to an e-mail message marked "urgent." He had added several pages to the story, asking those who read it to help the Shan, but the plea was out of context and ruined the artistic effect. He also asked me to correct the story and send it back to him right away. Correcting Sai Sai's grammar and syntax was easy. Not overcorrecting was the challenge.

I wanted it to remain his story, to retain the flavor of a beginning English speaker. It began: "There are many mountains and many plants. Among them a beautiful house issuing. I live there, my name is Sai Sai." Not perfect English, but interesting. I did nothing with that language, correcting only a few later instances where the syntax was tangled to the point of difficult reading.

In the story, Sai Sai said that when his father had brought him to his grandparents he had left a letter for Sai Sai saying, "I am a Burmese soldier. When you know that, you will hate me. But son you are my son and your mother is my wife. I love your family too much. This word comes from my heart. I love you so I separate from you. If I stay with you, your family will get many troubles."

It must have been difficult for Sai Sai to live among Shan students, knowing he was part Burmese. Shan armies fight against Burmese occupation. In return, Shan rice fields are seized, their houses burned, their women raped, and they are sent to relocation camps, where small houses are clustered together on land too barren to afford hiding places for warrior sons and fathers.

When I sent the corrected story back, Sai Sai wrote to thank me, saying he had never told the story to anyone but me, and adding, "I shall love you and respect you until the end of my life."

A few days later I got an e-mail message from the German woman who had taught English at the Shan School before I did and had returned to Germany a month after I arrived. She said she had gotten a wonderful story from Sai Sai and had corrected the English for him. I wrote back asking her to send it to me and telling her I, too, had corrected a story for Sai Sai.

She sent me the same story, now highly revised—an American might have written it. Sai Sai's original opening lines, "There are many mountains and many plants. Among them a beautiful house issuing," had been changed to read, "I see a beautiful house among lush green plants." The German teacher had over-corrected the piece.

I was angry and my ego was bruised. I had been busy with writing and deadlines of my own when the story arrived and had set everything aside in response to Sai Sai's feeling of urgency.

I wrote telling him he should have let me know he was sending his story to the other teacher, too. That was enough for sensitive Sai Sai to feel criticized. For a while his e-mail messages were brief. He wrote once to say he had been accepted for further training with an environmental organization, and he wrote several times to say Thai police were searching out illegal immigrants and deporting them. He was worried and could not sleep.

When I returned to Thailand and the school for Shan State refugees in December, 2002, the school director said Sai Sai had left his training because he was frightened. He had returned to live at school for a while and later moved in with former classmates who lived and slept in the office where they worked.

That winter Sai Sai joined the English class I taught at a monastery. He sat next to Ying at the rough table nearest the blackboard, but he was no longer as conscientious as he had been in the School for Shan. He was preoccupied, forgetting to do his homework, forgetting what we had studied from week to week. He was still quick to volunteer when I asked students to take over a class or project. Sai Sai had taught in Shan Sate when he was fifteen years old. He was comfortable and skilled in front of the class.

Near the end of the course, students asked for a final exam. I gave them one to complete at home. Sai Sai forgot to turn his in. What he brought to class that day was a request for a recommendation letter. He was applying for a journalism internship. I recommended Sai Sai to the journalism school based on how well he had performed at the School for Shan and on his excellent writing ability. They chose Ying, for whom I had also written a recommendation letter. I had struggled to keep the letters fair, extolling the best qualities of both Sai Sai and Ying, and when a Journalism School administrator called me in Minneapolis for a verbal recommendation for Ying Tzarm, I asked her if they might also accept Sai Sai. She remembered him and said they might accept him later, but I suspected what had swayed her in favor of Ying was my emphasis on her stability and consistency, qualities I had not mentioned in the recommendation for Sai Sai.

* * *

Several months after I left Thailand, I got an e-mail message from Sai Sai's German English teacher. She said he had asked her for a recommendation letter to another environmental organization. Soon afterward I got a message from Sai Sai saying he had been accepted.

In August 2003, Sai Sai wrote about his training, and I realized he was no longer stinging from my admonition that he should not have had both teachers correcting his writing without telling us what he was doing but that, more importantly, he had mastered self-discipline and perseverance:

Dear Teacher,

Now I am at an environmental school. I am learning a lot here . . . In my opinion now I can give training to the others. I have self-confidence more than before. I can give Environmental Training, Human Rights Training, and Non Violence Training . . . because here I have to learn many subjects . . . I am very happy because after this school, I can help a lot of people with my knowledge. I have plan to go back to Shan State. I will give some workshop to my friends. I am very happy with my dream. Thank you for helping me and courage me forever. I love you and miss you.

Bye bye, your love Sai Sai

SHANG PHUN, GAO, AND THE SWEAT SHOP

Winter 2003

A lasting solution, the possibility to begin a new life, is the only dignified solution for the refugee himself. —Poul Hartling, UN High Commissioner for Refugees, 1978-1985

I had gotten an e-mail from Shang Phun in the summer of 2002, thanking me for twenty dollars I had sent him to get an aching tooth fixed. He said that after having the dental work, he bought a volleyball for the school with the remaining money. And he told me not to worry. They were fine, he said. They were fine. This among many messages from other students telling me how frightened they were, how bleak their prospects.

I spent nine months in Minnesota that year, wondering how best to help the students. Maybe I was reverting to old ways, making life easy for myself, for I decided finally that there was little I could do. Still, I wanted to follow up with Shang Phun. He had told me about his past and about how he had applied for refugee status from the United Nations High Commission for Refugees and was turned down. Maybe I could help him reapply.

When I returned to Bangkok in December 2003, I rented a room in the Atlanta Hotel in the Sukumvit area, common to call girls and expensive high-rise apartment buildings, and with a few low-priced hotels for budget-conscious travelers like me. In that city of six million people, it took three weeks and multiple phone calls to locate Shang Phun. When I did, he said, "I will come to you, Teacher."

Sukumvit Soi 2, dead-ends at the Calvary Baptist Church. The Atlanta Hotel is next to it. On the morning Shang Phun was to visit, I stood in the street, my back to the church, waiting for him. When I saw him walking toward me, my insides turned mushy with relief. I had been worried about connecting with him in this huge city.

He looked different. Smaller. When he was directly in front of me, he bowed his head slightly, and clasped his hands prayerfully below his chin.

I wrapped my arms around his narrow back. He was so small. At 5'1"
and 110 pounds, I am about the same size as most Thai women. Twenty-
six-year-old Shang Phun felt like a child in my arms. In gray slacks and a
blue plaid shirt that hung outside his trousers, he looked look like a boy
wearing clothes he hadn't grown into.

"Hello, Teacher," he said. "I am very happy to see you." He put his
small hand in mine and we went into the Atlanta Hotel, where a sign next
to the front door proclaimed "No Sex Tourists Allowed." The hotel clerk
looked at us suspiciously. Bangkok, and especially the Sukumvit area, is
notorious for sex tourism. I had seen a number of old men tottering down
the street holding hands with young Thai beauties, and although I had
seen few women flaunting their young men, I knew that, too, existed.
The clerk might be wondering if Shang Phun and I fit the "sex tourist"
equation. Looking her in the eye, I said, "My student."

* * *

Shang Phun had been an outstanding student in the school for Shan
State refugees, not for his academic skills, which were average, but for his
kindness, compassion, and generosity, and for his loyalty to his country
people. In the classroom he was spontaneous, volunteering answers to
questions, being the first to deliver a speech, becoming deeply involved in
language games. He gleamed with cleanliness. When I asked each of the
students to choose one adjective to describe him or her self, Shang Phun
said, "I am a tidy boy."

Like most of the students, Shang Phun was Buddhist and he embodied
the belief that teachers deserved almost as much respect as the Buddha
and one's parents. He always added a respectful "Teacher" at the end of
his sentences, and he made sure I always had something to drink when
we talked.

One day, as I sat on the school floor, my back against the wall, listening
to a song on the tape recorder and writing down the English words for
the students, Shang Phun brought me a small cup of hot, sweet coffee and
squatted at my side. He was wearing camouflage army pants and told me
he had been a medic, working with the Shan State Army as they waged
jungle warfare against the Burmese military regime. His eyes fixed on a
spot above my head and he said, "Sometimes we had to fight, Teacher." I
remembered how a sad look would come over his face whenever there was
a lull in classroom activities and thought it might be the firsthand knowledge of misery that made him more compassionate than most.

In a "What if?" game, the students talked about what they would do if they won the lottery. "Buy a motorbike," "Buy a stereo," "Travel," the voices called. Shang Phun said if he won the lottery he would "help marginalized people," and when I asked who that was, he said it was women who had been forced into prostitution by parents who could not afford to feed their children.

On an evening that I stayed late at school, Shang Phun told me about how he had trekked through the jungle for three months, backpacking medicine and food to Shan who were hiding from the military. "Until my money ran out, Teacher," he said. He could never return to Burma, he said, because he might be beaten, tortured, or imprisoned.

* * *

In the Atlanta Hotel dining room, I asked Shang Phun if he wanted a fruit shake. "I never had one, Teacher," he said. The Shan students had eaten rice three meals a day. It was filling, and it was cheap. I ordered two mixed fruit shakes, and, sitting at the last table in the restaurant, next to the kitchen, Shang Phun and I talked over the buzz of the blender.

He was back at his job in the garment factory, he said, the job he had left to attend the English language school in Chiang Mai Province. He had told me something about the job when he was my student, told me about the long hours and low pay, but I had little memory of the details.

A waitress wearing a white blouse and long black skirt, her head bowed demurely downward, brought us tall glasses filled with fruit shakes frothy with cantaloupe-colored bubbles. Shang Phun sipped his drink tentatively, smiled, and said "Is good, Teacher," and I remembered my son Brent's first taste of Kentucky Fried Chicken, of how he had marveled about it, saying "It really *is* finger-licking good!" and I felt like a young mother again.

Shang Phun told me about his life during the eight months since I had seen him. He had had an opportunity to apply for medical training after he'd completed the six-month English and computer course, he said, but he had no hope of being accepted. He had worked for a Shan medic after returning from his three-month stint as a medical backpacker in the Burmese jungle; the medic would have to recommend him for further training, but they were not on good terms when Shang Phun left the clinic; he was afraid to ask him for help.

With several other students who did not get further training, Shang Phun stayed at the school for one month after the session ended. The students slept together on the floor, kept the building and the school grounds clean, and helped the cooks. But, he said, "I could not stay with no work, Teacher." He returned to Bangkok and to the garment factory where he and his sister, Gao, worked long hours to make money for their parents in Burma. "They are hungry," Shang Phun said.

"Do you want to see my work, Teacher?" he asked. "Meet my sister?" Of course I did. We sipped the last of our long, cool fruit drinks and walked out into the humid Bangkok heat. Shang Phun's long sleeved shirt was buttoned at the cuffs. "Aren't you hot?" I asked. He unbuttoned a cuff and rolled it back, displaying rows of blue letters and symbols inscribed on his brown arm. "Is for this, Teacher. If they see, they know I am Shan."

Then I remembered having seen the tattoos after school one day when he was freshly showered and shirtless in the evening air. It looked as though someone had written and drawn symbols all over his shoulders, chest, back and arms. He laughed about them, said, "They are for good luck, Teacher. Our people believe they will protect us." Seeing them, a knowledgeable person might have deduced that he was Shan. But maybe the tattoos had served their purpose. Maybe they had protected him.

Shang Phun had managed to elude the Burmese military which was forcing young men from his village into unpaid labor as porters, carrying heavy loads of supplies through Shan territory and serving as human mine detectors and body shields when they neared Shan military outposts. He had escaped to Thailand and had survived two terms in illegal immigrant detention centers so crowded he could not lie down to sleep at night and where sympathetic monks furnished the only food he had to eat.

Outside the hotel, Shang Phun put my handbag over his shoulder, shaded me with the umbrella I carried, and took my hand in his. We walked through the muggy heat toward a taxi stand, past a high-rise apartment building where a doorman controlled a gated entry to the garage, past families on the sidewalk, sitting on bamboo mats and eating rice, chicken, and mandarin oranges, past construction sites on either side of the street, where caterpillar tractors moved earth, and helmeted workers sweated under the tropical sun.

Beyond the workers, enticing food smells emanated from charcoal-burning grills set on high wooden tables, where Thais sat at round, umbrella-shaded tables, eating grilled fish balls and small, skewered pieces of meat, dipping the delectables in hot, green chili sauce and sweating profusely. Several taxis were parked next to the food stalls, but I did not want to take one.

Shang Phun had traveled two hours by bus to reach the Atlanta. It seemed almost decadent to take a taxi now. I asked him if we could take the sky train to his factory. "I don't think so, Teacher." I convinced him we should try and led him to the boarding station. Checking the map outside the turnstiles, we selected the most westerly destination, bought tokens, and entered the streamlined train that zoomed over the city quickly, coolly, and efficiently. It seemed like another world, or at least another country, in the antiseptically clean, air-conditioned train where people looked straight ahead or stared fixedly out the window at a city that looked so Westernized only the occasional gilded Buddhist temple and the small friend at my side reminded me where we were.

As we sat on benches that swayed with the train along its curving route, Shang Phun's head started to nod. He had awakened at 5 a.m. to finish some work before coming to my hotel. He sprang into wakefulness at our destination and led me to a concrete pedestrian overpass. Perspiring under the relentless sun, we crossed to the other side of the street, where he led me into a Big C department store, and we climbed several flights of stairs to a food bar. There he asked for two bowls of noodle soup and insisted on paying. After a few bites, he said, "I cannot eat much, Teacher."

He was slim when I met him. He had become much thinner, and he had a persistent cough. When I asked if he was well, he said, "Not so much, Teacher. I cannot eat." He had not seen a doctor, he said, because he worked twenty-eight days per month from 7 a.m. to 9 p.m. There was no time.

Leaving noodles still floating at the bottoms of our bowls, we left Big C and went to the bus stop, where we stood in clouds of carbon monoxide as the passing cars, buses and pickup trucks coughed their unmuffled way through the huge city. "Now we must take a taxi, Teacher. Only pickup trucks go to my factory, and you will get very dirty. I don't want that, Teacher." He hailed a taxi. Inside he said, "I have to tell you, Teacher. My factory, it's a little bit dirty."

Driving through progressively shabbier areas of the city, where dogs loitered lazily on sidewalks and bare-bottomed children peered from doorways, we neared an area of tall concrete buildings. More than two hours after we left the Atlanta Hotel, we arrived at the street where Shang Phun worked. We walked along the little-trafficked, potholed remnants of an asphalt-covered roadway, where pedestrians of all ages stopped to stare at me, or perhaps at the strange combination of an older woman, a pale-skinned *farang*, the uncomplimentary Thai word for "foreigner," and a young Asian man. Shang Phun took my hand and led me past dog droppings and discarded plastic wrappings to a tall building at the end of the street.

"A little bit dirty" was an understatement for the factory entrance. Mounds of discarded fabric spilled from huge plastic bags and tumbled into everyday debris: plastic wrappers, soft drink cans, and scraps of paper on a filthy floor. The unsightly mess affected me physically. I felt shaky with disgust, sadness, and fear. Fear for Shang Phun. We skirted the debris and mounted steep, narrow steps with a railing that might once have supported a leaning hand but was now loose and wobbly, ensuring a dangerous or fatal fall for the unwary.

The thick, hot air grew thicker and hotter as we climbed. On the second floor, Shang Phun led me to a cooking area, where the starchy smell of boiling rice filled the air, and a perspiring young woman stood over a hot plate laden with two steaming kettles. "She is the cook for our group, Teacher," he said.

Shang Phun opened the door to a five-by-ten-foot plywood-partitioned, windowless cubicle across from the cooking area. "My friends' room," he said, unrolling a quilt from the corner of the floor and motioning for me to sit down. I sat awkwardly cross-legged on the quilt, while Shang Phun fell into perfect yogic posture at my side. "Do you sleep here?" I asked. "No, my friends. Three of them."

The friends appeared and sat across from us, staring at me. Shang Phun said something to them in Burmese. Then he turned to me. "I tell them you are my teacher." It was several months before I realized Shang Phun had been showing me off.

I heard excited female voices coming from the steamy cooking area. Shang Phun peered through the doorway, then motioned to me to follow. Two women stood talking to the cook. Shang Phun pointed to one of them. "My sister," he said. "She is Gao."

Gao was a surprise. She was big for an Asian woman, much larger-boned than Shang Phun, and everything about her seemed round. Even her high cheekbones were rounded, whereas Shang Phun's cheekbones were angular and his face seemed squared off. Then I remembered that his mother had divorced one man and married another. They must have different fathers.

Gao stood staring at me, her hands pressed to her chest, as if in prayer. Shang Phun explained her silence: "She doesn't speak English, Teacher." But she knew a few words, and her sign language was excellent. "Come," she said, taking my hand. She led me up another steep flight of stairs, Shang Phun following behind. My despair deepened and the heat grew more intense with each upward step. And I understood why places like this were called sweatshops.

At the top of the stairs, we turned right and walked through mounds of thread, unassembled sweater backs, fronts, and sleeves, through rows of small sewing machines and monstrous manually operated knitting machines, quiet during lunch break. Shang Phun stopped at the knitting machines, pointed to one at the end of the row, and said, "This is mine, Teacher." It dwarfed him. Spindles stood ready to be loaded with thread; a huge shuttle waited for his small arms to set it in motion. We turned and followed Gao to a row of plywood cubicles along the wall. Taking a key from her pocket, Gao unlocked the padlocked door and led us in.

She had created a Buddhist shrine at the end of the room, eight or ten feet from the doorway. Fresh flowers lay wilting and burned candles stood under a picture of Buddha. At either end of the room stood matching plastic wardrobes. In the middle of the floor, a sleeping space about five by six feet wide had bedding rolled at the side. Gao unrolled a quilt, unlocked her flimsy wardrobe, got a pillow from it, and motioned for me to sit on the cushioned floor. Shang Phun sat at my side. He and Gao spoke together in Shan; then Shang Phun said, "I must go now, Teacher. Gao wants to take care of you. I will come back later." Gao took care of me by motioning for me to lie down, and massaging my arms and legs.

When I sat up, she sat on her haunches across from me. By way of conversation, she pulled two one hundred baht coins from her blouse pocket, the equivalent of $2.50 U.S. Holding out the coins, she spoke as though she could not hear herself, like a deaf person. "Mothah, fathah," she said. That was why she and Shang Phun subjected themselves to life in this factory: To make money for their parents. I felt like crying, pulled out what money I had with me and handed it to her. "Mother, father," I said. It was a mistake.

Gao looked offended. "No," she said. "**NO**," and pushed my moneyed hand against my chest. She pressed her own hand against her chest and in her deaf person's voice said, "Me. Me." In a burst of energy she dug through her wardrobe, surfacing with handfuls of Thai baht. She thrust the money toward me, saying "Me. Gao. Mothah, fathah." I was embarrassed, wished I had words to apologize. She counted the money. Six thousand baht. One hundred fifty dollars.

Shang Phun had said he made one hundred twenty-five dollars per month. Gao sat on a stool at a sewing machine with a circular track that guided the needles and sewed sweater seams shut. Her work was considered more skilled than Shang Phun's. She made a few dollars more each month. I felt both sad and gratified, as I posted Gao's name next to Shang Phun's on my mental honor roll of worthy people.

Gao forgave my presumption and started pulling canned fruit out of a cardboard box near the shrine: rambutan, something that looked like translucent white radishes, pineapple. With an expectant smile, she pointed to the fruit and to me. She wanted to give me the fruit. I started to shake my head "No," then realized I might be insulting her again. She filled a paper bag with canned fruit and set it beside me. Then she insisted I lie down again.

When I was stretched out with a pillow under my head, she pressed her hands to her cheek and closed her eyes, indicating I should sleep. She held up one finger, and then pointed to herself and to the door. I guessed she meant I should sleep for an hour while she worked. It seemed important to her, so I closed my eyes and heard the door shut. It was stifling hot in the windowless room, and I was wet to the skin with sweat. It seemed ridiculous to think about sleeping while metal slapped against metal as the hand-propelled knitting machines were set into motion, but my body had a different plan. It was 3:00 PM, five hours since we had left the Atlanta. Physical and emotional exhaustion conspired to lull me to sleep.

* * *

A hellish symphony of sound still emanated from the clanging and clanking knitting machines when I woke to see Shang Phun sitting cross-legged on the floor across from me. Beside him were two cup-like paper containers. "I made rice soup for you, Teacher." He had left work early to go to the grocery store across the street, where he bought the soup, added water, and heated it in the store's microwave oven.

As we sat on the floor spooning soup into our mouths, I realized Shang Phun was unaware of my dismay at his surroundings. This seemed normal to him. He had brought me here because he wanted me to meet Gao and because he was proud of his work, proud that he could operate a strength-taxing monster of a knitting machine.

We chatted a while, and I asked Shang Phun if I could see his room. "It isn't very nice, Teacher," he said, and realizing it embarrassed him, I did not persist. He said the room was a little bigger than the one in which we sat and that he shared it with four other men. "Some of them smell bad, Teacher," he said. "I don't think they use soap when they wash their clothes, and I don't know how to tell them." I felt sad remembering how in English class Shang Phun had described himself as a "tidy boy."

It was 7 p.m. and dusk had fallen when Shang Phun guided me back through the knitting area, where men and women grasped hand-operated shuttles and swayed their bodies to and fro, propelling thread from oversized spools into the bellies of the machines and onto myriad wires that held more thread and partly finished shirts and sweaters. The men were bare to the waist, sweat rolling down their faces and their chests.

Shang Phun stopped at the last machine next to the shaky staircase we would soon descend. A wild-eyed perspiring man was filling in for Shang Phun. He swung the shuttle back and forth, his body moving rhythmically from side to side, and I wondered how little Shang Phun could possibly handle the machine. It was at least a foot higher than he, and his arms would have had to be almost fully extended to reach the handles at either side of the shuttle.

Shang Phun held my hand and guided me down the steep stairs. On the second floor, Gao sat at a stool sorting knit shirt and sweater parts from a large heap into smaller heaps. She came running out to say good-bye, holding her tee-peed hands below her chin, and Shang Phun and I proceeded down two more flights of stairs to the street, where the hot Bangkok air seemed cool by contrast to the sweat shop.

We walked to the main road, and Shang Phun said he would get a taxi for me. I was ashamed to spend money on a taxi when Shang Phun had so little. "I will take a truck to the bus stop," I said. "No, Teacher. You might get lost. I will worry. I will pay taxi for you." A taxi to the Atlanta would only cost $5.00 U.S. dollars, but that was more than Shang Phun earned in one day. I convinced him that as his elder and his teacher he must allow me to pay. Underway in the taxi, I glanced back and saw Shang Phun still standing on the corner, looking after me.

It was 9 p.m. by the time I got back to the Atlanta. I was tired despite the long nap in Gao's room, but my bed seemed hard and uncomfortable that night. Between brief waves of sleep, I lay open-eyed, worrying, crying, and trying to figure out how to help Shang Phun and Gao.

* * *

In the morning, I called the woman who had hired me to teach for the 2002 Burma Volunteer Program. I told her how Shang Phun had applied twice to the United Nations High Commission for Refugees (UNHCR) and how he had twice been turned down for refugee status, which would have exempted him from the dangers of being an illegal immigrant in Thailand. With a trembling voice, I told her about Shang Phun's living and working conditions. She told me about the International Rescue Committee (IRC), which sometimes furnishes lawyers for those who want to appeal their treatment by the UNHCR.

Later that morning I took a taxi to the IRC and asked to see someone in charge. A small man led me to a round-faced woman I remember only as Rita. She said she was from the Mon ethnic group in Burma, that she had gotten refugee status and was now attending a Thai university. She listened to me relate Shang Phun's story and asked me if he had family in Bangkok. Then she said, "I'm sorry. We are only helping women who have no family."

Her sympathetic manner had made me hopeful. Now she was telling me Shang Phun did not qualify for help. Weakened by disappointment and lack of sleep, I slumped in my chair, tears rolling down my face. "His work is so *hard*," I whimpered. "And he is so *small*. He can't last." It was not a plea for special favors but a hopeless outpouring.

Rita looked distressed. "Can he come to see us?" The question shocked and delighted me—there was hope. "Yes!" I said.

The next day Shang Phun came to the Atlanta and we took a taxi to IRC. There, he told Rita he wanted me with him during the interview, and she reluctantly agreed. They spoke in Burmese, Rita asking questions, Shang Phun answering. I did not understand a word, but as the interview progressed, Rita's face softened and I grew hopeful. When they finished talking, she smiled and nodded to us. I turned to Shang Phun. "Yes?"

"I must talk to the attorney," he said. "They will call me." Talk to the attorney! A minor victory. If the UN accepted him, he might even be able to come to the United States. In time, he could apply to have Gao live with him. I wanted to kiss Rita. Instead, I tee-peed my hands under my chin, bowed my head, and thanked her.

"It is not for sure. It will depend on the attorney," she said. "But he is very kind. Does his best for everyone." And she added another caution, "Even if the attorney represents Shang Phun, it could take up to a year to find out if he gets refugee status."

* * *

Two days later I left Bangkok for northern Thailand where I would be teaching English to a new group of Shan refugees from Burma and a more advanced English class to Shang Phun's former classmates who had access to a monastery. I settled into a nearby hotel and resumed teaching. Two months later, I received a phone call from Shang Phun.

He had seen a doctor who said his lungs were clear. He coughed little as we spoke, and told me the attorney had agreed to appeal his case to the UNHCR. Now all we had to do was wait.

Soon the unrelenting March heat reduced my fastest pace to a stroll and forced its way through the thick cork soles of my Birkenstock sandals. Even the *songthaews* I took to the monastery were oppressively hot.

* * *

On March 17, I flew from Chiang Mai to Bangkok and returned to the Atlanta Hotel. My flight to Minneapolis would leave March 20. At 11:30 p.m. on March 19, the phone rang. It was Shang Phun. In an excited voice, he said, "Teacher, your country is going to war with Iraq."

"No!" I said. "They're going to let the weapons inspectors in."

"Yes, Teacher. They're going to war! I heard it on the news." I wondered why he was so excited, till he said, "Iraq isn't far from Burma, Teacher. Maybe they will go there next."

Standing under the whirring overhead fan, I shivered and hugged my skimpy nightdress to me. "No, Shang Phun. They won't go to Burma."

"But Burma is worse than Iraq, Teacher," he said, meaning Burma committed more offenses against its civilian population than Saddam Hussein committed against Iraqis.

He may have been right, but I knew the U.S. military would not intervene in Burma—there was nothing to be gained. No one would help Shang Phun.

* * *

Summer 2003: Near Shang Phun's factory is a shop where twenty baht, or fifty U.S. cents, will buy an hour's Internet time. Occasionally, Shang Phun sends me e-mail messages. He does not mention the war with Iraq, but has written to say the IRC attorney has appealed his case to the United Nations. He must wait for a hearing. His messages are filled with love and a sense of indebtedness.

> *Dear my love teacher,*
>
> *I am feeling in my heart on your helping me too much. I also think about you every time how to give back for you . . . I never think someone kind me like you. Teacher I want take care you by my heart one day. Teacher if I cannot go to your state directly I can go step by step. I am understanding my poor life. I am refugee.*
>
> *Your student, Shang Phun*

PART THREE:

Travels in Shan State and Burma

The greatest human rights abuses take place away from foreign view . . .
—The Burma Debate

KENGTUNG: AN INTRODUCTION TO SHAN STATE

The World is a book, and those who do not travel read only a page.
—St. Augustine

<u>December 3, 2004:</u> I struggle out of my lady-sized backpack—that's what the fellow who sold it to me called it—and stash it next to the big, strong-guy models on the floor of Burma's government tourist office in Tachilek, across the Sai River from Thailand. The place is crowded with Western tourists, most are European men in their thirties or forties with muscular legs and broad shoulders—and with more than enough money to spend. Cameras dangle round their necks, and they wear expensive travel pants, the kind that zip off above the knee and convert to shorts.

I look up at them. They look back—polite, dismissive glances—and although I am thirty to forty years older than most of these men, I feel the way I did in first grade: the smallest, youngest kid in the one-room school. Powerless—with only good behavior to protect me. Carlene Hermann was the only other girl; the rest were big strong boys, husky like the travelers in this room.

* * *

Looking at the young men who surround me, I wonder if I am out of my mind to be traveling alone in Burma. This past year I tore the medial meniscus in my left knee; at the same time my back started aching—a deteriorated disk in the lower spine, the doctor said, the result of lugging too many heavy backpacks across too many countries for too many years. A touchy metatarsal arch in my right foot is a bigger problem. I have a tough time walking when it becomes inflamed and am counting on the cortisone shot I got between my toes to keep me mobile. If the cortisone wears off, I will have to fall back on Extra Strength Tylenol.

I could have stayed home, safe in the cocoon of my Minneapolis condo, but that is not the kind of life I want. I will not give up my lust for travel before I have to, will not settle into the mediocrity of coffee circles where caffeine highs encourage complaints about why we older people cannot do what we used to do. I want to see Burma, have wanted to see it since I first heard about Americans working on the Burma Road during World War II and later when I read Kipling's unforgettable "Road to Mandalay, where the flying fishes play" and the writings of Orwell, Maugham, and Maurice Collis. I especially want to see Shan State and the city of Kengtung, where four of my Shan refugee students lived.

They have urged me to visit Shan State since I met them in Thailand in 2002. "It's safe for you, Teacher," they said. Safe for me—a lucky accident of birth—but I am nervous.

In 2001, a French man who worked in a Thailand refugee camp rode his motorcycle across the Mae Sot border into Burma and was never seen again; an American woman who visited Aung San Suu Kyi, when visits were still allowed, was pushed into traffic afterwards, presumably by a military intelligence man; and a few months ago, an eighty-one-year-old American man who protested in front of government offices in Rangoon was beaten and imprisoned before being sent back to the U.S. Every week Burmese who have escaped to Thailand report new outrages committed by the Burmese government. Their vehicle is *The Irrawaddy News,* a Thai publication I get on-line. In Burma, opposition political leaders and journalists who publish articles derogatory to the regime are imprisoned for years.

That knowledge may be the reason most backpackers travel in twos, and here I am, alone. And I have a secret to keep: The government would not look kindly upon my involvement with Shan refugees in Thailand. My stomach is fluttery with excitement, anticipation, and fear.

* * *

A table near the door holds haphazardly stacked passports. The disarray is alarming. I don't like handing over my only means of identification to a regime I have learned to hate on behalf of the Shan who fled to Thailand to escape military persecution.

Aung San Suu Kyi, who has been under house arrest most of the time since her National League of Democracy Party won eighty-five percent of the vote in the 1990 elections, has asked travelers not to visit Burma, not to feed money into the oppressive military regime. I honored her request, a decision I started questioning after meeting a Dutch journalist in Bangkok.

He had been living incognito in Rangoon during 2003, passing himself off as a teacher, while writing about and photographing abuses of the regime, including documenting the military rape of an ethnic woman. "Her vagina was like ground meat," he said. "I could not look through the lens when I took the photo." He urged me to visit the country, to talk with the people and see for myself what was going on. "You can avoid giving money to the government," he said.

As though he were listening to the conversation I was remembering in my head, Burmese Army General Than Shwe, head of the ruling junta since 1992 and the man who controls the army, looks down on me sternly from his portrait on the wall. At seventy-one, Than Shwe firmly opposes the release of Aung San Suu Kyi. In 2003 he instigated an attack on her convoy and then oversaw her arrest. Yet Suu Kyi remains an icon of democracy to the people of Burma, a model of passive resistance.

Looking at the general's firm visage on the wall, a quiver of fear runs through me, and I remind myself that "Teacher of Shan Refugees" is not written across my forehead. I am a small unobtrusive woman from Minneapolis—the military should not feel threatened by me.

* * *

Long-limbed, slim women staff the tourist office, their faces dusted with yellow thanaka, a wood product used as sun protection and beautifier. Sometimes it is subtle, reminding me of childhood attempts to beautify myself by patting flour on my face. Some workers have painted their cheeks with deep yellow triangles or circles. They are beautiful in spite of not because of the designs, the way some American women are beautiful despite highly rouged cheeks and eyelashes dripping with mascara.

Because the morning is cold, the women wear windbreakers over sarong-style skirts, unisex garments the Burmese call *longyis* (lon-jees). The office operates like U.S. workplaces did in the 1940s. The clerks insert carbon paper between two copies of legal-sized forms and complete them by hand. No typewriters, no computers ease their tasks. It takes them three hours to complete my paper work. Then I am assigned to a driver who, for a ten-dollar fee, will carry me ninety-eight miles, a five-hour trip, from Tachilek to Kengtung.

* * *

If this were the early 1900s, I might be visiting the palace of Kengtung's Prince, Sao Kawng Tai. Burma was under British rule then, and Shan State's system of feudal governance was so successful it was allowed to continue. Kawng Tai ruled the Kengtung area from his palace, which my *Lonely Planet* guidebook calls an outstanding work of architecture—not a universal opinion.

British writer Maurice Collis, whose book, *Lords of the Sunset,* revolves about the murder of Kawng Tai, contains many photos of Shan State, none of the palace. Ugly or outstanding, thousands of Shan protested when government workers tore it down in 1991. Erecting a large government hotel where the palace had stood was another attempt to eradicate the Shan culture.

* * *

A young Thai woman applied for entrance to Burma at the same time as I. Aside from the clerks, she is the only other woman in the office. Now she smiles broadly, pointing to herself and then to me, indicating she wants to make the trip together. We have no common language, and I feel no affinity for her, but I am leaving control behind with my passport.

We walk with the driver down the dirt streets of Tachilek to a battered old Toyota Corolla. I have agreed to pay the equivalent of fifty cents more for a front seat because I am prone to motion sickness; the Thai woman sits behind me.

In Thailand, steering wheels are on the right and drivers use the left side of the road. In Burma, steering wheels are on the right and drivers use the right side of the road, and I wonder how they can judge their distance from oncoming vehicles.

We drive a few feet to an open-air grocery, where a middle-aged man joins us. He speaks English, says his name is Sao Sing Sai, and he tells me both he and the driver are Shan. I like Sao Sing Sai immediately; maybe there is a likeness to my refugee friends; maybe it is one of those complicities of character that form the beginnings of spontaneous friendships.

He says I am "very brave" to travel alone. "Brave or foolish," I say. By the time I return to Thailand, I will know.

At an apartment building, we pick up a hefty man who shoves Sao Sing Sai to the middle of the back seat, where he must sit with raised knees. Based on his rudeness, I guess he is Burmese, but realize I am prejudiced on behalf of Shan friends who have suffered under the Burmese—a ridiculous prejudice, since Aung San Suu Kyi, herself Burmese, has suffered as much as they under the military regime.

Leaving the dirt streets of Tachilek behind, we travel up and down and round and round through deforested mountains. Occasionally we see Burmese soldiers cutting standing trees and rolling them down the eroded road banks. Only the distant mountains are heavily wooded.

It is through that dense mountain jungle that my former student Shang Phun now travels, bringing food and medicine to outlying villages and to displaced persons hiding in the jungle. He climbs the mountainsides with soldiers from the ragtag Shan State Army, which is supported by twenty baht (fifty cents U.S.) contributions by migrant workers in Thailand. When Shang Phun enters Burma, only he and his army escort know where and how he is. I will not rest freely until he returns to Thailand.

The driver zigzags around piles of rocks that have slid down the eroded mountainside. Herds of brown cattle walk leisurely along the road; long-horned water buffalo graze in the ditches. Long-snouted, short-bodied pigs that look like wild boars scamper out of the way. Before we left the tourist office, I took half of a Dramamine pill to quell motion sickness. It has made me drowsy, but I do not want to fall asleep. I hold my eyes wide open, for I love the foreignness of this place; which, foreign though it is, reminds me of my childhood on the farm.

*　*　*

In the front seat of the Toyota, I fall into a reverie where I tramp through the pasture on my daily task of getting the cows and jump from log to log on the corduroy road, picking clumps of yellow marsh marigolds, though I know they will wilt before I return home. Inhaling the marshy swamp smell, I dream about the future: In my child's mind the Burma Road I hear my father talk about is tied up with Jason and the Golden Fleece, a book Aunt Marie left at our house, one that forms the base for a magical world inhabited by monsters and kings and the visiting Princess, Bernice.

I hear the cowbell tinkle and follow the sound, unheeding of the thorns and thistles that nick my legs, for at day's end I will count them badges of adventure. The bell leads me to another swampy place where the cows loll in cooling mud and jack-in-pulpits grow. Still holding the marsh marigolds, I peer one-by-one into the depths of the plants, looking for the unsuspecting insects they have lured into their sticky traps. Such unique and lovely murderers they are.

I linger too long, shoo the cows onward, for we must be at the barn by five o'clock. I follow behind the cattle, the wilting marsh marigolds clutched tightly in my hand, hoping that this time I will be able to revive them when I return home, that I will be able to watch them raise their pretty faces to another day.

It was only as an adult that I realized I had loved the pasture. With its flowers and swamps, the creek, and the big pine tree where grandma and grandpa built their first house, it was a playground where I could create imaginary worlds and adventures and still do my duty. I had loved the pasture the way Shang Phun loves the jungle I see in the distance.

* * *

Most traffic on this road is military, new trucks filled with armed Burmese soldiers, some with their heads turned to the sides and rifles at the ready, others staring straight ahead, looking for rebels and for people like Shang Phun who try to help the needy Shan.

Forced-labor crews trudge along the roadside, carrying hoes and shovels, an armed soldier walking behind them. The workers look thin and tired, and I wish we could stop to give them water. More fortunate crews stand in pickups with their guards. I question my decision to travel here, as I have done so many times before—this time because I wonder if being in a country where forced labor exists is a way of implicitly condoning it. I have been reading *Schindler's List,* and detest the armed Burmese soldiers the way I detest the now-dead SS men who relished the power their guns gave them.

Shan women, wearing *longyis,* walk at the road's edge, bent under huge baskets of firewood affixed to their foreheads with leather straps. Broad-shouldered, slim-hipped men in *longyis* carry hoes and bamboo poles into wilderness. Villages announce their imminence with gold-spired pagodas that jut skyward. Shan and Burmese share the same gentle Buddhist religion, which forbids killing, as does Christianity, a tenet we Americans ignore in Iraq; a tenet the Burmese ignore in driving the Shan from their land.

Farmers wade through muddy, lime green rice fields, tending young plants; plumes of smoke rise from the fallow fields. The odor reminds me of my youth on our northern Minnesota farm when we burned the fallen leaves, and I feel nostalgic for the simpler days and simpler ways of childhood when we lived much like the rural Shan with dirt streets, outhouses, no electricity, no running water—an irrational yearning, for life was difficult then.

* * *

The road to Kengtung has been recently improved; it is one of the better roads in Burma. Despite the switchbacks that wind us higher and higher up the mountains, the ninety-eight-mile trip should not take five hours. Three toll booths and three military checkpoints slow us down.

The pink identity card issued to me at the border lies on the dash, folded within two legal-sized documents. The three other passengers' identity cards are at the other end of the dash. At each checkpoint, the driver carries the three Asians' papers into an office, returns with them in hand, drives to another office and carries mine inside, for some sort of approval stamp, I suppose, a cumbersome, time-consuming system. No one comes out to see if our faces match the photos on our documents.

Two hours into the five-hour trip, we stop for lunch at an open-air, thatched-roof restaurant crowded with Burmese soldiers. The cooks and waiters are Shan, and the restaurant looks clean despite the dogs that roam the floor, looking for scraps. "You will eat with us?" asks Sao Sing Sai. Food appears on the table: two bowls of meat broth, small bits of meat fried with chilies, two vegetable dishes pungent with red-hot chili peppers, a bowl of freshly washed greens, a huge bowl of rice.

Sao Sing Sai gestures for me to help myself, but I do not eat meat, and chili peppers throw me into fits of coughing. "*Ma pit*," I say, Shan for "no spicy." "*Ma neu*," I say, "no meat," hoping I do not seem as fussy as I am.

A tiny, dimpled waitress brings me a bowl of clear broth with garlic, ginger, and onions floating in it and a dish of fried greens. They are fresh and delicious, and I am relieved not to be sharing the meat broth with fellow travelers, who dip their eating spoons into the communal dishes. My meal costs the equivalent of one-dollar U.S. I am allowed to pay with Thai baht because I have no Burmese kyat (pronounced jaht), with its exchange rate of nine hundred to one dollar.

Behind the restaurant, are unisex outhouses with squat toilets. Users slosh them clean with buckets of water scooped from a tank with a hose running into it. The surrounding ground is muddy, and I am fast losing my nostalgia for the simple days of childhood.

* * *

At 3 p.m., five hours after leaving Tachilek, we arrive in Kengtung. The city was named for the abundant tung oil in the area, according to the *Lonely Planet*, which describes the region as "one of the most remote inhabited mountain valleys in Myanmar."

We stop at two guidebook-recommended moderately priced hotels.

The immaculately clean Harry's Guest House, where prices are quoted in U.S. dollars and range from $6.00 to $20.00 per night, is too far from the city center. My knees could not handle the walk. The Thai woman stays behind at Harry's and we drive on.

At the top of a steep hill is the Noi Yee, an elegant old white and blue building referred to in the guidebook as "a former royal residence." The room I see is large, light, and very cold. There is no restaurant, and it is a ten-minute walk to the nearest teahouse. I shudder, imagining dragging myself out of bed into the cold morning air to search for breakfast.

"I think you will like the Sam Yweat Guesthouse," says Sao Sing Sai. "It is near the market."

Back in the Toyota, we pass the large government hotel on the site of the former palace. Flooded with anger absorbed from Shan friends, their anger at the palace's destruction, I want to spit at the guard who stands at attention near the street entrance. Instead, frustrated by a feeling of total impotence, I look straight ahead.

We wind past Buddhist temples and stands selling bread, cassette tapes, wool hats, stockings, jackets, and sweaters. Ten minutes later we are at the Sam Yweat.

The guesthouse gets only one line in the *Lonely Planet*: "decent rooms and friendly staff." It deserves more. It is a charming old wooden building with highly polished teak floors. The owner welcomes me like a mother, though she is younger than I, as most people are these days. Ten dollars per night includes breakfast.

As Sao Sing Sai and the driver prepare to leave, Sao says he will "show me around," whenever I wish. He lives in a nearby village, but the hotel owner "knows me," he says, instilling me with a sense of welcome and good will that, together with the hotel owner's welcome, are soothing my fears about visiting Shan State.

I am given a cozy wood-paneled room on the second floor. Washing the day's dirt from my hands, I feel water pouring down on my feet through a hole in the plastic tubing used to drain the sink. Oh, well. Other things are more important. I am hungry.

The desk clerk, a smiling young woman, takes me by motorbike to a nearby Chinese restaurant.

On an English-language menu, I point to fried vegetables. *"Ma neu,* no meat,"I say. *"Ma neu?"* the waiter asks incredulously. *"Ma neu,"* I say.

One side of the restaurant is open to the outdoors. I sit on the open side; waiters sit at a table next to me, watching television. The waiter who took my order sits with his left foot crossed at right angles across his right knee so he can pick at a callous on his heel. Clean feet, I reassure myself. He brings me chunks of fatty meat fried with vegetables. "No," I say. The cashier, who speaks some English comes over. I point to the meat and say *"Ma neu."* Fifteen minutes later, the foot-picker brings me fried vegetables topped with cashews. They are delicious.

I have eaten half my food when Foot-Picker starts setting two large tables with glasses, chopsticks, and soup bowls. He spills a box of toothpicks on the floor, crawls nimbly under the table, collects the picks from the unswept floor and puts them into a plastic container on the table. I finish my meal and do not use a toothpick while waiting for symptoms of foot germ poisoning to set in.

Walking back to Sam Yweat, I am met with smiles and stares of amazement. "Where you from?" "Where you go?" "Beautiful, Madame." The people of Kengtung have seen few Americans—the city was off limits to Westerners until 1996. Here, as in Thailand, my seventy-two-year-old presence is considered beautiful. I love it.

* * *

December 4: It was cold last night. My windows would not close, and I am getting a head cold. I may leave tomorrow, but today I want to see the lake at the center of the city, which students have talked about, and the Roman Catholic Mission and orphanage on a hill where the city was founded one thousand years ago.

The desk clerk tells me her name is Tin Te Ye. She speaks some English. "You are very beautiful," she says. This is fun.

"How do I say 'thank you?'" I ask.

"Akha," she says. The Akha are a nomadic hill tribe that wanders between Burma and the highlands of Thailand—Ye and I will not be having lengthy conversations.

"Akha?"

She nods. "My mother, my father Akha." She opens a small album and points to photos of women in elaborate silver beaded headdresses—Akha women carry the family's wealth on their heads.

* * *

Using a map Ye gave me, I follow a winding dirt road toward the lake and happen onto an open-air hut where four small children and their male teacher sit on stools at a two-foot-high table. He teaches the children English and Shan, he says, for only Burmese is taught in schools, and he asks me to join them. The runny-nosed child next to me is five-and-one-half years old, the teacher says. The three other children are five years old. He pulls out an English First Reader and asks the runny-nosed boy to read, "A pen. A pencil. This is a man. This is a woman." He does not miss a word.

"Am I a man?" I ask, pointing to myself.

The children laugh: "Nooo!"

"Am I a woman?"

"Yesss!"

I lead them to a small open space to teach "Head and Shoulders." They are a quick study. Twice, I touch my head, shoulders, knees, and toes, saying the words at the same time, and they are laughing and singing with me, delighting the crowd that has gathered outside the hut.

When we sit at the table again, a woman brings me a glass of amber liquid. "Plain tea," she says. Then, pointing to my cheeks, flushed red from the sun, she says, "Very beautiful."

I know that when I look in the mirror I will see the same aging face, my father's long, narrow nose, high forehead, and small mouth, my mother's manner, but I like the B word, which I have not heard for years in the States, where aging women are considered attractive at best. "Thank you," I say.

"How old are you?" asks the teacher. "Seventy-two," I say. He repeats the question three times. When my answer does not vary, he holds up six fingers, points to himself, and says "I am sixty years old."

"I am seventy-two years old."

"Ohhh," he says. "Very young," and he says something in Shan to the crowd of onlookers who have gathered to stare at me. I don't understand him, but the chorus of ohhs and ahhs must mean he told them how old I am. Boasting about age is common in Asia, where being old and mobile is greatly admired.

Leaving the children, I walk to the lake. It is small, with a long, narrow shape and stagnant green water. Men standing on bamboo rafts cast fishing nets into the waters. In Thailand, a Shan refugee said, "The lake used to belong to the people, Teacher. Anyone could fish. Now the government charges money every time." In this poor country, charging money to fish is just cause for resentment.

A third of the way around the lake a young man walks up behind me:

"Where you from?"

"America."

"Ohhh. Do you need a guide?"

"No. I'm just walking."

I am sure he travels by motorbike, and although there is little traffic in Kengtung I don't want to have a leg scraped by a passing car and end up hospitalized in a country with one of the world's worst medical systems. "Thank you," he says, and turns around.

A hundred feet later, I stop for a cup of tea at a roadside restaurant. Kengtung has a teashop in nearly every block, but this place serves only Coke and coffee. "Tea?" I ask again, and the waiter points back the way I came. "Back there," he says.

At the teashop, the fellow who wanted to be my guide is sitting on a stool at a low outdoor table, drinking tea and eating sunflower seeds. I join him. We chat a few minutes, and it is obvious he is a bright young man. "I just finish tenth standard [tenth grade]," he says. "Now I study English and Shan. In school is only Burmese language. Next month I go to university. Then I want be tour guide." I assure him he will be a good guide, because his English is very good. "But next year will be exam for nine months English and computer school in Thailand, Chiang Mai Province. I want to take exam."

Knowing it may be a foolish thing to do, I tell him I have taught English at the school he mentioned. "Do not tell anyone," I say.

"Noooo," he says, smiling broadly. "Ohh. I am very lucky." Talking with a teacher is lucky in this culture where teachers are highly respected. He turns sober. "Is it hard—the exam?" It won't be for him, I say.

I search for money to pay for my tea, realize I still do not have Burmese kyat "I will pay for you," he says. Tea is cheap, the equivalent of pennies, but I know this boy has little money and I am humbled. He rides off on an old motorbike, and I walk back to the center of town.

* * *

At the intersection next to the Sam Yweat is a platform for motorbike taxi drivers. It is vacant, so I sit down. Women passing by and a few men are heavily powdered with thanaka. Some have completely yellow faces; others have patterned themselves with lines, squares, triangles, circles. Some look as if they are wearing white masks. Skin whitening creams and powders are popular in Southeast Asia. A recent article in the *Bangkok Post* said many of the creams have dangerous side effects, but women continue to use them, for fair skin is prized.

Traffic policemen in white uniforms and gloves direct motorbikes, bicycles, and old trucks carrying tired-looking workers, their skin burned dark brown by the sun. I have seen three traffic policemen on the little-traveled streets of Kengtung.

A motorbike stops next to me. A young man wearing a vest with the word TAXI lettered on the back dismounts and sits beside me. *"Mai soong, ka,"* I say, the Shan greeting students taught me. He does not respond, looks at me curiously. *"Mingala Ba,"* I say, the Burmese greeting. He smiles, and says his name is Pau Sa Win. I ask if he is Shan. "No," he says emphatically. "I am Burmese. My father is soldier." Later, he says his mother is Shan, but it is his Burmese ancestry he is proud of.

I am dismayed, remembering Sai Sai, who wrote a story about his home being burned by the military. When we discussed the story after class, Sai Sai hung his head and said his father had been a Burmese soldier. He had done his part to Burmanize the Shan by impregnating Sai Sai's mother. He had not planned to fall in love with her, but he did. Sai Sai had been ashamed of his Burmese ancestry.

Truckloads of armed soldiers course through the town. "Why are there so many soldiers?" I ask Pau Sa Win, knowing the answer but wondering what he will say. "They are visiting," he says.

In reality, this is an occupied city. Kengtung and Baghdad, I think, picturing U.S. soldiers, patrolling the streets of that ancient city. The thought is shaming. I wish I could dissociate myself from the war in Iraq, but know the taxes I pay help to fund it.

Pau Sa Win takes a wad of pulverized betel nuts from his pocket, stuffs it into his mouth and chews until red juices flow. Betel chewers are disgusting to look at, with their maroon stained teeth and sloppy mouths. I am also irrationally disgusted with Pau Sa Win for saying he is Burmese rather than Shan and for his dumb remark about "visiting soldiers." I get up from the bench and start toward the Sam Yweat.

In the block next to the guesthouse, workmen are renovating an old hotel. Flimsy, ladder-like bamboo scaffolding tied with plastic bands supports barefoot workers scraping paint from the walls. I marvel at their agility, at the way their bare feet curl around the bamboo high above the ground. Most chew betel nut, spitting the red juices onto the ground. Betel nut is a stimulant—it may give them courage.

* * *

I have moved to a first floor room at the Sam Yweat, one where the sink water does not pour onto my feet. The key to my first room is missing. Ye is alarmed when I say I cannot find it. I ask her if I can get a key to the new room, but she says it must be cleared by the Immigration Office.

The Burmese occupation of Kengtung has seemed relatively benign—until now. I think about my passport, probably still stacked on a table in the tourist office at the border, and I think about my identification papers, which have never been in my hands. The taxi driver kept them until we arrived in Kengtung. There he gave them to the immigration authorities. I cannot get a key to a different room until the Burmese authorities have approved my move and the last key is accounted for. I am indignant, wonder how the Shan maintain such a calm countenance. Buddhism, perhaps—or maybe they have just grown used to this way of life.

* * *

December 5: Last night was even colder than the night before. In this room, I do not have to wash my feet when I wash my hands, but there are many windows—none close tightly. I slept with two heavy blankets, doubling one over the other in the middle of the night.

I remember winter mornings on our Minnesota farm, times when the wood fire went out during the night. I would jump out of bed those mornings, grab my clothes, tuck them under the quilts, and warm them next to my body before tenting the quilts and dressing under them. I no longer have an iota of nostalgia for the old days and old ways.

I pull my slacks over pajama bottoms, leaving on the turtleneck top and socks I wore to bed. Wearing the light jacket and knit cap I brought with me, and with a wool shawl wrapped around my shoulders, I go to the outdoor table where guests eat breakfast. Ye approaches, huddled into a heavy jacket, and wearing a wool cap. "Breakfast?" she asks, and in a few minutes serves hot instant coffee, scrambled eggs, and white Wonderbread-like toast.

Two guests I haven't seen before approach the table. They arrived late last night, they say, and introduce themselves as Gregg and Michael of San Francisco. They have month-long visas and will fly from Kengtung to Mandalay. We chat, and Gregg says he met some of my Shan friends in Chiang Mai. "They told me you were in Kengtung," he says. "I wondered if we would meet." He says he would like to work with the Shan, give them additional information about computers perhaps. Such coincidences make me want to believe there is a pattern to life. So far I haven't found it.

Gregg and Michael ask me to have dinner with them and leave to explore the city. The guesthouse owner's daughter, who speaks fluent English and has flawless, fair skin, sees me shivering in the morning sunshine and offers to take me to the market to buy a coat.

* * *

The market is huge, perhaps two square blocks. I wish there were chairs in the middle, so I could sit and watch the morning happen: Women in conical bamboo hats carry heads of cauliflower, holding them up for view; Akha women in heavy silver headdresses and black and white dresses shop for coats and sweaters, some of them with babies at their breasts; monks draped in saffron-colored robes and wearing matching wool hats wander through the crowd. There are stalls upon stalls of tinware, enamelware, plastic wear, coats, gloves, hats, and underwear, all imported from China. Other stalls sell jades, rubies, sapphires, diamonds, gold, and silver—Shan State is rich in minerals and gems, one reason for the Burmese occupation. Still other stalls sell imported Thai silk and Mandarin-style Shan shirts.

The south side of the market is redolent with the odors of frying ginger, garlic, onions, and chili peppers. The strong fumes set me coughing. Next to the cooked-food stands are tables covered with rows of fruit and vegetables, cauliflower, onions, apples, imported Chinese pears, papaya, mounds of red chili peppers, and deep red and gold flowers, the hardy kind, similar to Minnesota chrysanthemums.

We stop at a coat stall. "This is the best place," my companion says. "The best quality." Coats, all of them made in China, hang on three sides of the stall and are mounded in front of the vendor. At five-foot-one and one hundred ten pounds, I am a big person in Shan State. I try on a coat labeled XL. It is too small. The XXL fits in the body but is too short in the sleeves. The XXXL is too large. This will not be easy. Digging among the heaped coats, we find a leather one. It fits, but while I cannot smell anything unusual my companion says it stinks. Good thing she is here—my sense of smell seems to be fading. She leads me to several other coat stalls. Nothing fits.

Most vendors sell only one thing. I buy gloves at one stall and a free size made-in-China sweater at another. The military regime is on good terms with China—it values the protection of its powerful neighbor. China values the stagnant Burmese economy, which produces little.

* * *

Back at the guesthouse, I read *Schindler* until evening, when Gregg, Michael, and I walk down unlit streets to a Shan restaurant they have found. The men have greasy, unappealing meat dishes, and we share several plates of vegetables, a huge bowl of rice, and a large bottle of Myanmar beer. The beer is mellow, the vegetables fresh, and I am content.

In Kengtung, Michael says, people guess he is older than he is, and he hates it. He is forty years old and Gregg is forty-two. I tell them I am seventy-two and am pleased when Michael says he thought I was in my fifties. I have pondered this age business often, embarrassed that I feel so good when others say I look young, and though I would like to think I am unique, I know I share the Western obsession with youth. Living a full life is another obsession. When I look young in others' eyes, it places me further from the edge of the grave, gives me more years to wander the earth.

Four Chinese men, arrogant with the power money brings, arrive in a new Toyota van, accompanied by a guide. I suspect they are drug dealers, the kind of men who earned Kengtung its *Lonely Planet* description as a strategic "Myanmar government stronghold . . . [for] the illicit drug trade."

We finish our food and start back, three abreast, to the Sam Yweat, stopping briefly at a grocery store, where Gregg buys a large bottle of Myanmar beer and a bag of deep-fried fruit chips. We ask directions back to the Sam Yweat, for it is 8 p.m. and the rough dirt streets are dark, as are the buildings lining them. The clerk points into the night, but we soon lose our sense of direction. I am glad the men are with me as we walk one way, turn around, and walk another, meandering back to the Sam Yweat.

Michael gets a small DVD player from his backpack; Gregg unbags the Myanmar beer and fruit chips, and we settle into large handmade lobby chairs to watch the video *King Arthur*. Excited by the opportunity to watch an English language film, Ye sits next to me. I grab a heavy blanket from my room and spread it across our knees.

King Arthur has the usual Hollywood dose of sex, battles, and blood. Ye turns her head aside during the sex scenes, walks outside during the bloody battles. The chairs grow harder and the air grows colder as the film progresses. I run to my room for another blanket, a hat, and gloves, and settle down to watch Lancelot die on the battlefield—truer to history than the usual King Arthur stories, according to Michael—and Arthur and Guinevere marry.

* * *

<u>December 6:</u> This morning I tell Ye I would like to see Sao Sing Sai again, tell her he has promised to show me around. She talks to the guesthouse owner, who says Sao Sing Sai lives in a different village and she does not know which house is his. I am disappointed until I realize this means I will have another day in the market.

As I walk toward the market gate, a young man emerges from a doorway and says. "I see you every day. You here long time already. Where you from?"

His name is Wan Thit (Tit), he says. "It is Burmese name. I am university student. It is easier for teacher to remember if we have Burmese name." I don't like his placid acceptance of the name, ask if he has a Shan name. He says, "Yes. Shan name, too," but does not volunteer it.

"This used to be Shan State," he says, "but it is change to Burma." I think of the refugees in Chiang Mai who are proud of their Shan names and their ethnicity, who teach the Shan language at a monastery, celebrate Shan holidays, and learn as much as possible in Thailand with the goal of returning to Shan State to pass their knowledge to their country people, and I feel an unreasonable dislike for Wan Thit.

His grandmother is sitting in a rocking chair, watching us from the doorway of a dark, barren room, a colorful crocheted afghan on her lap, a knit cap on her head. *"Mai soong, ka,"* I say. One of the few people who has understood the Shan greeting in this Burmese-dominated city, she answers, *"Mai soong ka."*

After two hours wandering through mounds of Chinese merchandise in the market, the aromas of frying ginger, garlic, and onions, set me walking toward the Shan restaurant where I ate with Gregg and Michael. I sit at an outdoor table, overlooking the busy street. Women and children walk past dressed in flannel pajamas, street wear in Kengtung, as in parts of Thailand. Two women with hair rolled tightly into permanent-wave curlers chug past the restaurant on a motorbike, a strange sight in this country of straight-haired women. Men walk with arms wrapped around each other's shoulders.

Across the street, a bare-chested woman in a *longyi* pulls a sweater across her pendulous breasts when she meets motorbikes. From her flighty frightened demeanor, I suspect she is demented, wish I had the gumption to run to her and wrap a blanket around her shoulders. The men she encounters look aside, and I wish she would flutter home.

Feeling a presence at my side, I look up to see a young man who says, "I know you are here." His words shock me. I had worried about being followed by the military—instead, I have been followed by a smiling teenage boy.

"My name is Francis," he says. "This morning you talk to my friend, Wan Thit. He say Mommy [meaning me] speak English very well." Gesturing to a waitress, he says, "That is my sister. She is in university, but I have not passed 10th standard. I am very stupid." I tell him he is not stupid or he could not speak English so well. He smiles broadly. "I speak well?"

"Very well," I say, and ask if he is Catholic.

"How you know?"

"You have a Catholic name."

"Yes," he says, "Francis Catholic name. I study at mission." He asks if I am Catholic, looks disappointed when I say "No." He has followed me to practice speaking English, but I do not invite him to sit down. My food has grown cold, and I am relieved when he leaves to talk with his sister.

* * *

December 7: According to the *Lonely Planet,* a huge tree on a city hill deserves a visit. The guesthouse owner points out the hill. I cross the street and bend my back to the road, climbing higher and higher.

In the inside loop of a switchback, a small shack overlooks the city. It looks like a refreshment stand, and I think about stopping for cold water. Then I see soldiers leaning back in chairs with their boots on the railing. It is a military overlook.

On the other side of the switchback is a long row of barracks. A sign in round Burmese letters and in English says: "Our motto: Safe, Swift, Secure." Swift to kill, safe and secure for the military, I think. A soldier walks past me on the road, and in the distance I see him following a narrower road to the right. He turns around and gestures with his arm for me to follow.

I remember the stories in *Licence to Rape*, stories about young girls, who were left bloody and weeping, stories about middle-aged women raped and killed while looking for food in the jungle. I remember the Dutch journalist and his story about the woman whose vagina looked "like ground meat" after being raped, and wonder if it would be foolhardy to turn right where the soldier did.

At the bend of the turn, is another large barracks. Soldiers are playing soccer in the yard. Someone yells. They cluster at the gate and stare at me. Boys they are, and I see no evil in their faces. A handsome young fellow smiles broadly and throws me a kiss, as Kengtung children have done. I have to remind myself these soldiers are of the same ilk as the raping brutes I have read about, and I pity the people of Kengtung who have to cope with these smiling, kiss-throwing oppressors. I turn onto the path the soldier took.

A few feet past the barracks I see a groomed garden with flowerbeds. On the right is a monastery where a saffron-robed monk climbs a tree, looking for fruit. The soldier who beckoned me forward has disappeared. In the distance I see the huge tree.

A sign at the tree base gives details in Burmese and English:

Botanical name	- Diptero Carpus Alatus (ROXB)
Planted Year	- 1115 [Burmese calendar]
	- 1753 [English calendar]
Height	- 218 Ft.
Basal Girth	- 39 Ft. 10 Inches

Two teenage girls stand hand in hand, looking up at the enormous tree. A mother and daughter stand at the other side. They agree to have their photos taken, laugh with delight when they see their images on the digital screen. They do not look oppressed.

I hear military music in the distance, walk up another incline and follow an arbored path. An overhead sign reads "Peaceful Estate." On the other side, a rope bridge swings across a ravine.

From a clearing at the ravine edge, I see more army barracks and soldiers marching on a groomed green parade field. Trumpets join the thrumming drums, and the music segues into *Auld Lang Syne*. I struggle with a jumble of feelings: fear, anger, and then nostalgia at the strains of *Auld Lang Syne*. I feel like laughing. Would the smiling soldiers arrest me if they heard me laughing at their music?

* * *

At the Sam Yweat, Ye asks me to teach her some songs. I sing *You Are My Sunshine* and *Twinkle, Twinkle, Little Star,* and write the words for her. We move to tongue twisters: "Peter Piper Picked a Peck of Pickled Peppers" and "Sally Sells Seashells." Ye is laughing and struggling with the S and Sh sounds, when the owner tells her sixteen Thai guests will be arriving. That is the end of our English class.

The Thai guests, an extended family, have been traveling through Burma. The oldest fellow sits next to me at the outdoor table and speaks Thai, while I repeat "*Nitnoy Thai, nitnoy Thai.* (Little Thai.)" One son speaks English and translates his father's questions. Where am I from? How old am I? A daughter says "*Suay*," Thai for beautiful, and the English-speaking son tells me I am very strong.

The old man speaks to his children in Thai. He glances at me repeatedly, uses the word *farang*, foreigner, commenting no doubt on why and how we foreigners are thus and so. To him, Germans, Scandinavians, British, and Americans, all who are foreign and pale-skinned, are one.

They are tired from their travels and go to bed early. Ye has lit coals in a charcoal burner, which she places at my feet, and I sit at the outdoor table reading *Schindler.* Gregg and Michael have left for Mandalay—no more comfortable conversations, no more videos. When the charcoal burner loses its heat, I go to my room and snuggle fully dressed into a cocoon of blankets, wrapping a woolen shawl around my head.

* * *

December 8: Ye has notified the Immigration Office that I will return to Tachilek today and want a front seat. I am filled with regret: I have spent too much time in the market and have not visited the Roman Catholic Mission. I think about asking Ye to take my papers back to immigration. Then I remember the weight of the many blankets that could not keep me warm at night.

At 10:30 a.m. an old Toyota Corolla with a cracked windshield stops at the hotel. A soldier is driving. I hate the idea of riding with a Burmese soldier—it seems like a betrayal of my Shan friends—but I have no choice in this military state. Reluctantly I take my seat behind the cracked windshield. My identity papers are on the dash.

The soldier stops at a dirt-floored shack with tires stacked in the yard. The Toyota is jacked up and a tire replaced; several liter-sized soda bottles of gasoline are emptied into the gas tank, and we are on our way. Near Harry's Guesthouse we pick up three loud, giggly teenagers, a heavy-set Burmese girl, and two skinny Thai boys. The girl is obnoxiously loud; the boys giggle at her running chatter.

We go through the same checkpoints, the same tollgates. It costs three thousand kyat, more than three dollars U.S., to travel the road between Kengtung and Tachilek, three days' wages for Burmese laborers. There is little traffic.

A soldier stops us at a checkpoint, asks the driver if we can add a mother and her three children to the five people already in the Toyota. The child in her lap looks sick, and I am relieved, and shamed by my relief, when the driver rejects them.

Reading *Schindler's List*, I had wondered how I would have reacted as a German citizen in the midst of Jewish genocide, wondered whether I would have helped the Jews, as Schindler did, or turned a blind eye. My reaction to the woman and her children has answered my question: I am not a Schindler.

ONE WEEK IN MANDALAY

We are all travelers in the wilderness of this world, and the best we can find in our travels is an honest friend. —Robert Louis Stevenson

January 21, 2005: The sun has risen over Mandalay. At the street corner across from the Nylon Hotel, men in unisex *longyi* skirts push trishaws, bicycles with attached wooden sidecars, into a line. They smile through betel-stained teeth, pat the nearest of the two back-to-back seats attached to their bikes, and say, "Where you from?"

"America."

Thumbs up. "America! I like."

"Where you go?"

"To the Lashio Lay."

Another pat of the cushioned seat, "Ride, Madame?"

"No." The Lashio Lay Shan Restaurant is four blocks from the Nylon—I need the exercise.

Turning left on 83rd, I see two skinny men dressed in *longyis* and turbans squatting next to large plastic sacks, the kind farmers use for grain. The sacks drip blood that flows into the street, filling the air with a sweet, cloying smell that attracts swarms of flies. A man in a white apron hoses blood and flies from the ceramic tile floor of the building where the men squat. One of them sticks a brown hand into a sack, as if to make sure everything is there, and I see dark gray horns attached to a furry gray buffalo forehead. They have probably killed their transportation.

The men look weak and sickly. I hope the meat will restore their health, hope they get it safely home. This is the cool, dry season in Mandalay, but even now the midday sun is hot. I imagine the bloody buffalo chunks rotting under the midday sun, imagine them regurgitating it onto the street. I try to stop imagining and walk on.

Continuing north on 83rd, a broad one-way street, I meet a small gray-haired man wearing a tattered brown *longyi*. After passing him, I glance back and see him looking back at me, worried perhaps that I have seen his wrinkled brown body through the holes in his *longyi*.

Except for some East Indians who deal in currencies, a few successful Chinese business people, and top Burmese military officers, most everyone in Mandalay is poor. They live in lightless hovels, carry water from community wells, and wash their bodies and their clothes in the Irrawaddy River. Rice, a Burmese staple, has become so expensive many cannot afford to feed their families. The thoughts make me angry, but do not dull my appetite. I hurry toward the restaurant.

Eighty-third Street is one of the city's main thoroughfares. Sputtering, clanking, overloaded Mazda pickup buses spew exhaust fumes; motorbikes and trishaws merge easily, for this is not a heavily trafficked street—few can afford cars.

At the Lashio Lay, vegetable and meat dishes rest in stainless steel containers on a hot table. This is the same kind of Shan food my refugee friends in Thailand prepare, and I wish they were here to share it with me. "*Ma pet, ma neu*, no spicy, no meat," I say, hoping the waiter will understand my Shan. The man behind the counter points to sautéed mushrooms, bright yellow corn, and spinach. I nod. He piles the vegetables onto a plate and I carry it to a round table, where a waiter brings me a large stainless steel bowl of rice and a glass of amber-colored tea.

The restaurant is clean, as my *Lonely Planet* guidebook promised, no spittoons underfoot, no litter on the floor. I am surrounded by Burmans speaking with a lovely, unintelligible rhythm. Burmese is softer, easier on the ear than most Asian languages I have heard. To my uneducated ear, the rhythms sound a bit like French.

I am the only Westerner in the place, the only person eating alone. I like traveling alone—sights and sounds are more intense when not filtered through another's perceptions—but the fresh, flavorful vegetables make me long for Shan friends, who cannot travel freely in their own country.

* * *

Back at the Nylon, I lie on my bed, my feet and legs propped high against the pink-and-green-ceramic-tiled wall, and consider my prejudice against Burmans, a prejudice I absorbed from Shan friends driven from their land by the Burmese military. That prejudice is hard to reconcile among the polite and poverty-stricken people of Mandalay.

I fall asleep, and, upon waking, slide my legs down toward the bed, sit up, and start reading *The Bridge on the River Kwai* where I left off last night. An ironical portrait of a British officer who refused to surrender his dignity to Japanese captors, the book details the struggles and suffering of Allied prisoners of war during the Japanese occupation of Thailand and Burma when they forced prisoners to build bridges and rail lines to facilitate transportation of arms and troops between the two countries.

When the sun falls lower in the sky, I think about dinner. This evening I will eat at the Marie Min, an East Indian vegetarian restaurant described in *The Lonely Planet* as having "one of the cleanest kitchens" in Mandalay. The Nylon Hotel is on 25th and 83rd Streets—the Marie Min is three to four miles away. Even if my arthritic knees were up to the walk, it would be dark when I finish eating and I could not find my way back.

I see a trishaw driver who does not seem to be chewing betel and ask him what he would charge to take me to the Marie Min. "And back?" he says, and I notice his betel-stained teeth. Oh well. I answer his question with a nod, and he says, "One thousand four hundred kyat (one dollar and fifty cents U.S.)." It's probably too much. Trishaw drivers usually start high and come down slowly. I do not argue—I've seen too much poverty today.

We bump over Mandalay's rough roads, past the train station where wooden-benched passenger cars clang along the tracks, and through double lanes of traffic where snub-nosed Mazda pickups, Toyota Corolla vans, motorcycles, trishaws, and bicycles vie for position.

The driver stops in what looks like a residential neighborhood, and points to an alley. "Down there," he says. "I will be here when you are done."

At the Marie Min, five tables look across the alley at a puppet and antique store. More brown-skinned puppets line the walls of an adjacent shop. The restaurant looks clean, no soiled napkins or orange betel juice splotches on the floor. I order a mixed fruit lassie, dhal, and chapatti. The lassie is rich with yogurt and the juice of mangoes, papaya, bananas, and strawberries. I ignore my guilt about leaving the trishaw driver, who is probably as hungry as I, waiting in the street, and scoop the dhal onto chunks of chapatti.

It is past six and dusk has fallen when I finish eating. The trishaw is waiting for me at the alleyway. In Mandalay, traffic continues on unlit streets after dark. The driver stands on his bicycle pedals, maneuvering his trishaw around cars that honk their way through the darkness, sputtering motorcycles, silent bicycles, and other trishaws, all of which swerve to avoid the potholes memorized in daylight.

Bumping along the street, I ask the driver if he thinks the government is better now that they have a new prime minister. "Maybe," he says. "A little better." Then he brings up his mother, as though she were part of the government conversation. "Now my mother, she is very sick. She was in rest home for many years. It is very hard."

"What is wrong with her?" I ask, thinking he will ask me for money.

"I don't know," he says. "It is very hard."

I say I am sorry, but I want to know how he feels about Aung San Suu Kyi, so I ask.

"*She* is my mother," he says.

I am puzzled. I know the Nobel laureate is *not* his mother—her sons are in England.

"Your *mother*?" I say.

"Jess," he says, the Burmese pronunciation of yes. "I call her my mother, because I love her very much. She is very intelligent, very kind. I love her very much." We have reached the corner of 25th and 83rd streets, next to the Nylon Hotel.

"Can I give you a paper I wrote for her?" the driver asks.

I tell him I would love to have his paper and get out of the trishaw.

It is 7 p.m., and the streets are dark. He guides the trishaw closer to the hotel, so he can see by the generator-produced electricity that shines through the hotel windows. "It is in my secret box," he says, lifting the cushion I was sitting on. He raises a cover on the wooden seat and gives me a typewritten story titled "Martyrs Day."

"It is about her father," he says. "He is our national hero." In Burma, it is acceptable to write and talk about Aung San, who engineered the country's independence from England. Writing or talking about his daughter, Aung San Suu Kyi, could land you in prison.

I am in Burma not only because I have dreamt about this exotic land for years, but also to find out if the government is as repressive as I have heard and read. This young fellow, a university student, he says, feels he must disguise his conversations by calling Aung San Suu Kyi his mother, by writing a story about her father when it is she he reveres. Repressive? Yes.

* * *

January 22: At the Nylon Hotel, the six-dollar-per-night room rate includes free breakfast served on the 6th floor. I am on the 2nd floor. I climb four flights of stairs to a large dining room overlooking the corners of 25th and 83rd Streets. Breakfast is a pot of instant coffee, tasteless scrambled eggs, equally tasteless toasted white bread, and a small banana. I eat enough to start the day, vowing to find a tastier breakfast tomorrow, leave the hotel, and ignore the calls of trishaw drivers as I walk east on 25th Street toward the former Mandalay Palace, which has been re-built using forced labor.

King Mindon built the original palace in 1857. In his historical travelogue, *The Trouser People,* Andrew Marshall paraphrases British imperialist George Scott's description of the royal compound as "a fairy-tale collection of exquisitely carved teak pavilions with tiered golden roofs, protected by a thick red-brick wall and a moat." Maugham traveled here in 1923 and wrote about the palace's mosaics of "innumerable little pieces of mirror and of white and brightly colored glass."

When the British deposed King Thibaw and occupied the city in 1885, the compound was renamed Fort Dufferin and became the site of Burma's government house and British Club. It was theirs for less than sixty years.

From 1942 to early 1945, Japanese forces held the compound. During the fighting that preceded their ouster by British and Indian forces, the fairy-tale palace caught fire and burned to the ground. The twenty-four-foot-high walls that guarded the compound remain; the two-hundred-foot wide moat has been restored. Now the Burmese military occupies the fort, a stronghold in the center of the city, where generals plot punishments for those who dare to speak the name of Aung San Suu Kyi.

I walk three blocks east on 25th Street, past overloaded Mazda pickups where red-robed monks cling to bars on either side of the rear platform, clutching their begging bowls, past trishaw drivers who repeat the familiar "Where you from?" "Where you go?" "Ride, Madame?" A littered street where children play with discarded garbage meets Moat Street next to the palace. I weave through fleets of bicycles and vehicles to a sidewalk next to the moat that reflects the walls King Mindon built; then I turn north and walk toward the east entrance.

Crossing a bridge that leads into the compound, I see soldiers standing guard near a large red sign: THE TATMADAW [the military] AND THE PEOPLE IN ETERNAL UNITY. ANYONE ATTEMPTING TO DIVIDE THEM IS OUR ENEMY. I ask if I might take a photo of the sign and am granted permission; I cannot take a photo of the soldier who grants permission.

A trishaw driver is waiting at the entrance. He hurries over, says, "Cannot go inside. Cannot go inside. To Mandalay Hill, Madame?" I decline, think about asking where I might enter the compound to see the reconstructed palace, but in a spate of inner anger, I decide not to tour the replica, my disgust triggered by the knowledge that the military used forced labor to replace the teak palace, parts of it with concrete and aluminum. I will return to the Nylon and from there go to the Irrawaddy River to find Ohn Win, a young Burmese woman who attends an English language school, her tuition paid by Gregg, the American whom I met in Kengtung earlier this year.

I feel good this morning—I walk. After two or three miles, I stop at a canal that intersects 26th Street. I am getting tired, want the canal to be a river, but cannot turn the stagnant waters into Kipling's "Road to Mandalay." There is not a flying fish in sight.

Summoning all my energy, I walk a few more blocks and then climb a hill. Beyond its crest lie the blue-green waters of the Irrawaddy. The riverbank is littered with paper and plastic debris, but it is a thrilling sight nonetheless. Sand deltas extend into the water; ferries line the shores, and the air smells fresh. Turbaned women squat on the high riverbank, their washing spread to dry beside them.

I want to absorb the river and take it back to dream about, but there are no chairs, no shade from the midday sun. I walk past heaped-up clay water jugs placed to form a shelter for a couple who sit within their shade, and I wish I could join them. I will look for the girl I came to find and stay no longer.

"Just go to the river and ask for her," Gregg had said. "Everyone knows Ohn Win."

"Ohn Win?" "Ohn Win?" I ask everyone I meet, but they look at me blankly. A trishaw driver thinks Ohn Win is a destination. I will try another day.

Horse cart and trishaw drivers line the street next to the riverbank. "Where you from?" "Where you go?" they call through betel-stained teeth. I cannot bear to look at them—sore knee be damned, I will walk. A handsome young man squats at the crest of the hill I climbed to get here. "Pretty, pretty," he murmurs as I pass, and the pain in my knee disappears.

* * *

Tonight I will see the Moustache Brothers. The three performers, two brothers and a cousin, poke fun at the government, a risky business in Burma. One of the brothers, Par Par Lay, and the cousin performed for Aung San Suu Kyi in 1996. They joked about government cooperatives, calling them thieves, and sang a comic song about the Burmese generals. When they returned to Mandalay, they were arrested and imprisoned for five years, together with two members of the National League of Democracy (NLD) who had invited them to perform. The government no longer allows them to perform in public, but the brothers have turned their home into a theater and attract guests by word of mouth.

I invite a very tall and very shy young French woman to accompany me, and we ride in one of the snub-nosed noisy Mazda pickups for twice the normal price, a "service" provided by the Nylon Hotel.

At the home theatre, we enter a puppet-adorned room. The walls display large photos of Aung San Suu Kyi and the Moustache Brothers and signs reading "We Are Under Surveillance."

Brother Nu Law speaks better English than the other two men; he is the main performer. "You know the KGB in Russia?" he says. "We have the same thing. Here it is called MI, military intelligence." He grins mischievously. "They follow us. Watch us. Well, the government fired those guys. Now we have the same men without uniforms. They follow us. Watch us." He puffs a cheroot, offers a box of the brown cigarettes to the audience. "We know it's them. They talk on cell phones. Talk on walkie-talkies," he chuckles, holding a cupped hand to his ear.

He recounts the arrest of his brother, Par Par Lay, and their cousin. "They have show for Aung San Suu Kyi. Come back to Mandalay," he says, holding his wrists together, "they arrest. Seven years. Not me. I am lucky. I only have KGB. Watch me, watch my father."

He turns to an electrical box behind him, unplugs an unlit red light bulb and holds it up. "This is government light," he says. "No good. No light. We have generator."

He turns dramatically, gesturing toward a television set at his right, and says, "Have generator. Now we watch video, *About a Boy*. Talk about us!" Lu Naw's daughter switches on the television and the screen comes alive with an image of Hugh Grant in his role as a playboy who tended telephone lines for Amnesty International. Grant tries to get a date with a female caller, while the man next to him educates another caller: "Did you know, for instance that in Burma you can get seven years for telling jokes! Next time you laugh, I want you to think of Par Par Lay, the Burmese stand-up comedian."

The repressive government and spousal abuse are the focus of Lu Naw's performance. "Daytime I cooking, washing clothes. Two hours I massage my wife. No good. No good. Nighttime I get revenge." His speech is thick with American idioms. "I married the pick of the crop. Get out here in a jiffy," he says, looking off stage. "Shake a leg!"

Lu Naw's wife, a Burmese woman with glossy black hair piled high on her head, glides onto the stage. Before the performance she was a dowdy, big-hipped woman who served tea to the French woman and me. She has transformed herself into a beauty, a wild, high-stepping beauty, who prances and pounds across the small stage. Lu Naw looks on proudly. "My revenge," he murmurs.

Lu Naw calls his brother, Par Par Lay, who was the star of the show when performed in the Burmese language. Lu Naw introduces him as a trader. He speaks an unusual language at great length, managing to be funny while incomprehensible. At the end of his brother's monologue, Lu Naw says, "What does it mean?"

"I don't know what it means! I don't know what it means!" says Par Par Lay to an appreciative audience. If the question had been about his imprisonment, he might have answered the same, for the "KGB" might be in earshot. His five years in prison, much of it at hard labor, has made him chary of his words.

* * *

January 23: Today I will try again to find Ohn Win. As I walk west on 26th Street toward the Irrawaddy, a trishaw driver stops at my side, "Would you like to ride, Miss?" It is 11:30 a.m. and the day is heating up. I will ride. I tell the driver I am looking for a girl named Ohn Win who lives near the river. There are many girls by that name, he says, but he will try to find her for me.

Remembering my unsuccessful attempts to ride a bicycle while wearing a skirt, I am impressed by the way the driver's *longyi* stays neatly in place, covering his body like trousers, as he pedals gracefully along the wide street and over the canal bridge. A few minutes later he pushes the bicycle and me up a steep incline, and we are at the Irrawaddy.

We stop next to a woman lounging in a plastic chair near the brick wall that separates the road from the riverfront. She looks at me curiously, then bares betel-stained teeth and speaks Burmese to the driver. "She is Ohn Win's aunt," he says.

The driver says his name is Maung San; he will stay until the aunt finds Ohn Win's mother. He finds a plastic chair for me, places it next to the aunt, and in a few minutes a handsome woman with dark brown skin and a terrycloth red turban wrapped around her head walks up the riverbank and stands in front of me. Maung San speaks to her in Burmese, and she inclines her entire body toward me as she takes my hand and arm to lead me across the street. She speaks no English. "She will take you to a tea-shop till Ohn Win returns," says Maung San. I ask him to stay, and the three of us sit at a low table shaded by a leafy tree.

She asks Maung San questions, and he interprets. Where am I from? How do I know Ohn Win? She smiles broadly when I say I'm a friend of Gregg's, which is probably stretching things—I didn't know who Gregg was until two months ago when we met in Kengtung, but I can think of no other word to describe our unexpected and comfortable three-day companionship. We exchanged e-mail messages after that meeting, and when I said I was going to Burma again, he told me about Ohn Win.

Gregg's name elicits a strong reaction from Ohn Win's mother, who gazes at me long and lovingly, as if trying to memorize each detail of my face. She speaks to Maung San, and he says, "Ohn Win will be here soon—she is riding her bicycle. We will have coffee." The two of them order coffee and I order tea, free when something else is ordered.

By now, the entire neighborhood is aware of my visit. A boy hurries to our table, says, "She is coming. Ohn Win is coming." A few minutes later, a teenaged girl appears riding a white bicycle. She is the only Burmese woman I have seen with short hair. It frames her face like a cap, a modern version of the 1920's Flappers' bob. She parks her bike next to the tree, and walks straight toward me.

"Hello, Ohn Win," I say. Her mother smiles joyfully, when I say the girl's name. "Gregg told me about you," I say.

"You are Gregg's friend?" she asks, and I can tell that by saying "Yes," I am assured of her affection.

She must be the star of her English class, I think, as she chatters on. We will go to Mandalay Hill tonight, she says. "Get a trishaw driver to bring you to Mandalay Marionette School. I will meet you there at 5 o'clock." I look at Maung San. He nods.

* * *

Keeping a steady and graceful rhythm, Maung San maneuvers the trishaw east along 26th street, through heavier traffic at the clock tower corner and the large indoor market, then along the bumpy side streets leading to the Nylon. I dig through my wallet for his fare, come up short two hundred kyat, about twenty cents, a lot of money in Mandalay. "Okay, okay," says Maung San. "Is enough. Tonight. 4:30."

* * *

At 5 p.m., Ohn Win and her classmates are waiting for me outside the puppet theater. Henry, an English student who has a law degree but says he can make more money as a car salesman, pats the back of his motorbike seat. "You will ride with me?" he asks. I say I will ride with Maung San, who motions for Ohn Win to sit behind me on the double trishaw seat.

Her classmates mount motorbikes, three to a seat, while others furiously pedal bicycles. Ohn Win and I sit back-to-back on the trishaw. She twists her small body toward me and holds my hand, as Maung San pedals effortlessly past the south palace wall toward Mandalay Hill.

We are going to talk to "foreigners," people like me who visit the Buddhist temple at the hill's summit overlooking Mandalay. They go for the view and to watch the sunset; the students go to practice speaking English.

Maung San dismounts at the foot of the hill—it is too steep even for his strong legs. He will wait for us here. Ohn Win's classmates stand clustered together, waiting for us. Henry, who acts as their unofficial leader, says we must take off our shoes here: the temple entrance is at the bottom of the hill. This is sacred ground. If I were desperate, my bad knee might allow me to hobble to the top if I did it with my shoes and orthotic inserts. Without them, I would be in big trouble.

Henry sees me hesitating, and says. "Come. Come with me. We will go on the motorbike. It is very safe—there is no traffic." I climb onto the black leather seat behind him, and we zigzag around sharp turns on an eroding asphalt road. The only traffic we meet is a man in a *longyi*, descending the trail with the aid of a walking stick.

We stop near the top of the hill at another, more important, temple entrance. Here, we *must* take off our shoes; I sit on dirty marble stairs to untie my laces while Henry pushes his motorbike to a parking lot.

Watching his broad-shouldered young body receding from me, I notice his athletic beauty, the outline of his strong legs under his *longyi*. Lacking the ability to let my thoughts simply be what they are without nagging them for answers, I wonder if I have become the female equivalent of a dirty old man who lusts after young bodies. No. I do not want to take Henry to bed—I just like to look at him.

Henry returns for my shoes, says he will leave them with the motorbike, but it is impossible to cash travelers' checks in Burma, and I have hidden hundred dollar bills under the orthotic inserts. "No," I say, and pull a plastic bag out of my shoulder bag. "I would like to carry them."

Henry puts the shoe bag in his backpack and leads me up the unwashed marble stairway to an elevator where tourists stand waiting. Most are German—big, loud Germans who seem oblivious to our presence.

The only other American I have met in Mandalay is an expatriate who says she is Spanish, preferring to identify with the country where she has lived for forty years. When it comes to the war in Iraq, I do not like to be identified with the United States either, and have been surprised by my acceptance here. In Burma, the war news that makes me cry with shame, frustration, and anger is not so available—there are few televisions and radios. Maybe that is why the people are so friendly. Or maybe Burmans have the same gracious attitude as a Malaysian man who told me, "Cannot judge the person by the country."

Waiting at the elevator, I realize how guilty I am of judging people by their country, and even worse by their country's history. Although I am half German, the guttural voices of the German tourists send shivers of anger and disgust through me, anti-Hitler feelings ingrained in early childhood, and I am even more grateful for the simple acceptance of the students. They have joined us at the elevator, but we are too late. The Germans claim it.

Henry points into the distance. "We call those the Shan hills," he says, pointing toward blue-gray, haze-covered hills. The sight thrills me. My Shan friends lived in those hills; I've read many books set in those hills. "I am half Shan," Henry says.

"Half?"

"And half Mon." Good. I remember the betel-chewing motorbike taxi driver I met in Kengtung, who said his Burmese father was a soldier and who only reluctantly admitted to being half Shan, and I am glad Henry's mother was not a victim of the military campaign to Burmanize the Shan through rape and marriage.

Ohn Win has squeezed next to me and holds my hand as we board the returning elevator. At the hilltop, Henry guides me to the right. "If we go that way, you must pay," he says. I glance left and see men in the brown uniforms I have come to fear and despise on behalf of my Shan friends. I am sure the ticket-taker soldiers wear guns, but I will never know because I refuse to look at them.

We walk on the right side of the platform, Henry at my left and Ohn Win clinging to my right hand. The evening breeze is cool—this is a perfect time of year in Mandalay. Warm days, cool evenings. We are on a large circular platform that overlooks the city. Enshrined in the center is a huge Buddha. Layered with gold leaf, it towers twenty feet over the few red-robed monks at its feet.

We walk on and are soon surrounded by a crowd of young people wanting to practice English. I teach them the alphabet game, where one person thinks of a word starting with the letter "a," another with the letter "b," and so on. The difficult part is remembering the words that went before: "a, animal, b, bird . . ." We chant them together, helping those who choose letters near the end of the alphabet. They are good at this, a consequence perhaps of the chanting and rote learning practiced in Burmese schools.

A young monk has joined our group. He chooses the letter "r." "Renunciation," he says, looking at me triumphantly. "Do you know it?" he asks. The students say nothing. "It means going into the jungle," he says. I say it also means giving up anything or anyone. He looks at me with disbelief.

We continue chanting: "q, queen, r, renunciation." I am impressed. They sense it and chant louder. After "z" zebra, we walk slowly around the circular platform, Ohn Win and Henry on either side of me. I hear someone speaking French, but most people lined up along the western edge of the platform speak a guttural German while looking toward the hazy orange sun. The students approach them and ask, "Where are you from?" "How do you like Mandalay?"

"Cannot ask how old they are," Ohn Win whispers in my ear. "Our teacher tell us."

All of the tourists speak English, but the students are soon intimidated by their strange accents and return to me.

Henry points out the buildings below us: the prison, the university. They are of equal size and house many of the same kinds of people. University students were at the forefront of the 1988 protests for democratic reform. Thousands were killed; some escaped to Thailand; some are still imprisoned.

After the uprising, most universities were closed. For years, distance learning was the only option. Slowly the schools are reopening. Alice, who has joined the students on the hill, is now studying at a branch of Mandalay University. She has fair skin and a familiar sweet manner. When she says she is a Shan from Kengtung, I wonder if she is related to a former Shan student in Thailand, but that is a question I cannot ask her. We are near the soldiers now. They might overhear us and arrest me.

The foreigners stare intently at the western horizon, waiting for the sun to disappear. "Do you like to watch the sun set?" Henry asks. When I say

I do, he asks why, and I realize I am not sure. This is the most colorless sunset I have ever seen and there is nothing pretty about the flat and hazy horizon. "I think it is a way of celebrating the day," I say.

"You mean like 'now our work is over?'"

"Maybe," I say.

"We don't watch. It happens every day," he says, and I understand that watching the sun set is a luxury most in Mandalay do not have the time or enthusiasm for. How could you appreciate the sunset at the end of a day when you have not earned enough money to buy rice for your family?

When we are ready to leave, a different group of German tourists is waiting at the elevator. Their bulk and loud voices are intimidating—they crowd into the elevator first and we squeeze into the little remaining space. The elevator stops at the parking lot; we put on our shoes, and Ohn Win joins others who ride to the bottom in a pickup.

Henry and I mount his motorbike, and I hold the metal bar behind the seat instead of clinging to his waist. His broad back breaks the cool evening air as we zoom across the switchbacks that bring us to Maung San, standing respectfully next to his trishaw. He could not see the sunset from his vantage point at the bottom of the hill, but says he does not care. It happens every day.

* * *

January 24: Last night before Maung San and I left Ohn Win, we arranged to meet today to see the American film, *Around the World in Eighty Days*, and I asked Maung San to be at the Nylon by 9:30 a.m.—the movie starts at 10:00. They both arrive early, and Ohn Win and I ride back-to-back across the bumpy betel-splotched streets of Mandalay to a theatre with a billboard of Jackie Chan's befuddled face against a background of hot air balloons and seductive-looking women.

We are fifteen minutes early. I buy three tickets for less than four dollars, hand them to Maung San, who tucks them into his shirt pocket, and we walk across the street to a teashop.

Maung San orders Indian chapatti bread and chickpeas, Ohn Win orders coffee. I reach for the spouted tea thermos on the low table. Maung San gets it first, takes a small cup from a stack on the table and pours a small amount of tea into it, rinsing it and tossing the excess into the street. Then he fills the cup with tea that has a smoky aroma and hands it to me.

We sit at the edge of the teashop, waiting for the theatre to open. It is cool this morning. Ohn Win wears a red hat pulled low on her forehead,

"Gregg give to me," she says. Gregg is her champion. He encouraged her to quit her waitress job in a restaurant-bar where Maung San says drugs changed hands, and he is sending her to English and computer classes. Gregg is never far from Ohn Win's thoughts. "He is my father," she says. Her real father left years ago; she never thought someone else would assume his role.

Maung San is scooping chickpeas onto chapatti when we see a crowd surge toward the theatre door. "Is open," he says, stuffing one more piece into his mouth, and the three of us walk across the street.

Maung San gives the tickets to an usher and we select seats near the back. Ohn Win clutches my hand. "Is dark," she says. "I never been here before."

For the next two hours we watch Jackie Chan's athletic antics, as he travels the world, playing buffoon to a dignified investor while carrying out a secret mission of returning a stolen Buddha to his home village in China. Maung San and Ohn Win chuckle with delight.

* * *

Outside the theatre, Ohn Win grips my hand and looks into my eyes. "Can you come with me?" she says. "My mother prepare food this morning." Her mother cannot be there she says. She is washing clothes on the banks of the Irrawaddy River, one of the lowest paid jobs in Burma.

Maung San cycles to the house of Ohn Win's friend, a girl who calls herself Ann, and leaves us there. Ohn Win and her mother live in the basement.

Clutching my hand tightly, Ohn Win says, "I am scared. I am really scared."

"Why are you scared?"

"I am poor. I am very poor," she says. "Would you like to go to a restaurant?" I wonder at the sudden change of plan. "If you would like to," I say.

"No," she says decisively. "Come with me."

She leads me down steep concrete stairs littered with orange peels, plastic bags, discarded slippers. We duck through a rectangular opening and half slide into a small dirt cellar that is her home. A few boards are laid across the floor; a strong urine smell fills the air. It nauseates me. I want to vomit, to cry.

Eat now, cry later, I tell myself, and settle down on a log next to a wooden box with a tin washtub turned upside down on top of it. Ohn

Win lifts it off to display pickled tea leaves, shelled and unshelled peanuts, mandarin orange slices, small bananas, and an empty pink bud vase set upon a white cloth.

She gets a basin of water from the floor, pours it over my hands, and gives me a rag to dry them. "Now we can eat," she says.

I sprinkle peanuts on top of pickled tea leaves and bring a forkful to my mouth. "This is delicious," I say, meaning it.

She looks gratified. "Gregg like this very much," she says. "I am dutiful daughter. When he is here, I cook for him." The urine stench seems less strong, and I suspect she does not smell it at all.

At one end of the small room is a wood platform bed, a large mosquito net suspended above it. "I'm glad you have a mosquito net," I say, hoping it keeps out mice, rats, and other stray animals. "Gregg buy for me," she says, and I have a deeper respect for the friend I made in Kengtung.

Ohn Win points to a metal box beside me. "That is my box, that is my box," she says, the way another person might say, "That was my grandmother's porcelain vase." She stands up, rummages in the box, and comes up with a small book, *A Guide to Myanmar.* She wraps my hand around it: "For you," she says, looking pleased with herself. Thanking her, I glance through a few musty pages: The population of Burma is about fifty-two million; travel agencies offer cruises on the Irrawaddy River.

Ohn Win watches me intently. "Beautiful, our country," she says.

"And the government?"

"They take care of us," she says. "They are like our father."

Earlier she told me her father abandoned her and her mother, that for years they had lived under plastic sheeting on the banks of the Irrawaddy before finding a place in Ann's cellar, but I know she was not referring to a father like hers. She meant the government takes care of its people like a kind father—or she was afraid to say anything else.

She hands me another book titled *Intermediate English.* "This is my school book," she says. "My teacher say I need cassette player—there is tape with our book. I must listen." She resumes her position at the table.

"My mother is working very hard for me, so we can buy one," she says, and I imagine her mother on her knees at the edge of the Irrawaddy, heaps of unwashed clothing on the riverbank beside her. She lifts blouses, shirts, and *longyis* into the water, soaking and soaping them, slapping them against rocks, lifting them out and placing them to dry on the riverbank, wishing the unwashed pile were even higher, so she might buy a cassette player for her daughter at day's end.

"I would like to see some cassette players," I say.

Ohn Win pops up, walks to a rough wooden altar on the wall at my left. The altar holds a plate of oranges, three small glasses of water, and a picture of Buddha. She kneels in front of it, flattens her body so her buttocks touch her heels, presses her forehead to the ground three times, and rises to her feet again in one fluid movement. She empties the water glasses onto the floor and refills them from the basin of water she poured over my hands.

"Excuse me," she says. "I will change my clothes." She gets a red skirt from her metal box and sets it beside her. Then, she unwraps her *longyi*, and pulls it to her chin, holding an edge of the fabric between her teeth, reaches for the red skirt and pulls it on under the tent of her other *longyi*, which she drops to the floor.

"This is my lucky skirt," she says. "A little bit short. When I am in sixth standard, I win a prize. My teacher, she know I have no clothes, cannot come to award ceremony. She give me this."

The long skirt emphasizes her slender body, makes her look taller than her five feet, and I silently bless her teacher. "I am ready," she says. Then she looks down at the skirt and laughs apologetically, "A little bit short," she says.

Trying to get out of the narrow cellar opening, I inadvertently knock my head against a wooden support. "Oh, no," says Ohn Win, stroking my head. "Are you okay?"

"I am playing Jackie Chan," I laugh, but she looks troubled.

She holds my arm tightly as we walk down dusty 26th Street toward the Nylon Hotel. The cassette shop is on the way, she says.

Ohn Win has high expectations of her English class, but says, "I don't care if I am rich. I want to be noble woman. Noble woman. You know?"

A noble woman? "Do you know a noble woman?" I ask.

She looks at me from the corner of her eyes. "Jess. I know. But cannot say."

"Aung San Suu Kyi?" I say. "Is she a noble woman?"

"Oh, oh!" she gasps. "Cannot say her name. Cannot say her name." Her fear of being overheard runs deep—no one is near. Later I realize she may have meant "a Nobel woman," referring to the Nobel peace prize Ms. Suu Kyi won in 1990, but she would never say that, for she has made it clear that she is loyal to the Burmese government.

The cassette shop clerk shows us three recorders. We settle on a Sony that will allow her to record as well as listen to tapes: twenty-six thousand kyat, thirty dollars U.S., a small price to lessen my shame about my plenty and her need.

Ohn Win walks me to the Nylon, pulling me sharply aside when vehicles approach. "Don't worry," she says. "I am with you. I take care you," and I trust that she will.

* * *

Ohn Win has asked me to attend her English Class this evening and speak to her classmates. Maung San is waiting outside the Nylon at 4:30. The route is becoming familiar—the Marie Min Restaurant is on the way—and Maung San is growing more comfortable with me. I ask him if he thinks the government will be better now that they have a new prime minister. "Maybe," he says in his melodious voice. "We cannot know what is happening unless we have radio, and they are very expensive."

"What about Aung San Suu Kyi," I say.

He takes his eyes from the road, looks into my face. "You must be careful," he says.   Looking from side-to-side, he crosses the four-lane highway and weaves through the thick traffic. At the other side of the street, he returns to our former conversation. "You must not talk about Aung San Suu Kyi. Some trishaw drivers, they are spy. Sometime they follow you."

I shouldn't be shocked—I've read and heard so much about people in Burma being followed—but I am. "Do you think I'm being followed?"

"I don't know. Maybe. Must be careful."

I remember reading about the eighty-one-year-old American man who was beaten and imprisoned in Rangoon recently, remember thinking he was foolish to protest government policies. Now I realize asking questions about Aung San Suu Kyi may be equally foolish.

Maung San delivers me to the Marionette Theatre and says he will wait in a nearby teashop. Still dressed in her red skirt and a white blouse, Ohn Win grabs my bag, shifts it to her shoulder, and leads me to a stage at the front of the hall. The room is filled with young adults—thirty or forty people are waiting to hear my short presentation.

I introduce myself, tell them I teach English in Thailand and traveled to Mandalay from Chiang Mai, tell them that in the United States I have two grown sons and two granddaughters, that I am happy to be in Mandalay, and that I have read about Burma for many years and have longed to visit. Then I ask for questions.

"What do you think of our school system?" someone asks. This is what I know about Burma's school system: that one must complete ten grades before attending university, that tuition is charged even in the lower grades, that the universities are closed for long stretches of time without warning, that instructors use chanting and rote learning, that most of them teach only part of what students must know to pass exams and extort tuition from students for additional after-class tutoring. Remembering Maung San's admonition, I say, "I don't know much about your school system, but I will tell you about ours."

The next question is from Ohn Win, who is sitting next to the stage. She looks up at me, wrinkles her short nose and smiles. "Was it your goal to become a teacher?" she asks.

Yes," I say. "But I worked many years before I went back to school and became a teacher."

The students nod and smile, liking my answer, and I remember Irma Brunko, my first grade teacher, whose smiling face beamed a light of approval at me when I was five years old and my feet could not touch the floor as I sat in one of the wooden desks in our one-room schoolhouse. I wanted to be like her then, and I still do. I hope these bright and curious students sense my approval as I return their smiles.

"What do you think when you hear someone speaking broken English?"

"I think it's great that they are speaking, trying to learn the language."

"I worry about my accent."

"It's okay to have an accent. Just try to pronounce clearly so you are understood. I speak Spanish with an American accent. I cannot change that."

"Teach us Spanish."

"*Hola*, hello," I say. "*HOLA*," they chant.

"*Bienvenido*, welcome," I say. "*BIENVENIDO*," they echo.

"*Buenos dias*, Good morning," "*BUENOS DIAS*."

"Now you know Spanish," I say. "And it doesn't matter if you speak it with a Burmese accent." The students laugh and I am grateful.

I turn to Ohn Win. "Where is your teacher?" She says nothing. I turn back to the class. "It is time for your teacher to speak now," I say.

Silence. Then, "She is not here," someone says.

I wasn't prepared to speak for an entire hour. I improvise, fall back on teaching "Head and Shoulders," which English students of all ages seem to like. Thirty or forty people stand and laughingly chant in unison as they touch heads, shoulders, knees, and toes, eyes, ears, mouth and nose.

One more game and an hour will have passed. I tell them I will teach them a dance, and ask Ohn Win if we can go into the street. The question worries her, "No, no. Cannot." Could the military be watching us, could they possibly take offense at the Hokey Pokey?

"Okay. We will do it here," I say, gesturing for the students to rise. They stand in the small space in front of their seats and I ask them to raise their right and then their left hands and feet, show them briefly what we will be doing, and sing a few bars of the Hokey Pokey. Every move I make elicits smiles or laughter. They mimic me perfectly as they dance and sing the Hokey Pokey in the space in front of their seats, concluding with uproarious laughter as they jump their "whole selves" into an imaginary and very small circle, like the circle of their restricted lives.

* * *

January 25: At a crowded teashop two blocks from the Nylon Hotel, I sip tea and eat a banana pancake, the batter rich with condensed milk, while young boys hover around me, curious about the pale-skinned woman sitting among the crowd of Burmese men. They look very young. I wonder why they are not in school, then answer my own question: Their parents need the money they earn.

They look at the book I am reading, Barbara Kingsolver's *Small Wonder*, essays she wrote while trying to find hope and give it to others after the 911 attacks. I hold the book up so they can see the camellia on the cover.

There are plastic-lined spittoons under every table. Trying not to look at them, or at the wads of betel men chew and expel before drinking tea, I concentrate on my pancake, wondering whether life in Burma is better now than it was during British rule. Yes, it is, I tell myself. During the Brit's time, pale-skinned foreigners like me would have been the norm in the teashop. The Burmese would have been home, polishing our shoes.

* * *

At the Nylon, Maung San is standing beside his trishaw, dressed in the same red, white, and blue flannel shirt he has worn every day since I met him. He must wash it at night, for he always looks clean. Today he is wearing a different *longyi*, a small purple check with an embroidered black line running from waist to hem. He has invited me to his house today, but first we will visit the candy factory where his wife and son work.

We cycle down 26th street, past the canal I had tried to turn into the Irrawaddy River, and he says, "Do you want to see a small market first? Is close to my house."

The vendors look astonished when they see me. "*Mingalaba,* hello," I say. They look at each other and at me as though I had said something clever. "*Mingalaba, mingalaba, mingalaba,*" they echo, the way parents mimic a child's first words. "Where you from?" "Where you go?" "Beautiful, Madame." We walk past mounds of cabbage, fragrant cardamom seeds, tangerines, green vegetables, red chilies, lengths of *longyi* fabric, and piles of musty smelling used clothing. Someone nearby is frying chilies. The strong fumes sting my eyes and throat and set me coughing, and we walk toward the other side of the market, Maung San speaking to everyone along the way. He is explaining me, showing me off. More than once he turns to me, says, "She say you are beautiful."

I love Mandalay. Burmans have different standards of beauty than Westerners, standards that are not dependent on youth and freshness. At seventy-two, I am showered with compliments that a puritanical part of me says I should not glory in—but I do. I can be puritanical in the grave.

I buy *longyi* fabric for Ohn Win's mother, and we continue our journey on the trishaw, turning right at the canal.

Small children defecate next to the water; fishermen dangle bamboo poles into the murky green sludge. "Do you eat fish from the canal?" I ask.

"Not safe," says Maung San. "Polluted."

Maung San is forty-six years old, between the ages of my two sons. I have grown attached to him, admire his wisdom, his fine manners, his desire to show me Mandalay. "You will see how the common people live," he had said, when inviting me to his home.

He stops the trishaw and I dismount next to a huddle of bamboo buildings. "This is the candy factory," he says.

Near the entrance, a young man with thick black hair falling over his forehead stands barefooted on the dirt floor, stirring a metal bowl of caramel-colored liquid inserted into a tub of water. "Sugar cane," says Maung San. A blast of heat from the rendered sugar hits my body. "A difficult job," I say.

"Jess," says Maung San. "People they don't finish high school must take a bad job like this." He was one of those who did not finish high school. Before becoming a trishaw driver, he had a bad job in a paper factory for twenty-two years. "Every day I use acid many times," he says, pointing to a film on his left eye. "This happen."

I back away from the hot liquid and walk past a man and woman squatting on the dirt floor next to a plastic sheet covered with caramelized sugar. They wince as they cut the hot mixture into strips. Deeper in the factory, muscular men tug the cooling candy into long, thin ropes, looping it round and round their arms so it doesn't touch the dirt floor.

Maung San points at a far table where a woman snips lengths of cooled candy into smaller pieces and bags them. "My wife," he says. She is probably in her early forties, and has a lovely oval face, an Aung San Suu Kyi sort of face, but unlike the noble woman she resembles, Maung San's wife has no teeth—a candy factory is a bad place for hungry people.

She looks up briefly as he introduces us, finishes bagging six lengths of sugar cane candy, and says something to Maung San. "She will go to our house," he says.

A seventeen-year-old boy with the same beautiful face takes the seat she vacated. "My son," Maung San says. "They work together." A few minutes later his wife reappears.

"Would you like to visit my home?" says Maung San.

"Your wife?"

"She must work." I do not like leaving her at the factory but suppose she has no choice.

We walk through the candy factory to a dusty courtyard fringed with discarded plastic bags, past two children mixing water with dirt and patting mud into a toy tea set. A conscientious parent slathered their faces with yellow thanaka to protect them from the sun. Now they are slathered with mud. Next to them, a woman stirs a kettle over an open fire surrounded by large earthen pots. Maung San points to a semi-circle of woven bamboo shanties. "My home is there," he says. Stopping next to one of the huts, he says, "Here is my home. Please enjoy my home."

His bamboo home has only three sides; the side facing the street is open. Several feet of brickwork form a lip onto the dirt floor. A rough table covered with a ragged white cloth holds a vacuum pot of tea, three pieces of cake on a small plate, a bowl of cookies, and another of small bananas. "My wife prepare," says Maung San.

The room holds a platform bed, a small wooden cupboard, a bench against the wall next to the entrance, the table that holds our lunch, and two small wooden chairs. There is no color here. Only the dull grays and browns of poverty. The home affords no privacy, no shelter from mosquitoes and the misery they bring.

His conditions would have dismayed me if I had not first visited the hole in the ground that Ohn Win calls home. Maung San's hovel is a relative palace, and he is princely, as always. Gesturing to the chair nearest the entrance, he says, "Please sit down." The table legs are uneven. It rocks when I bump against it, and I have to grab it to save our lunch. I sit and reach for a banana. Maung San gets it first, peels it, and hands it to me.

A young woman, another Aung San Suu Kyi look alike, stands at our right staring at me. "My niece," Maung San says. A comb with a handle is tucked into the thick loop of black hair atop her head and her back is to the platform bed with its bundle of gray blankets. He speaks to her in Burmese. She gets a mosquito coil from the cupboard, and although there are no bugs this time of day, she sets it near my feet and lights it.

Two more sons return from school; their little sister walks behind them wearing a bright pink sweatshirt with the word *Jasmine* scrawled over the image of a black-haired girl. All of the children carry bright green book bags, all have their mother's lovely face. They join the niece and stand staring at me.

A man and woman walk into the house without saying anything. They sit on the bench, looking me over. The woman says something that sounds like "Chore-day." "Hla-day," says the man. "They say you are beautiful," says Maung San. By now, I should be tired of this, but I am not.

* * *

On the way back to the Nylon, I tell Maung San I want to look at radios. He takes me to a vendor near the clock tower, speaks to her in Burmese, and she pulls two radios out of a glass case. One is small enough to fit into the pocket of his blue plaid shirt. The other is larger. I ask which one he likes. "You must choose," he says.

The smaller radio costs four thousand kyat, a little over five dollars; the larger one is eight thousand kyat. It does not fit into his pocket but is a better radio he says. Looking at the larger radio, I realize that it is short-wave: It would bring in Voice of America. I have read about Burmese who were imprisoned for listening to the program. I buy the smaller one.

Maung San looks old for his age. His skin is stretched so tightly over his face that his skull seems indecently evident, and his filmed-over left eye looks like that of a much older man. I cannot imagine him as a son or a nephew, but holding the radio in his hand, his face has the same look of excited anticipation theirs had when getting a childhood toy.

The giving humbles me. In a just world, his strong legs would have earned him the cost of this radio—he would have bought it himself.

He lifts the trishaw seat cushion and the wooden cover of a box under-neath, tucks the radio inside, and takes me to the Nylon. I try to pay him for touring the sugar factory, but he refuses. "No," he says. "I am happy with my radio."

* * *

In my room at the Nylon, lying with my legs propped on the ceramic tile wall, I think about Maung San. I am dismayed by his poverty and by the knowledge that if worth dictated worldly circumstances he would live like a prince. Maybe he is comforted by his Buddhist beliefs. Kind as he is, he must surely feel that he will be reborn into a better life.

* * *

Maung San picks me up at 5:00 p.m. and takes me to the Marionette Theatre for a puppet show. Wearing her lucky red skirt, Ohn Win comes running to meet us. She grabs my arm, and I ask Maung San to get me after the performance.

Ohn Win and I stand outside the theatre surrounded by her classmates. They stir and bow their heads toward the street: Ma Ma Naing is approaching. Ma Ma Naing owns the theatre and is one of their English teachers. In a long red silk dress, she looks as glossy and perfect as the puppets that line the theatre walls. She extends long, thin fingers in welcome. "You will sit in the front row with Ohn Win," she says.

We take our places as Burmese musicians warm up with a clanging of cymbals, gongs, and drums. Ohn Win holds my hand and stares into my face, looking at me as intensely as her mother did the day we met. Her eyes flicker from my hair to my chin, as if she is trying to memorize me.

On the wall across from us, a *Time* magazine cover shows Ma Ma Naing, wearing the same bright red dress she wears tonight. I am surprised to learn she is a woman of renown. Maybe she has some influence with the military, I think, and am glad she is Ohn Win's teacher.

For one hour we watch puppets prance across the stage, sometimes with the curtain raised to show the puppeteers manipulating their strings while the Monkey King reenacts part of the Ramayana and saves a wooden maid.

After the performance, one of Ohn Win's classmates says he will bring her home on his motorbike, and Maung San emerges from the night, pushing his trishaw toward me. There are few streetlights in Mandalay. As we cycle toward the Nylon, I am amazed at the way Maung San maneuvers through traffic and around potholes, for we are moving through total darkness. Approaching vehicles emerge suddenly; ghostly images of trishaws, bicycles, and trucks veer to avoid us.

Several blocks away from the Marionette Theatre, he says, "Now I have something to talk to you about. I can listen to the radio and tell my family about!" His excitement reminds me of my father, and I see him again with my child's eyes, wearing a plaid flannel shirt like Maung San and sitting next to the large walnut radio in our living room, listening to a Joe Louis boxing match. And I know then that, in memory, Maung San will be synonymous with Mandalay.

We cycle past a man wearing a *longyi* and military jacket. The light from a nearby house reveals his stern face, and I wonder if he heard us talking, if simply owning a radio is a crime in this country of many crimes and few freedoms, if the military man will follow us and lock us into the yellow prison buildings I saw from Mandalay Hill. Nothing happens. We rattle along the dark streets to the Nylon.

I ask Maung San how much I owe him. "Cannot say. Nothing. I am happy with my radio."

I tuck one thousand kyat into the pocket of his blue plaid shirt, and we arrange to meet tomorrow. He wants to take me to Amarapura, Burma's capital before King Mindon moved to the fortified Mandalay palace, a move that did not prevent the British from marching on his son and successor, King Thibaw, and sending him into exile. "We must leave at 9 a.m. See monks eating," says Maung San. "Very quiet. Very peaceful."

* * *

January 26: Returning from the teashop at 8:30 a.m., I see Ohn Win standing next to her spotless white bike outside the Nylon Hotel. "Good," I say. "You can come to Amarapura with Maung San and me. We are going by trishaw."

"No!" she gasps. "Cannot. You will get too tired. Very bumpy. Very far. We must take bus."

I am easily convinced and so is Maung San when he joins us at 9:00. We walk toward the clock tower, stop when Maung San says, "Get bus here."

The only Mandalay buses I have seen are small, battered pickups, so overloaded that people must stand on the tailgate holding onto vertical bars affixed to the back. Several drive past loaded with red-robed monks, five or six standing on each tailgate, holding onto their begging bowls. "Too many people," says Maung San. Then he flags a pickup that looks almost as crowded. He takes my arm and leads me to the cab, where a fat Burmese man fills the passenger seat. "She will sit here," he says. The fat man squeezes toward the driver, and I turn my body sideways to sit beside him. Ohn Win and Maung San squeeze into the pickup box.

The fat man says he speaks English and tries to talk to me, but I cannot understand a word he says. He has no body odor, but I am overwhelmed by his girth, and the cab window becomes an out-of-focus camera lens. Nothing is distinct among the blurred masses of people in *longyis* and battered old pickups on the streets.

A half-hour later, the truck stops, and Maung San opens my door. I feel like running around him in circles, like a dog set free. Ohn Win stands on the sidewalk behind him.

"First, we will go to monastery," says Maung San, and we walk toward a long wooden footbridge that spans a lake. It is one hundred fifty years old, says Maung San, and was built by a famous monk.

We stop at a shaded teashop and I breathe deeply, expanding myself into a white plastic chair with no fat man at my side. Ohn Win and Maung San sip coffee and I drink tea until I am recovered from the bus trip, then we walk toward the lake.

A narrow bridge with tall, uneven pilings extends into the distance, but we have walked only a short way when we come to workmen repairing a broken expanse. We detour down stairs toward the lakeshore and a fleet of crescent-shaped boats. Maung San negotiates a round-trip price and we are ferried across, Maung San in the prow, Ohn Win and I sitting side-by-side in the middle.

We cross a lagoon before the lake proper begins and disembark in tall grasses at the other side. In Thailand, I read that Burma has the world's highest incidence of death by snakebite, a fearful statistic for someone like me who dislikes the very sight of snakes. I ask Maung San if he thinks the statistic is accurate. "Maybe," he says. "I don't see, but snakes can be anyplace."

My eyes are glued to the ground as we walk toward another stairway to the bridge, where artists display pen and ink sketches of crescent-shaped boats, the teak poles of the bridge rising in the distance and barefooted monks walking along the planks, black and white renditions of the colorful sights around us.

The bridge seems to grow longer as the sun moves higher in the sky, and I am relieved when we reach the opposite shore, where we spend a long afternoon, walking through the quiet grounds of Mahagandhayon Monastery. With its wide streets and elegant colonial buildings, I suspect the complex was once part of the royal compound. It is now a teaching monastery, says Maung San, and most monks from Mandalay come here for two or three weeks each year.

We stop at a sign listing ten goals resident monks strive toward, ordinary goals, such as being "clever in conduct, speaking, and walking." I am surprised to see that the last goal is "to be literate," a strange order of goals for a teaching monastery, and I wonder if the military government's desire to keep people uninformed is the reason for the emphasis on good conduct over learning.

Maung San leads us to an open-air kitchen where huge cauldrons of rice are cooking over steam created by wood fires and an elaborate water piping system. Two men in *longyis* sit on the floor, chopping dried fish into small pieces. "They are villagers," says Maung San. "They work here when they have time and get their meals. Monks cannot eat fish."

We wander through the monastery grounds and nearby temples until I am weary, and then retrace our path across the footbridge, down the stairway and into the grassy area where I am convinced snakes lie coiled and ready to strike, into the crescent-shaped boat, and back to the opposite shore. Walking along the dusty streets of Amarapura, we find a Chinese restaurant Maung San spotted from the bus.

A large wall poster shows a bottle of Spirulina Beer, "the anti-aging drink for health." In Kengtung, an American tourist had told me about Spirulina, the latest health food craze. Maung San's eyes light when I ask if he would like to share a large bottle.

A waiter brings a jug of water and three glasses. Maung San pours one for himself and one for Ohn Win. "Okay for us to drink—not for you," he says. "Is not pure, but we are used to it." I wait for the beer.

Maung San and I order vegetables and rice; Ohn Win orders a meat dish. When it arrives, I say, "I'm glad you are not having chicken. I have read that there is bird flu in Burma—your government does not tell you." They laugh and talk together in Burmese. "We say we don't worry," Maung San says. "Chicken very expensive. Cannot buy."

Our food arrives quickly. The vegetables are crisp and fresh; the Spirulina Beer is mellow. Maung San chuckles, and says, "We are having a little party," and I am grateful for our chance meeting on the streets of Mandalay, grateful that these two fine people have erased my prejudice against the Burmese.

At the street corner, an overloaded pickup stops beside us. "You and Ohn Win go in," says Maung San, helping me onto the high platform at the back. "I will stand here."

I remember an old photo in *Life Magazine*: a phone booth stuffed with people during some sort of contest to see how many could fit in. The people stuffed into this pickup could easily have won. One person's knees and elbows fit into the crook of another's, whose knees and elbows fit into the crook of another's, and on and on like a jigsaw puzzle along the two benches that run the length of the cab and a third bench in the middle. People stand between the rows of seated passengers. A seated woman turns her hips sideways, looks at me, and pats the few inches of space she vacated. Afraid I will fall if I remain standing, I squeeze onto the bench beside her. She grabs Ohn Win, who is standing in front of us, and holds her on her lap.

Having ridden crowded, malodorous buses through Latin America, I am surprised by the lack of body odors. The thought is running through my head, when a foul stench emanates from a baby across from us. Ohn Win wrinkles her nose, and looks at me with a worried smile. "Baby can't help it," she says, and seems relieved when I return her smile.

The bus delivers us to a stop near the Nylon, and I try to pay Maung San before we part. He refuses money. "No. We have a party. Cannot take money."

Tomorrow I will leave Mandalay. I kiss Maung San and Ohn Win on their cheeks and make my lonely way to the Nylon Hotel.

MAYMYO, FRIGID HOME OF THE "TRIUMPHANT ELITE"

Education is not preparation for life; education is life itself. —John Dewey

<u>January 27, 2005:</u> I am riding in a Toyota Corolla van with three other passengers enroute to Maymyo, a town that grew from a British campsite used during the conquest of the adjacent Shan States. Named after British Colonel May, it became a haven from the heat for British soldiers.

During the generals' renaming game, when Burma became Myanmar, Maymyo became Pyin U Lwin, a difficult but reasonable mouthful: Pyin U Lwin was the town's name before the British renamed it after their colonel. Yet Shan refugee friends resist the renaming. To them and to me, it is Maymyo.

Later I will visit Yawghwe, home of Burma's first president, Sao Shwe Thaike, who married Sao Hearn Kham, Princess of Hsenwi, who had attended St. Joseph's convent school in Maymyo, but finished her schooling at the age of sixteen in Kalaw. In 1932, the year Sao turned sixteen, and I was born, her brother decreed she had enough education and ordered her home. Sao's dreams were shattered—she had hoped to attend university. I rest my head on the Toyota seatback and think about the young girl who was sentenced to wait for a likely husband, comparing her to myself at sixteen.

I was a bright child, and my third grade teacher, Miss Tolppi, decided I should skip fourth grade and zoom through the lower grades, which meant I started ninth grade when I was twelve years old and graduated from high school at sixteen, knowing nothing except how to type and take shorthand and smile sweetly when approached by boys.

Sao had been a more serious student—she had the highest grades in her class—while I, having received ten minutes of career counseling from our high school principal who foretold my future as an office receptionist or a "hostess in a restaurant," played away my time. The principal's assessment had served as confirmation that college was not for the likes of me.

Like the high school principal, my parents did not see the value of advanced education for me. Their parents had been farmers, clearing trees from northern Minnesota fields where Sioux Indians still roamed, bending their backs to tug rocks from the reluctant soil. Children had more important things to do than attend school. My father had completed sixth grade. My mother completed eighth grade. Further education was a privilege and self-indulgence of the wealthy—farmers did not have time or money for such foolishness.

But, in the end, it was expectations that forestalled my education: the principal's expectation that looking pretty and greeting diners in a restaurant was the best I could expect from life, my parents' expectation and mine that I would marry young and have a family. At the age of sixteen, I got a job in the local bank, and though neither my parents nor I openly acknowledged it, I, too, waited for the right man to appear.

I rouse myself from my Dramamine-induced stupor and look out the window as the Toyota winds around a twisting road where white Buddhist stupas dot the hilltops. The air is cooler. Maymyo is at three thousand six hundred feet. Stupas, heavy toward the bottom, light and graceful at the top, and pointing always to the heavens, are said to represent the Buddha seated for meditation. The first eight stupas were built in India to house the Buddha's ashes and to inspire his disciples to give up materialism and free themselves from suffering, to attain enlightenment.

In the Theravada Buddhism practiced in Thailand and Burma, enlightenment is even more difficult for a woman to attain than it is for a man. Women must first be reborn as men, a distinction that angers Shan women friends in Thailand, as it angers me. Pressing my head back against the seat, I close my eyes, think about how Sao Hearn Hkam and I overcame the restrictions placed on us.

Sao Hearn Hkam exceeded the limitations of her role as a lowly woman when Shan Prince, Shwe Thaike, whom she was forced to marry, became the first president of Burma. Sao thrived in the role of first lady, visiting Prime Minister Nehru and Indira Gandhi in India, befriending the widow of assassinated Aung San in Burma.

As for me, when I finally entered college at the age of thirty-eight, my world became one of infinite possibility. No longer distracted by boys and frivolities, I excelled in my studies and felt empowered. I could do anything I wanted to do—I could even dream of traveling in Burma one day.

No one in the car speaks English, and the Dramamine I took before leaving Mandalay is lulling me to sleep. Occasionally, I raise my eyelids to see ever more white stupas. They inspire me not to the difficult task of attaining enlightenment but to despair at the distortions men make in religious beliefs to assure ultimate bliss in the afterlife, while practicing ultimate horror in the present life.

I remember the fictional Burmese magistrate in Orwell's *Burmese Days*, who plotted to defame and disgrace a fellow Burman as well as an English lumber merchant. He chuckled at their downfall, and planned to build pagodas to offset his evil deeds and attain nirvana. "Nothing has changed," said a Burman who had read Orwell's book. "The leaders are worse today."

Photos of today's Burmese generals show them donating goods to Burmese monasteries while their soldiers slaughter unsuspecting villagers in the jungle. My thoughts veer to George Bush, who God blesses America while American soldiers slaughter innocent Iraqis in "friendly fire" incidents. Unsettling thoughts, but they do not lower my spirits—I cannot feel depressed, for my dream of visiting Burma has come true.

Nearing Maymyo, we pass a giant military academy, with a glittering gold sign that announces the cadets' motto: THE TRIUMPHANT ELITE OF THE FUTURE. I dislike this monument to the military, but Maymyo has more to offer. There is a huge botanical garden here, developed by British General May using Turkish prisoners during World War I.

We stop on Maymyo's impressive main street. On one side of the street is an arcaded colonial building with a watchtower at the top; Queen Victoria donated the clock tower across the street. They are impressive only from a distance. The clock does not work; the paint is flaking on the arcaded building, which appears to house offices.

I look at two nearby cheap hotels, settle on the Grace, which charges five dollars per night and looks clean. After stashing my backpack in the room, I walk to the market to see stall after stall of sweaters. Maymyo's main industry is knitting, but despite the large volume of sweaters, there is little variation in patterns, and most are too large, too small, or too ornate. I buy a lime green cardigan for five dollars, and then I find a pony-cart—Maymyo's only taxi system—to take me to the botanical gardens, and we bump along a dirt road lined with sturdy-looking, tin-roofed brick structures where British colonizers once lived.

We arrive at the garden at five o'clock. It closes at 6:00. I will have sixty minutes to see the two-hundred-forty-acre site—long enough for my bad knee, not long enough to absorb the beauty of the place.

The flowers that line the entrance road are like those of Minnesota, pale blue lupine, moss roses, petunias, pink and purple fuchsias, small-petaled daisies, begonias. My yearning for the exotic is gratified when I see bushes heavy with tropical cup-of-gold flowers, like large inverted trumpets, drooping toward the ground next to flowering red poinsettia trees. Black swans float on a lake at my right—reminders that I am still in Burma, the exotic land I dreamed about while reading Kipling and Maugham.

I do not remember when I first heard Kipling's *Road to Mandalay* or how I knew Mandalay was in Burma. But there seemed to be a part of my brain that had always known about and longed to see Burma. Not the Burma of today, not the Burma of depraved generals and frightened ethnic people, but a Burma of gilded temples, of exotic foods and faithful friends.

The gilded temples remain and so do faithful friends, I think, remembering Ohn Win and Maung San in Mandalay, but the Burmese people have gone from the arrogance of British colonialism to the equally arrogant uncaring rule of military generals. Military rule and the arrests of those who speak against it must seem even more oppressive than British rule did—it must be doubly painful to suffer at the hands of your own people.

I wander through the grounds in a large circle, inhaling air that smells like flowers and water and earth, and stopping next to a plaque that gives credit for this garden to Burmese General Than Shwe, no mention of British Colonel May. I remember my surprise that most Shan refugees did not know who Aung San Suu Kyi was: Now I attribute their ignorance to this kind of historical re-writing where arrogance replaces fact with fiction.

Near sunset, I find a bench near the lake where big, black crows squawk in anger as they vie for position in the trees, and I liken them to Burmese generals, sleek and well fed on the decaying remains of this country, a vile thought that does not destroy my delight in the garden.

The pony cart is waiting outside the gate. We jolt along the rough road past a large sprawling guesthouse, where a few guests sit reading on the patio. It looks obscenely luxurious for this poor country, but I wish I were staying there instead of at the humble Grace. It looks so easy.

At a restaurant next to the Grace, I eat cardamom-flavored fried rice before climbing the stairs to my second-floor room, which feels like a refrigerator now that the sun has gone down. The hotel clerk said the bathroom had hot water, but I cannot stand the thought of removing my clothing to shower. I take off my jacket long enough to put the lime-green sweater over my tee-shirt, replace the jacket, pull on gloves I bought at the market, put a woolen shawl over head and shoulders, and climb into bed to read *The Bridge on the River Kwai.*

I should have lifted the blankets before I chose this hotel: There is no top sheet, and I am obsessed with the thought of dozens of dirty bodies sleeping under these same rough blankets. I take the shawl from my head and shoulders, tuck it between my body and the blankets and read about the proud British captain whose ego blinded him to common sense and ultimately led to his destruction while he labored for the Japanese who marched through Thailand during World War II and conquered Burma.

I had hoped to see the convent school Sao Hearn Hkam attended in Maymyo, but I cannot stand the thought of another frigid night in a single sheeted bed.

HSIPAW, WHERE OXEN GRAZE
AND PRINCES DISAPPEAR

Hsipaw was an attractive place with a deceptive air of tranquility.
—Andrew Marshall, The Trouser People

Something terrible has happened. Inge Sargent (former Princess of Hsipaw)
—Twilight over Burma

January 28, 2005: With shoulders slumping under my heavy backpack, I look around in confusion. Could this be the first class compartment on the train from Maymyo to Hsipaw? The seats are narrow, unpadded wooden benches; there is no glass in the upper portion of the windows. I hand my ticket to a military man standing in the aisle, sure he will send me to another car. He points to a nearby bench. This is it. This wooden bench will be home for six hours.

A tall man in a military jacket, sitting on a bench across from me, stands and reaches for my backpack, saying he will "hep" me. He lifts the pack from my shoulders and stashes it on a metal overhead rack. Sitting, he says he will take cae-ah (care) of me on the train. This is what I have read about: the Burmese military dogging the footsteps of ordinary citizens and tourists. Realizing I am stuck with it simply by being here, I take a deep breath, sit, and survey my surroundings. With the exception of a ten-person tour group from the United States, most passengers are soldiers. First class fare is four dollars; ordinary fare is three dollars. For soldiers it is no doubt free.

The train rocks from side to side and bounces up and down, and my overactive imagination hears a weird chant in the rhythm of its wheels and the wind that swishes through glassless windows: *It's death we bring; it's death we bring; it's death we bring.* It is a chant born from reading human rights reports about women raped and entire families killed by Burmese soldiers, and I wonder how many of the straight-backed, polite, military men around me are murderers.

I walk the length of the car, saying hello to fellow Americans: They are here to see the Gokteik Bridge built more than a hundred years ago over a one-hundred-foot-deep gorge. Pennsylvania Steel won the bid for material, design, and building of the bridge, and Americans worked on its construction, completing it in 1900, when it was touted as the highest railway bridge in the world.

I return to my seat followed by a silky-haired man from Georgia who is coming to talk with two Americans sitting across from me. As tour-group tourists are prone to do, he recounts various trips he has made, including five trips to Russia. Then he starts talking about Burmese politics. Most of his words are submerged in the train's clanging chant, *It's death we bring; it's death we bring, it's death we bring,* but I hear him mention Aung San Suu Kyi. "They can't do anything about her," he says, shaking his head, and I wonder if he can possibly feel sympathetic for the heavily armed military battalions that guard the small, unarmed pacifist woman day and night.

* * *

We are now in Shan State. The train chugs through the smoky hills, past terraced rice fields. Wind fanning my face through the open windows carries the scent of fires that consume after-harvest debris, and I inhale the smoke, remembering grass fires my father lit to clean weeds and underbrush from our farm. Orange clay soil becomes a sickly brown, soil my father would have measured with his farmer's eye and pronounced "Poor land." Oxen huddle in the shade of woven bamboo stilt houses; the ubiquitous plastic bags that litter the world float over neatly tended yards.

As we near the Gokteik Bridge, the soldier across from me stands, looks out the window on the opposite side of the train, and says, "Come here. Look." And reluctant as I am to be befriended by a soldier, I follow him for a better view of the deep gorge and the bridge that spans it.

The Americans "Oooh" and "Ahhh." Soldiers, who have seen it before, doze using their rolled-up jackets as pillows. I look at them, wondering which of them has raped Shan women. The one wearing a brown-checked *longyi,* his bare feet curled under himself? The one who is showing me the view and said he would take care of me? The one who sprawls across an entire seat, sleeping with his head on the wooden armrest, his feet sticking out the window?

Soon we are on the bridge itself, and I gawk out the open window at the one-hundred-foot-deep ravine. I return to my seat, open my journal, and write. The caretaker soldier watches, asks what my business is, and seems relieved when I say I am a teacher. I wonder if he would have demanded to see my journal if I had said I was a writer, wonder what he would have done if he had seen my scribbling about the dreadful tatmadaw—the military's name for itself. Would this courteous, handsome man have roughed me up, like the 81-year-old American who protested against the government earlier this month?

The Americans leave the train at Kyaukme, where a bus will meet them, and they will continue their tour. "Fifteen minutes here," my caretaker soldier says. I leave the bus and stroll the long train platform, stretching backwards and sideways to relieve kinks induced by hours of sitting on wooden benches. Women with thanaka-decorated yellow faces stroll through the crowd, selling flat breads, oranges, a meat and vegetable concoction fragrant with garlic, and sticky rice wrapped in banana leaves.

Too soon, the caretaker soldier walks toward me, a worried look on his face. I made the mistake of writing my name for him, and he has assumed the last four letters are pronounced like the word nice. "Brr-nice," he says. "The train will leave." We hurry back. Glancing up at one of the railway cars, I see whole families crowded onto one narrow wooden bench, and I understand the luxury of first class: space.

I thank the soldier for getting me, but I refuse to like him, for as soon as we are underway, I hear the awful message of the rails: *It's death we bring, it's death we bring, it's death we bring.*

Seven hours of bouncing and swaying bring us to Hsipaw. My soldier companion carries my backpack to the coach door, where a trishaw driver speaking broken English invites people to Mr. Charles Guesthouse.

I climb onto one of the wooden trishaw seats. The driver settles my backpack into the other seat and pedals across rough roads covered with discarded plastic bags next to open sewers that smell of urine. Fifteen minutes later, we arrive at the guesthouse, a large white home, and two smaller teak homes set in a courtyard filled with wooden tables and white plastic chairs, all surrounded by white stucco walls, an island of cleanliness and order.

I settle into a high-ceilinged three-bed room, the only one available with attached bath. Washing the day's dirt from my hands, I watch black water flow down the drain and consider a quick shower, but I am eager to explore the town, to use my body after sitting on a wooden train seat for seven hours with wind from the permanently open window blasting my face. I want to see the former Shan palace, home of the murdered prince, to immerse myself in the mystique of the magical life he shared with a tall and elegant Austrian woman, Inge Sargent.

In *Twilight Over Burma*, Ms. Sargent's memoir, she writes about life with Sao Kya Seng, a Shan she met while both were students at the University of Colorado. She married him without knowing he was a prince until they arrived in Rangoon by boat and were met by throngs of people throwing flowers into the river. They had been married ten months by that time, and she scolded the prince for keeping his true identity a secret, but she learned to enjoy their life together—until the military takeover of 1962, when the prince was imprisoned by the military. The *Lonely Planet* says he "disappeared." Ms. Sargent has ample evidence that he was killed.

On a city map, I locate the palace, two or three miles north of my guesthouse, and walk toward it along a potholed road, across patches of crumbling asphalt and a bridge over a stream where women stand knee deep in water, washing clothes. I turn right at a dirt crossroad, then left before a monastery where monks chant singsong meditations, and then I stand befuddled. This weed-lined pathway does not look like a palace road, not like the road the prince and princess traveled in their Mercedes. An excited-looking villager walks to the fence bordering his yard. "Palace that way," he says, gesturing right along the path.

I turn a bend and see a padlocked chain link fence. Next to a deep ditch, a retaining wall provides a place to sit and rest. A motorbike approaches, bearing a slim, athletic-looking driver and a pudgy, moon-faced boy, who dismounts, unlocks the gate, and stays behind when the driver goes inside.

"Would you like to see the palace?" asks the boy in near-perfect English. My knee hurts—I tell him I am tired and will probably visit the palace tomorrow. "Mr. Donald is not here," he says. "He is in Yangon [the recently renamed Rangoon] doing business."

When I compliment the boy's English, he says, "I learn from Mr. Donald. He is my grandfather."

"I have read Inge Sargent's book," I say, and he choruses the title with me, *"Twilight Over Burma, My Life as a Shan Princess."*

"Mr. Donald, he is the prince's nephew," says the boy. "I am Mone Sageng Zing. I will write for you," he says and demands my notebook. He prints his name and explains the meaning. "Mone mean round, Sageng mean ruby, Zing mean clear." I print my name, telling him it means "bearer of victory." He glances at me out of the corner of his eyes, and it is clear that he is here to educate me, not to be educated.

"If you want to see the palace, you must pay me one thousand kyat," he says. He looks like a ten-year-old child but talks like a twenty-year-old, and is self-confident to the point of brashness.

"What do you say your town name?" he asks.

I correct him. "*How* do you say your town name," I say. He looks puzzled. "You said '*What* do you say your town name. You should say, '*How* do you say your town name.'"

"Same thing," he says, and I'm glad I'm not his teacher.

"My town is Minneapolis," I say. "I live in the state of Minnesota."

"Are you sure you don't want to see the palace?" he asks.

I have walked all this way only to develop a sore knee. "Maybe tomorrow," I say.

The boy points to two small brick houses, one behind the ditch outside the palace walls and another inside the gate entrance. "Soldiers live there," he says.

Two tourists approach. Mone Sageng Zing pops up from the retaining wall. "Do you want to see the palace?" he asks. They nod. He opens the gate and they start walking through. "Just a minute. Just a minute," he says sternly. They stop, send a puzzled glance my way. "If you want to see the palace, you must pay him one thousand kyat each," I say.

They are German and do not part easily with money. They sit next to me on the retaining wall and read the *Lonely Planet* blurb about the palace. Having read that a one-thousand-kyat fee is normal, they agree. The pain in my knee has eased a bit, so I join them. The young couple is not typical of most German tourists I have met: They are quiet and polite.

Inside the gate, Mone Sageng Zing says, almost gleefully, "Cannot see the palace. Only the grounds."

As we were sitting on the retaining wall, he had said he had a tennis court where he played with his uncle every day. I ask if the crumbling, weed-infested, concrete area on our right is the tennis court. He nods. No net, no posts to hold one.

Mone Sageng Zing points to the small brick house on our left. "A soldier lives there. That is his camera," he says, pointing to a wooden box appended to the house. "Inside camera. Take your photo."

"Is the soldier nice?" I ask, wondering if he is Burmese and has been planted there by the regime, or if he is from the Shan State Army North, which has signed a ceasefire agreement with the Burmese military, but it is a question not worthy of an answer, I guess, for the boy says nothing.

Neither do the Germans, who communicate only by unreadable glances. We continue toward the palace.

This is not exactly a murder scene—the prince was taken away from here and murdered in the jungle—but it feels like one. I remember the eerie feeling I had going to a K-mart Store in Minneapolis the day after a young woman had been found murdered on the grounds, remember wondering if I were some sort of horrible thrill seeker, or if I really had to be there. This place gives me the same feeling, a sort of shameful sadness.

The palace looks worse up close than from a distance. Paint on the wooden trim has flaked and faded. The boy looks at it. "No water. No electricity," he says; then he runs up steps to the kitchen entrance, sticks a hand through a missing panel in the screen, and opens the door, returning with a guest book. "Please write your name and country and how much you donate to palace upkeep," he says, for the admission fee is supposed to be used for that purpose. He leans over to form a writing table with his chubby back. "Write here," he says.

Standing, he says, "This way to the prayer house." He stops at a banyan tree with a girth so large the five of us could not reach around it and with a myriad of exposed roots extending like giant fingers into the ground. "More than one hundred years old," he says. "You like?" I like. The Germans smile.

Behind the tree is a graceful, two-story gazebo-like structure. Climbing an open stairway to the second floor, I realize it is in a dangerous state of disrepair. Floorboards are missing in the verandah that wraps around three sides. This time, the look the Germans exchange is obviously one of fear. We dare walk only near the core of the building, the doorways to which are padlocked. "Cannot see inside," the boy says. "No electricity. No water."

He points into the distance. "Prayer house; prayer house; rice fields." The deceased prince was generous, giving away part of his estate to local farmers and lending them the equipment to cultivate it. "Over there the river," says Mone Sageng Zing. We follow his chunky body back down the stairs. At the bottom he says, "Would you like to see the pool?"

The five of us retrace our footsteps along the garden path and walk past the palace to the pool. As we had sat together on the retaining wall, Mone Sageng Zing had said, "I have a pool. I can swim. Can you swim?" But this pool has not seen water for years; the concrete is crumbling. "No water?" I say, and he repeats his mantra: "No water. No electricity." The Germans exchange messages with their eyes—incredulity, I think.

The boy points to green sludge in the deep end. "I keep fish and frogs there," he says. Maybe. The muck is so thick nothing is visible beneath the surface.

The sun has set, and the sky is growing dim. The house looks abandoned, forlorn. I wonder if the boy's cocksure confidence sustains him indoors, or if he is pervaded by the house's gloom. The German tourists hurry away. I walk back to the guesthouse, feeling subdued. It's twilight over Burma.

* * *

I am reading in the guesthouse yard when an old woman with a towel wrapped turban-like around her head sneaks up behind me and starts massaging my neck and shoulders. She coughs, turns her head aside and spits onto the concrete. My neck and shoulders are sore, so I let her probe until I realize she cannot distinguish flesh from bone. Her fingers slide along my spine, ignoring the tension knots alongside. Probe, cough, probe, cough, probe, cough. She gestures to a bench, wants me to lie down, but I stand up. "No," I say. "No more."

"Two hundred kyat," she says, mumbling through toothless gums. About twenty cents. The woman's clothes are worn thin with washing; her feet are bare. I would give her more but fear it would encourage her to run her uneducated fingers down my spine and cough down my neck again.

She sits in a white plastic chair next to the guesthouse owner and her two daughters, who are relaxing in the sun. A French woman stops in front of them, asks one of the daughters if the old woman is a relative. "No!" she almost shouts. "She is dark skin. We are light skin!"

To my eyes, the mother and daughters have light brown skin. The difference in their skin color and that of the old woman is probably a matter of exposure to the sun, but a light skin fetish permeates Southeast Asia. In Thailand, refugee friends wear jackets even on the hottest days to protect their skin from turning deeper brown.

Recently, I read *In a Free State*, by V.S. Naipaul, a novel about skin color and degradation, about the condescension, pity, and shame of whites living among blacks, and about the rage and confusion of the blacks. Now I see it here and wish it were not so.

* * *

January 30: After spending the day at the guesthouse reading and writing in the concrete courtyard, I walk downtown, turning left at the guest-house and right on the main road where I pass teams of oxen lazing at the roadside and a mound of tangerines tended by a woman in a conical hat who refuses to sell me one but gives it to me instead. I walk over a urine-smelling wooden bridge that spans a garbage-strewn stream.

Two streams intersect the town, flowing toward the Dohtawaddy River, which borders the east edge. Hsipaw is a shady and seemingly peaceful place, with near-perfect weather this time of year, but the government fears what lies beyond its borders: travel to most surrounding areas is forbidden. Although the Northern Shan State Army has signed a ceasefire agreement with the military government, it is rumored that the Southern Shan State Army has outposts nearby, and although the Hsipaw branch of Aung San Suu Kyi's National League for Democracy Office has been closed, Burmese soldiers watch it carefully.

Yesterday I found Mr. Book, who handles English-and-Burmese-language used books, and bought an English-language copy of Orwell's *Burmese Days*. I had read it before but wanted to read it again while in Burma.

This afternoon Mr. Book, who speaks excellent English, waves as I walk past and invites me to join him in the courtyard of his home behind the dusty jumble of used books. I sit in a woven bamboo chair next to him, and he points to a light bulb hanging from the bookstall ceiling. It is lit. "It's curiouser and curiouser," he says. "Like *Alice in Wonderland*. Remember? It's curiouser and curiouser. In December, we have electricity three days only. Today light!"

He is watching an English language movie on a small television set nestled into the books. "A comical," he says. "No. A comedy, is it?"

Someone approaches. Mr. Book pops up, talks with him in Burmese for a few minutes and returns. "Police officer," he says. "He watch me all the time because I was secretary NLD, opposition party."

There are photos of Aung San Suu Kyi and the Moustache Brothers hanging on the courtyard side of the bookstall walls. I ask him if they are allowed, and he says, "Yes. Photos okay."

"Policeman ask if I have that book *Twilight Over Burma*—he probably saw you come here. I tell him, 'No. I don't have that book.' Many tourists try to give me that book, but I don't take. I know it is forbidden."

The light bulb goes out; the television screen turns black. "No electricity," he says. Then, "I am not afraid of the police."

We chat a few more minutes; then Mr. Book looks at me meaningfully and nods his head toward the street. "He is back," he says.

He walks toward the policeman, and I start to leave, aware that I am making trouble for him. "I like that book I bought from you, *Burmese Days*," I say. "Orwell was an excellent writer." Mr. Book glances back at me, says nothing, and turns to talk with the policeman.

I walk a few more blocks to Mr. Food's restaurant, where I sip a Spirulina, munch on fried peanuts, and read *Burmese Days*. Without asking permission, a man I have not seen before sits on a stool beside me and gestures to the book: In perfect English he says, "Orwell. Remember *1984*? When General Ne Win came to power in 1962, we said he had read only one book: *1984*. Because then our country become like *1984*." Burmese soldiers are eating noodles in a semi-private room nearby, but he seems oblivious to their presence.

Pointing again to *Burmese Days,* the man says, "Where you buy?" When I say I bought it from Mr. Book, he says, "He has trouble, but brave man. Every day police come, but he remember always what our leader [Aung San Suu Kyi] say, 'Do not show fear. Do not show respect.'" His words make me nervous. I glance at the soldiers in the nearby room, their heads bent over noodle bowls. His eyes follow mine: He rises abruptly and leaves the restaurant.

Twenty minutes later he returns and with his eyes trained on the soldiers who are still slurping noodles in the next room, he thrusts an upside down letter at me. "Please hide," he says. "Mail in your country. You can read." And he disappears again.

I finish my noodles and vegetables, leave the restaurant and walk out to the street, dark now except for the winking candles that light vendors' sidewalk tables and the bobbing beams of flashlights walkers carry. At a store across the street from Mr. Food, I buy the cheapest flashlight I can find, and hold it at my breast in the hope that drivers of wheeled vehicles, bicycles, motorcycles, and trucks, will see and avoid me.

The farther I get from the restaurant the darker it becomes. I cannot distinguish one building from another. When I reach a bridge, I see a motorcycle's single bright light, heading directly for me. I move to the edge of the road. The cycle swerves toward me; then stops suddenly about a foot from the hopeful pinprick of light at my breast. Fear ripples through me as I see a uniformed soldier straddling the cycle. "Do not show fear. Do not show respect," I think, an impossible task. I throw up my hands and say "Mr. Charles Guesthouse," and turn my head dramatically from side to side, trying to indicate I am lost. Only then do I realize I have been walking on the left side of the street—the soldier should have been driving on the other side. He detoured intentionally to frighten me. He chuckles and drives away.

I stand still until I see a young woman in a white blouse illuminated by a flashlight. Approaching her, I say, "Mr. Charles?"

She grabs my hand. "Come, come," she says, turning me around. Smiling reassuringly, she repeats, "Come with me," and in a few minutes delivers me to the guesthouse courtyard. I had walked past it in the darkness.

The guesthouse has generator-produced electricity until 9 p.m. I take a hot shower and look at the letter tucked inside my book. It is unsealed and addressed to someone in England. I open it and read. Most of it explains a numbers game played in Hsipaw, but a couple of lines say, "Now it is worse in Burma. The soldiers watch us all the time." That is why he wanted me to mail it outside the country: In Burma all incoming and outgoing mail is censored.

I settle into bed with *Burmese Days*, knowing I have experienced both the goodness and the evil of Shan State today.

* * *

January 31: I am riding a heavy one-speed bicycle I rented at the guesthouse this morning. I cross the wide stream, where washerwomen slap clothes against the rocks, and start up the hill toward the Shan palace. The sun is shining brightly, but the air is pleasantly cool. At the crest of the hill is a police station, which in Burma is synonymous with military base. A billboard outside reads, "May we help you" in English. I wonder if anyone has ever gone to them for help, or whether others feel the same mix of fear and anger as I do in passing.

I bike past the road to the palace, and, at the top of a second hill, a long stucco wall at my right encloses another military base, this one designated as such. An officer is swaggering down the road toward me. "Do not show fear. Do not show respect," I tell myself, and bike past the betel-chewing soldier—but only a few feet. The road ahead is empty: no houses, no bicycles, no oxcarts. I have read too many horror stories about Burma. I turn around and pedal back to the guesthouse.

* * *

February 1: I am walking on the west side of the street, across from Mr. Book and Mr. Food, when an even-featured man, handsome as a movie star, who is sitting on a curbside wooden bench, speaks to me. "Can I help you?" he says.

In this town where so many have adopted names dubbed by passing tourists, I now meet Mr. Knowledge. A young Irish friend who had traveled to Hsipaw told me about him, said he was an excellent tennis player though he was an old man—but he cannot be more than fifty.

"I see you before. You have kind face," says Mr. Knowledge. "Please come into my house. I will show you my coin collection." We sit at his desk near the front door of an immaculate teak home, and he shows me musty-smelling scrapbooks of paper money from many countries and leather bags filled with coins. On the desktop are photos of a man and woman on horseback. Pointing to the man, he says, "The Prince of Hsipaw. He was my father's friend." Shifting his finger toward the woman, he says, "Inge Sargent." It is a 50s era photo of a young and handsome couple, whose presence is remembered with a combination of pride, anger, and sadness in this seemingly peaceful town.

Behind us a shoe rack holds several pair of decrepit-looking tennis shoes. I tell him I have a young Irish friend who played tennis with him last year and lost every game. Mr. Knowledge chuckles, shows me the shoes' patched soles. "I fix with inner tubes," he says. "New too expensive. Cannot buy."

A canopy of sorts hangs over our head. "What is that for?" I ask.

"Holes in roof. World War II. Japanese bullet holes. Cannot repair—too expensive. Canvas catch pigeon feces. No money.'

He stands, asks me to meet his wife. Walking through the length of the house, he says, "No money and do not want to ask family. They have cheroot factory for many years." The cheroots contain fruit juices, he says, and are wrapped in banana leaves and sealed with sticky rice. I have seen many Burmese smoking the dark brown cigarettes and think they look like pure nicotine. Mr. Knowledge makes them sound like a fruity dessert.

In the kitchen, his wife stands stirring a kettle on a wood-burning stove. "My wife," he says. "She is calm. Stay in the kitchen." She turns a calm smile on me and keeps stirring, stopping only to ask how old I am, murmuring appreciatively when I say I am seventy-two. "Beautiful," she says, looking at me intently and stroking her cheek. It is my Minnesota-pale skin she admires.

Mr. Knowledge hands her a small bowl. She fills it with beans and sets it on a wooden table. Handing me a spoon, Mr. Knowledge says, "Please eat." The beans look like limas but are infinitely sweeter and more flavorful. Before we leave the kitchen, Mr. Bean tucks four beans into a small plastic bag, insisting I plant them in Thailand. Poking a hole in the bag he says, "We call Angry Beans. Must breathe or will not grow."

He walks me back through the living room, and as we pass his desk, says, "One minute, please. I have old money for you." Reaching into a desk drawer, he pulls out former banknotes with pictures of Aung San on them. "Ne Win [instigator of the 1962 military coup] he say no good. Worth nothing."

Ne Win, the Burmese general who led the country to poverty, confiscating land in the name of socialism, was a superstitious numerologist whose favorite number was nine. He demonetized the bank notes Mr. Knowledge has given me, and issued forty-five and ninety kyat notes, numbers divisible by nine, a ridiculous move that impoverished many. I tuck the notes into my billfold, say goodbye to Mr. Knowledge, and then I cross the street, turning right toward the river.

* * *

I met Australian-born Maureen at the guesthouse this morning. Although she had red hair and was younger than I, she reminded me of my mother, a woman who was comfortable with her role in life. She said she had lived in Hsipaw for most of the last eight years and wanted to exchange English-language books. I follow the directions she gave me to her home.

Near the general area of Maureen's home, I ask women at the roadside where she lives. Two of them raise their arms and point in the direction I am walking; a third woman says, "Three more doors."

Maureen is a small woman with fair skin, an English teacher, like me. She is sitting in the front yard of the garage-become-apartment she is renting while renovating an old teak tea storeroom on the riverbank. We chat a few minutes; she says she taught English at Mr. Book's for six months the first year she was in Hsipaw, and then shows me an array of books she wants to trade. I choose *The Book of Salt*, by Truong, a fictional memoir of Gertrude Stein's Vietnamese cook, and give her my copy of *The Bridge on the River Kwai*.

We walk a few more blocks to the Dohtawaddy River, and she points to a large teak house on the riverbank. "My new home," she says, and tells me of an arrangement she has with a local Shan man who is supervising construction. The property will be his, but she will live here and have a teashop.

Inside, Maureen opens the shuttered windows. Light illumines the cavernous first floor, and I imagine bags of tea packed up to the high, unadorned teak ceiling. We climb an open stairway to the second floor, which has lower ceilings and feels cozier. Opening the shuttered windows, we look east at the peaceful green Dohtawaddy River. Someone is paddling a small boat downstream, and for the first time I understand why Maureen wants to live here.

I leave her to deal with the workmen, who are constructing a concrete block building set at right angles to the house—when finished, it will house toilets and a shower.

I walk one garbage-littered block north along the river, then turn west toward the market, where I see a young trishaw driver who resembles Sai Soe, a refugee friend who lived near Hsipaw before fleeing to Thailand and who had wanted me to see the town. I wonder if they are cousins but cannot ask. Not only does the driver speak no English, but Sai Soe had a different name when he lived here. I am glad I do not know it—it would not be wise to talk about Shan refugees in this heavily fortified town.

The trishaw driver smiles sweetly but looks puzzled when I say, "To the palace." A friend lounging nearby says something to him in Shan and the driver nods, pulls his bicycle into the street and waits for me to mount one of the wooden seats. I want to meet Mr. Donald, who should have returned from Rangoon by now. We bump over the rutted roads to the hill before the turnoff to the palace. I get down and walk to ease the trip uphill, resume my seat at the top. A few more rutted blocks and we are at the palace.

A German man and his guide are sitting on the retaining wall where I sat with Mone Sageng Zing the first time I was here. The palace looks abandoned—there are no stirrings of activity within the compound walls. I chat with the German, ask him if he has read *Schindler's List,* which I read last month. The question upsets him. "No," he says emphatically. "We cannot read that book in Germany. Our country is like Myanmar. We will not talk about it," he says. This is an attitude I have not seen among other German tourists, who rave about their country's democratic attitudes, and I would like to hear more. But there is no prodding this stern-faced man—our conversation is over.

When twenty minutes have passed, I tell the trishaw driver to take me back to the guesthouse where I wonder what happened to Mr. Donald. Is he being interrogated by the military? Has he been imprisoned in Rangoon?

* * *

February 2: Today Maureen and I have arranged to take a bus to nearby

Lashio, another town refugee friends wanted me to see. In 1940, during World War II, Japanese troops descended on Burma through China on the north and Thailand on the south. That was when the allies built the Burma Road to supply China's Kuomintang forces fighting the Japanese in western China. In1940, the road terminated at Lashio.

I was a child at the time, but Burma, China, and the story of the road intrigued me even then. Today the Burma Road extends from Kunming, China, to Mandalay. I have walked across it in Hsipaw, but I want to stand on the original terminus in Lashio. Maureen wants to visit a Lashio medical clinic supported by a U. S. Burma relief group.

Maureen meets me at the bus stop at 8 a.m., says the bus will not be leaving until 10:00, and asks if I would like to see some jade. Most shops are still closed, but the jewelry shop's metal awning is raised: Workers bend their heads to gold and silver jewelry, setting translucent pieces of jade, ranging from dark green to almost white, into gold and silver neck-laces and rings. A round-faced man in a silk *longyi* meets us at a glass counter where we stand gazing at the jewelry. He and Maureen exchange a few English words—she has not mastered Shan—then he turns to me and asks, "A ring, Madame?" as if he has read my mind. Walking here with Maureen, I had decided an inexpensive jade ring would be a nice memento of Hsipaw.

He shows me several rings: Large stones set into rich eighteen-carat gold. Too showy, too ostentatious. I spy a small, translucent green stone in a simple deep gold setting and ask to try it on. It fits, and it is lovely. Although it is customary to bargain, when he says it is forty U.S. dollars, I peel off the bills and tell him I will wear the ring.

Walking back to a teahouse near the bus stop, I feel a twinge of guilt, triggered by my involvement with Shan refugees in Thailand and the knowledge that the money I spend on self-indulgences could mean the difference between hunger and satisfaction for the needy. In Thailand, forty dollars will buy one month's rice and cooking oil for a family of eight. But the deed is done: I have spent the money for the ring. Now I will enjoy it.

At a teahouse next to the bus stop, Maureen and I sit in a wooden booth and sip tea and munch on deep-fried bread twists. Around us men noisily sip tea from tiny cups and expectorate streams of orange betel juice into plastic-lined tin spittoons.

A teen-aged boy in a white satin shirt shows up at our table. A boy in a black leather jacket stands behind him. "This is Kyaw Kyaw and his friend" says Maureen, pronouncing the name Jaw Jaw. "He is my friend's son. The boys are coming to Lashio with us."

"Don't they have school?" I ask.

"Kyaw Kyaw isn't much for school," she says, a surprisingly indulgent attitude for a teacher, I think. Then I remember stories about Burmese schools, remember the rote chanting of the children in the school next to the guesthouse. The boys can probably learn as much in Lashio.

The bus is crowded, many stand or sit in the aisles, and I am glad we reserved seats yesterday. Women with terrycloth turbans wrapped round their heads crowd next to farmers in *longyis*, who carry broken machine parts. As always in Burma, I am surprised there are no offensive odors among such a large crowd of people. Only the fresh fragrance of oranges reaches my nostrils, as Kyaw Kyaw and his friend peel fruit in the seat behind us.

Two hours' travel over a narrow, wooded road brings us to the broad, asphalt streets of Lashio. We get off the bus at a broad intersection; Maureen asks the boys where they want to go first; then she tells me we will find a noodle shop Kyaw Kyaw knows.

The boys walk ahead of us, and I notice words scrawled across Kyaw Kyaw's friend's jacket: FUCK YOU. A mild-mannered, nondescript sort of boy, by walking through the streets in such a jacket he has assumed the persona of a rebellious teenager. Not much of a rebellion with two grandmotherly women walking behind him.

As we near the noodle shop, I am amazed to hear someone call my name, pronouncing the last syllable to rhyme with ice: "Brrr-NICE"!! I look right and see a tall man in a military jacket. He is sitting at an outdoor table at the noodle shop Kyaw Kyaw has led us to: the soldier who sat across from me on the train.

My first thought is that he has been spying on me in Hsipaw and followed us here. Then I remember there is a large military base here, and he had said he lived in Lashio.

He pops up from his chair, gestures to the man sitting across from him. "This is my friend. He own the shop. How long in Lashio, Brr-nice?"

I remember Sai Leng in Thailand, who told me he had worked for a charitable organization for children in Lashio and was followed by the police and the military wherever he went. "Just for the day," I say, and am thrown into deeper confusion when I notice his hateful Army jacket has a U.S. Army emblem on it. U.S. Army?

I join Maureen and the boys, who are sitting on low stools at a wooden table, and tell Maureen the soldier was on the train with me. "He was nice," I say. "But I thought he was following me. Now I see the label on his jacket says U. S. Army."

"Probably from a used clothing vendor," she says, and turns to Kyaw Kyaw. "Is that man a soldier?" she asks. He assesses him briefly, and says "No." And I regret all the energy I wasted trying to dislike him.

* * *

Leaving the noodle shop, we walk along the broad streets of Lashio. Maureen asks Kyaw Kyaw if he knows how to find the clinic. The boy seems to understand everything she says, but will speak no English. Instead, he acts as interpreter, stopping several people to ask directions in the Shan language, until we are directed to a street behind a school where a walled compound surrounds several buildings. We ring a bell, and a Burmese woman unlocks the gate. The clinic is at the left side of an immaculately neat courtyard. The woman leads us into a room with a long table and chairs in the center; the boys stay outside.

On the walls, poster boards are covered with photos of red-robed monks in classrooms and small children being inoculated. A tall woman with short blond hair enters. "I am Betty," she says. "My husband, Jerry, and I are working here." They are from Los Angeles and have been here three months, teaching monks and laypersons about HIV/AIDS and other health issues. Other volunteers teach English. I am immediately attracted to the place and the people, want to return next year and teach, but know I will return to Thailand and the refugee friends who have become my second family.

Dr. Jerry appears, introduces himself, and apologizes for not appearing sooner. He has been trying to complete a phone call to his ninety-seven-year-old mother in Los Angeles. No luck. Being in Burma is like dropping off the map.

We chat for a while before joining the boys who want to visit the market, then retrace our footsteps, past the school and the noodle shop, to a wide street bordering the market. Maureen plucks a wad of bills from her shoulder bag, peels off a few, and gives them to Kyaw Kyaw. We agree to meet here in one hour, and the boys walk into a shop that sells CDs and cassette tapes.

Within a few footsteps, Maureen and I are in a huge market where skirted men and women sell fabrics, jewelry, orchids and vining plants, sticky rice steamed in bamboo tubes, dried mushrooms, dried fish (a staple of Shan and Burmese dishes), mounds of bright red chilies, sweet-scented cardamom, anise, and cloves. Maureen buys a Chinese calendar for herself and one for her daughter in Australia. The vendor, a Burmese woman in a conical hat, looks at me, says, "Beautiful, Madame. How old ah you?" I am getting tired of the question. "Fifty-two," I say. She gives me a thumbs up, says "good," and I feel guilty. "No. Seventy-two," I say. She laughs, gives me another thumbs up. "Very good," she says, and we walk on.

An hour later, we meet the boys and take a pickup taxi to the bus station, but the bus has already left. "Wait one hour," says the clerk, gesturing to white plastic chairs lined up against the wall. Only then do I realize I have not stood at the terminus of the Burma Road.

"Oh. It was at the other bus stop. The one where we came in," says Maureen. I could cry with disappointment. I probably stood on it without realizing I was there, but it is not the same.

* * *

February 3: I finish my breakfast of *mohinga* and soy bread, and bring my instant coffee—the only kind I have had in Burma—to a courtyard table where I can sit with my back to the sun and read *Burmese Days*. Before I have finished one page, a middle-aged Japanese woman approaches. She checked into the guesthouse yesterday and somehow heard about Maureen. She sits beside me, says, "You are Maureen?"

"No," I say. "My name is Bernice. I am from the United States. Maureen is from Australia." She looks disappointed but continues. "You are working here? Teaching English?"

"No. I have been teaching English in Thailand."

"I want to do something," she says. "In Tokyo, I was forced to leave my job early. Now I have nothing to do. Maybe I can teach English."

Her face has a vacant, unhappy look, and her full skirt and dingy gray shirt need washing. She looks like one of the homeless women I see on Minneapolis buses, those who carry their possessions in plastic bags. I will tell Maureen about her and let her decide if she wants to meet the woman.

I frequently meet people looking for new lives in foreign lands. A month ago I met an American man in a village near Chiang Mai who wanted me to tell him exactly what he should do with the rest of his life. He seemed desperate. "I just want someone to point me in the right direction," he said. He had no interests, wanted something to happen that would save him from eternal boredom.

I suppose I should be more sympathetic toward such travel waifs, but it's hard to imagine being bored with life when you have your health and your senses, when you can read, write, walk, and talk without undue pain. Maybe what they are really looking for is meaning. If they would simply say that, our conversations might be different, but it could be painful to suddenly admit your life has no meaning. As for me, I realized it long ago.

I remember a university Humanities class where I happened onto the definition of existentialism reduced to its core: "Life has no meaning except that which you create for it." I found that comforting—maybe because it was the opposite of the Lutheran dogma I had been exposed to as a child, a choice between either believing a religious creed in its entirety or damnation, a choice that drove me away from church in the knowledge that by Lutheran standards I was damned. But I can hardly give the Japanese woman a definition of the meaning of life on first meeting.

I turn my chair to face the morning sun and bend my head to *Burmese Days*. Soon I am more involved in the story of Orwell's fictional Flory in love with an air-headed English woman than I am in the Japanese woman's dilemma—I cannot solve her problem, will not know the end of her story, but I can depend on Orwell to show me what happens to Flory.

I read until it is time to meet Maureen for lunch. We are going to have bean salad at the market, made, of course, by Mrs. Bean. As I walk toward Maureen's apartment, a Shan woman grasps my arm, and in an awed voice says, "You are so fair, so fair. So very fair." She has lovely light brown skin. Her comment saddens me—all this emphasis on skin color.

I stop to get Maureen, who is reading *Bridge on the River Kwai* in her front yard, her pale Aussie face turned to the sun, and we walk to the market to a raised platform with a small round table at one side and a tall wooden cupboard at the other. On the table is a blue vase filled with bright yellow flowers, smaller than poppies but with the same fragile, tissue-paper thin leaves.

Seated on a chair behind the flowers is Mrs. Bean. There are no overhead lights in the market and the daylight looks as if it has been specially filtered to backlight her pretty round face and blue sweatshirt. She looks like a painting by Vermeer, one of those where a calm, passive woman seems to be eternally waiting.

Maureen and I climb onto the platform, and Mrs. Bean acts as if she

has been waiting for us. She smiles broadly, says, "Please sit," and gestures to two small wood chairs next to the table. "I will get tea," she says,
and only then do I notice that her little oasis of hospitality is next to the
open sewer that runs through the market and along the streets of Hsipaw.
My sense of smell has faded over time, and since Maureen has been eating here for eight years with no ill effects, I decide to ignore the sewer.
Mrs. Bean busies herself at a small counter and brings us two small plates
mounded with a fine blend of beans, cilantro, minced garlic, lime juice,
and oil—one of the best salads I have ever eaten.

* * *

This is my last day in Hsipaw. I walk Maureen back to her apartment and
kiss her cheek, stop for a last brief visit with Mr. Book, not lingering long
enough to catch the eye of the watchful policeman across the street, bring
Mr. Knowledge a shiny brass and silver ten-baht Thai coin to add to his
collection, and walk over the bridge that spans a small stream, past the
tamarind tree where the tangerine vendor sits behind a pyramid of orange
fruit, past a pair of oxen lying in the shade, and back to the guesthouse.

There I ask Mr. Charles whether Mr. Donald, nephew of the former
prince of Hsipaw, has returned. "Still in Rangoon," he says. The words
shock me—I have heard rumors about Mr. Donald: that he is a Burmese
spy, that he is a Shan patriot who is closely watched by the Burmese
military. I have no way of knowing if either is true. And for weeks I have
been cut off from radio, television and newspapers. I cannot know what
evil the military regime might have committed during my short stay in
Hsipaw, how much has happened beneath the calm surface exhibited to
tourists, cannot help but wonder if Mr. Donald has met the same fate as
his famous uncle.

Addendum, Thailand, February 15, 2005: Tonight three refugee students
gather at my hotel to hear about my travels in Burma. They say ten top
Shan leaders were arrested the first part of February, one of them the revered Khun Htun Oo, cousin of the former Prince of Hsipaw.

Minneapolis, August 10, 2005: Today I received the following e-mail
message:

*Burma's military junta. . . arrested a member [of] Shan State Advisory
Council (SSAC) Sa Oo Kya [Mr. Donald] on 3 August.*

Oo Kya is the nephew of the last Hsipaw . . . prince, Sa Kya San . . . Although it is not known why he was arrested . . . it could be because of his political activities with Shan groups or taking foreign tourists to historic sites around Shan State.

The "historic sites" no doubt include the Prince of Hsipaw's Palace, which I toured with Mone Sageng Zing, the smart-alecky boy who got so much pleasure from his role as tour guide. I am glad I never met Mr. Donald, that I was not among the "foreign tourists" he entertained and who contributed to his downfall. I remember the death chant I heard in the rhythm of the rails on the train from Maymyo to Hsipaw and hope Mone Sageng Zing is safe.

The *Shan Herald Agency for News,* June 2, 2006: . . . *Oo Kya,* [Mr. Donald] *66, . . . went on trial for 2 charges.*

*Defamation . . . Two tourists were said to have written in the guestbook expressing their thanks for telling them "the truth"

*Violation of Library and Museum law: Asking for donations from tourists visiting the palace.

He received a 13 year jail term . . . 10 for the first charge and 3 for the second.

RETURN TO MANDALAY

Mandalay is rather a disagreeable town—it is dusty and intolerably hot ...
—George Orwell, Burmese Days

<u>February 4, 2005:</u> I am returning to Mandalay after visiting Maymyo and Hsipaw, lingering so long at the latter that I will have to limit the rest of my travels so as not to overstay my one-month visa. Burma's inefficient road system demanded I return to Mandalay before traveling southeast to Yawngwhe and Inle Lake and then south to Rangoon.

WELCOME TO MANDALAY THE GOLDEN CITY reads a sign at the city entrance. TATMADAW SHALL NEVER BETRAY THE NATIONAL CAUSE reads another. Tatmadaw: the military.

Passing under the Golden City archway, we are once again in the clatter of Mandalay, its broad streets filthy with refuse and covered with orange blotches of expectorated betel nut. I wish I were back in Hsipaw, Chiang Mai, or Minneapolis, anyplace but here, and wonder how I could ever have liked this noisy, dirty city. I know the answer, of course: Ohn Win and Maung San. But we have been driving five hours: I am tired and hungry.

The Toyota turns onto 83rd Street, where laborers with muscled backs and legs push carts laden with gravel; red-robed monks cling to the back of overloaded pickups; and trishaw drivers weave effortlessly through traffic. Soon we are at the Nylon Hotel.

They have only one available room—a gloomy, windowless cavern, so dark I cannot see if it is clean. Maybe tomorrow will bring better. I leave and start walking toward the Marie Min—I have been thinking about a cool, fresh fruit lassie all the way from Hsipaw.

I walk east for several blocks; then realize I do not recognize the buildings around me and fear I am on the wrong street. "Marie Min?" I ask two men chatting on the sidewalk, pronouncing it "Mary Min," as Burmans do. They exchange puzzled glances, and then one opens his betel-stained mouth revealing stubs of maroon-colored teeth. "That way," he says, pointing the way I came. "No," I say and keep walking east till I tire. Then I start looking for a trishaw.

"Bernice!" someone shouts. I look up and see Ohn Win, cycling through traffic on her perfectly tended white bicycle that she will "keep forever" because Gregg gave it to her. "And I love Gregg," she had said. "Love and respect Gregg." Meeting like this should be a happy event, but I am hungry and tired—I want to be alone and recover my strength.

She dismounts, weaves through three lanes of traffic and is at my side. "When did you arrive?" she says, grasping my hand. "Thirty minutes ago," I say. "And I am hungry and tired."

"What can I do for you," she says, emphasizing the "you."

"I am looking for the Marie Min Restaurant." She looks as puzzled as the men on the street corner.

Patting the metal carrier behind her white bike seat, she says, "Sit here. I will take you." But she obviously doesn't know where the restaurant is, and I am afraid of having a leg mashed in traffic or falling off and mangling my bad knees. "No," I say. "I will find a trishaw."

"Mary Min?" she asks a man standing nearby. He, too, points the direction I came. They chat a while, and she says, "I know. I know. I will take you." We start walking in what I fear is the wrong direction, till I see a trishaw driver with a seriously betel stained mouth and decide my knee is so sore I will ride with him. Ohn Win pushes her bike beside us, and in a few minutes we stop in front of the Min Min Restaurant, two blocks from the Nylon.

"No!" I say. "Not here! The Mary Min! Mary Min!" Now he says he knows it, will take me there for five hundred kyat, but I am tired, hot, hungry, and irritated. "I will eat here," I say, embarrassed at the irritation in my voice.

"I'm sorry. I'm sorry. I'm very sorry," says Ohn Win, looking like a child who has been scolded. "Never mind," I say. "This is fine."

I think of the dirt hole she calls home, the absolute poverty in which she lives. How could she know the Marie Min Restaurant where tourists pay as much for one meal as her mother makes washing clothes three or four days. "Never mind," I say again, but the scolded child look persists. "Come. We will eat."

I ate here one evening in January, but it was night and the dirt was not so obvious. The salt and pepper shakers and the jar of chilies on the table are layered with dust; the floor is littered with used napkins. I order

lemonade and vegetables tempura, a dish Burmans learned to make during the Japanese occupation.

Ohn Win refuses to order. Only then do I notice the black circles under her eyes. "Are you well?" I ask. "Jess. But a few days ago I was under
the weather," she says, smiling at her most recent American idiom. I ask
about her eyes. "They hurt when I read the dictionary in bed at night,"
she says. "And I have headache." I see her in her dirt hole, sitting beside
her sleeping mother at the side of the bed nearest the overhead light bulb.
"Maybe you need glasses," I say.

A Burman waiter with dirty fingernails brings me a glass of warm lemonade and the tempura, a tangle of feathery greens brightened by a few
carrot spikes. I ask for two sets of chopsticks. Ohn Win eats one green
thing and puts down her chopsticks. "You don't like?" I say. "Jess," she
says, meaning "No." She will order nothing, punishing herself, perhaps,
for leading me to the wrong restaurant.

I don't like the green stuff either but eat enough to restore my energy,
then, feeling guilty, I tell Ohn Win I will go to my room and rest—I
know she had hoped to spend the afternoon with me.

"Come to my hotel tomorrow morning," I say.

At the Nylon, I go to my dark, musty-smelling room, pull back the
blanket to see sheets that look as if they have been slept in, prop my legs
up against the wall and wish I could erase this last meeting with Ohn
Win, erase the exasperation I felt when we arrived at the Min Min, and,
most of all, erase the scolded child look from her face. I want to cry with
shame but am too tired.

* * *

February 5, 2005: I am eating a flaky banana pancake at the teashop near
the Nylon where young boys walk from table to table and shout orders to
the kitchen. Boys cluster around me, looking at the book I am reading:
Burmese Days. They fuss with the teapot, offer me toilet tissue napkins,
and try to read over my shoulder. I hold up the book to show them the
picture of a Burmese woman in a *longyi* on the cover and return to the
story of misguided love, disloyal women, and scheming Burmese magis-
trates.

A boy sidles up to me, slips a folded note onto the table, and quickly
walks away. *Excuse me? I see you are so pretty until now. I thaink you are
very beautiful right now. So I thaink you were so beautiful and nice woman.*
I suppose it is his way of saying, "You must have been very beautiful when

you were young," the kind of compliment I do not usually relish, but I am touched. I leave a generous tip, which he gives to his manager.

* * *

When I return to the Nylon, Ohn Win is waiting outside. She is on her way home from her 6 a.m. English class. She asks me where I will go today, and I say I want to find Maung San. "My mother will get him for you," she says. "I will call her." She uses the hotel phone, calls a friend who will look for her mother at the Irrawaddy, and returns looking triumphant. "She will go," she says. "She will send him to you. Now where will you go?"

I tell her I want Maung San to take us someplace where she can have an eye exam. "Okay! But first I must go to my mother. And I have another English class. One o'clock I am here."

One-half hour later, I see Maung San standing outside the hotel next to his trishaw with the red Honda seat cushions. He is wearing the same blue plaid, flannel shirt and billed cap he has worn every day I have seen him. He smiles as I approach, showing elongated, tobacco-stained teeth, and I feel as if I am meeting an old friend. "We will have tea," I say, and we return to the teashop I left a few minutes ago.

The boys flutter around our table. Maung San orders chapatti and chickpeas; I have tea. He has visited Hsipaw, so we share our impressions of the town, the pleasant weather, the peaceful atmosphere, the dingy, abandoned-looking Shan palace where spirit houses memorialize the prince who was murdered by the military.

Digging in his shirt pocket, Maung San pulls out three ticket stubs for *Around the World in Eighty Days*. Holding them up, he says, "I tell my wife, 'Did you ever see ticket for movie?'" He chuckles, tucks them into his pocket and pats it. "A memory for me," he says, and I get tears in my eyes.

He asks me where I want to go today, and I tell him I want to have Ohn Win's eyes examined when she returns from her second English class. He has seen an article in *The New Light of Myanmar*, he says, about an Australian ophthalmologist who is visiting a monastery outside Mandalay and giving free eye care. Patients must stay overnight at the monastery, but they can pay by donation. "Too far for Ohn Win, but I will go," he says, pointing to his left eye, which is red and has a thin film extending from the inside corner to the iris. "Many years work in paper factory. Must wash with acid every time. This happen," he says.

He will donate ten thousand kyat (eleven U.S. dollars) for the surgery, he says, two month's wages. I ask if I can help and he says, "Is too heavy for you. You are helping Ohn Win."

I ask him what American movie is playing now, and he seems to glow with excitement. "I don't know," he says. "Would you like to ride past the theatre?"

After paying the bill, less than one dollar for the two of us, I tuck five thousand kyat into his blue plaid shirt pocket, "For your eye surgery," I say, and he does not argue.

The theatre billboard is covered with images of square-jawed, bare-armed men holding automatic weapons. Judi Dench is the only name I recognize in the list of actors at the right, but decide even her fine acting could not redeem the violent film. "Too many guns in the world," I say. "I don't want to see more."

"Jess," says Maung San. I would like to think he is agreeing, but know he is conceding.

On the way back to the Nylon, he detours to show me an ophthalmologist's office. "Everybody say this one very good," he says. It is closed until 6 p.m. Maung San stands on his bicycle pedals and cycles across the battered streets back to the Nylon, where Ohn Win is waiting.

Her friend told her about an ophthalmologist on a one-way street a few blocks from the hotel. I ask Maung San to wait for us: Afterwards, we will eat lunch together.

Ohn Win holds my arm in both her hands, pushing, pulling, and stopping me as we weave through sputtering motorbikes, bicycles, Toyota Corolla vans, and Mazda pickups to the ophthalmologist's shop.

She speaks to him in Burmese, and he takes us into an inner office, where he has her look into a machine that magnifies her eyes; then she reads an eye chart. First, without glasses, then using lenses of varying powers.

The doctor speaks no English. Ohn Win tries to interpret his diagnosis for me, says her "optic is tipped."

"He is very surprise," she says. "My eyes they are different."

I watch the ophthalmologist write a prescription: 40+ for one eye, 25+ for the other. I hope he knows what he is doing.

Looking at frames, Ohn Win says, "Which ones do you want to buy for me?" I tell her to choose what she likes, but frugality sets in, and I say, "The frames are not important. What is inside is important." She chooses the cheapest frames, eight thousand kyat, about nine dollars and fifty cents U.S. I am surprised when she says the price includes the "mirrors," meaning the lenses, and that the glasses will be ready in three hours.

Now I hope she has not chosen cheap frames because of me. "Are you sure you like those?" I ask. "Jess!" she says. She looks cute in them, but nine dollars and fifty cents cannot ease my shame at the annoyance I felt when we arrived at the Min Min Restaurant yesterday.

Walking back to the Nylon, she says "He say I must wear them all the time. On my bicycle, when I read, when I play the computer." Then she looks at me joyfully, "Gregg is sending money for me to take computer next month. I want to play computer very well, like Gregg."

At the Nylon, Ohn Win and I climb onto Maung San's back-to-back Honda-cushioned trishaw seats, and he cycles effortlessly over the crumbling streets to the Lashio Lay Shan Restaurant. We stand in front of the hot table, inhaling mouth-watering aromas from an array of meat and vegetable dishes. We will each choose two dishes and share them, I say. I choose sautéed mushrooms and a cauliflower-broccoli dish; Ohn Win chooses two meat dishes, heavily spiced with red chilies, and Maung San chooses lima and green beans with tofu.

A waiter brings the food to a round table in the middle of the restaurant and mounds rice onto our plates, returning with a full bowl, which he places on the table. Maung San and I drink Myanmar draft beer and Ohn Win has a Star Cola, the cheap Burmese version of Coca Cola. This food is more interesting to Ohn Win than yesterday's feathery green tempura—she finishes one heap of rice topped with assorted vegetables and meat, and reaches for more. We stop to clink our glasses together, toasting good health and friendship, and I consider how fortunate I am to have friends who have completely erased my ill-formed prejudice against Burmans.

Maung San cycles back to the Nylon. I kiss him goodbye, in the sad knowledge that we may never meet again, and tell him I will go to my room and rest until Ohn Win's glasses are ready.

Earlier one of the hotel workers said he knew Ohn Win—they are in the same English class. "When she come to see you, I know her," he said. "But she does not remember me. She tell her story in class and I am almost cry. Say her father leave and mother wash clothes, but she is very pure." He is not a privileged young man, works long hours every day and sleeps on the hotel floor at night, but even he can cry for Ohn Win.

I tell Ohn Win to talk with him, and I will rest until her glasses are ready. In the sunny, ceramic-tiled room I moved into this morning, I prop my tired legs high against the wall. This is my last day in Mandalay. I came to find out how repressive the government truly was, and found a people afraid to speak the name of the woman who might lead them out of poverty and oppression. Yet, if the Moustache Brothers and Maung San, and Ohn Win are representative, they are a people whose spirit cannot be subdued, in whom kindness and the desire to succeed cannot be repressed, people who would agree with Aung San Suu Kyi: "The military can never win, because all they have is guns."

At 2:30, I slide my legs from the wall, run a comb through my hair, and go down to the lobby to meet Ohn Win.

At the ophthalmologist's shop, Ohn Win tries the glasses, which slip down on her snub-nosed face. I ask if she wants them tightened. "No. I like this way," she says, and I see her sitting in bed beside her sleeping mother. Oblivious to the urine smell, and to the crawling creatures and hordes of mosquitoes that share her dirt home, her glasses slide down on her nose as she reads the fine-print English dictionary in which she found the word "optimist" and decided it described her.

YAWNGWHE, HOME OF BURMA'S FIRST PRESIDENT, AND INLE LAKE, WHERE GARDENS GROW ON WATER

It is better to travel well than to arrive. —Buddha

<u>February 7, 2005:</u> At the Remember Inn in Yawngwhe (pronounced Yong-Whey), I pay five U.S. dollars for a room where the western sun shines through blue-curtained windows, illuminating delicate yellow flowers on the wooden table below. I plop my backpack onto one of the twin beds, my body onto the other, prop my legs up against the wall, and pull a blanket over my shoulders and chest. Exhausted though I am from a six-hour, bone-jolting ride from Mandalay, five minutes rest is all I can tolerate before the excitement of being in Yawngwhe propels me off the bed, onto my feet, and out the door.

The evening sun warms my back as I cross the dirt road fronting the guesthouse on the south and a former Shan palace on the north—my reason for being here.

An *Irrawaddy Newsletter* article said the Burmese government may have left the palace alone because of a superstition that evil would befall anyone attempting to destroy it, for this had been the home of a powerful Shan prince, Sao Shwe Thaike. In the minds of the superstitious Burmese, his ghost and those of his wives and children may wander here still.

In *The White Umbrella,* Patricia Elliott tells the story of Sao Hearn Hkam, who married Shwe Thaike and lived with him in the palace. In 1948 Shwe Thaike became Burma's first president and Sao Hearn Kham became Burma's very first first lady.

Shwe Thaike left office in 1952. Ten years later, Burmese General Ne Win's troops surrounded his home in Rangoon. He was arrested and locked up in Rangoon's Insein Prison. Pronounced "insane," the prison has become synonymous with the military regime that has ruled Burma since the coup. Shwe Thaike died in Insein. Sao Hearn Kham escaped to

Thailand with three of her children and founded the Shan State Army in Chiang Mai.

Many students in my English classes had ties to the Shan State Army: Their fathers, uncles, brothers had fought with them; three of the older students had been soldiers. This palace and its untidy yard are part of their history. I am their proxy, here at their urging, for they dare not travel in their own state. In 2003, Amnesty International reported the Burmese military execution of six Shan civilians and a four-month-old baby who were traveling from Shan State to Thailand. Such killings usually go unrecorded. Crossing the border in either direction is risky business for the Shan.

The palace is a sprawling teak, brick, and stucco building with a balcony that forms the center of an inverted "U" set back thirty or forty feet from the arms at either side. I had expected something grander—it is no larger and not so elegant as most houses on Lake of the Isles near my Minneapolis condo.

The staff has left for the day; the windows are dull and lifeless. Looking at it, my chest grows heavy with sadness, for I know the history of this ghost house and those who peopled it.

A sign outside the fenced compound says the palace closes at 5 p.m. and designates it as the "Museum of Shan Chiefs." It makes me angry: This was the home of Burma's first president; it should bear that inscription. Calling the palace a museum is the government's way of rewriting history. And they have renamed this town a tongue-twisting "Nyaungshwe" to give it further distance from the Shan prince-become-president. Only the pagoda-like, seven-tiered spire on the rooftop indicates this was the home of highest royalty.

Although it is well past 5 p.m., I walk through an unlocked gate. Barking dogs trigger visions of lying in a Burmese hospital being punched with used hypodermic needles, and I retreat to the cement courtyard of the Remember Inn.

In my room, the afternoon sun is filtered by dusty windows and reminds me of Vermeer paintings. A wave of sadness passes over me. The cortisone shot I got in Minneapolis is wearing off. Arthritis, and the meniscal tear in my left knee, means it hurts whenever I walk and for a long time afterward. I wonder how long I will be mobile and how I will endure life when I no longer am.

Then remembering how at eighty-nine my mother, who had a sore knee of her own, laughed about such minor ailments, I chastise myself for brooding. My mind flits from sore knees to passing time to Vermeer—but what does Vermeer have to do with Burma or my life?

When I look at Vermeer paintings of lone women and now at the pale light filtering across the yellow flowers, I feel regret and longing, a longing for what might have been. The same feelings I had looking at the weedy, untended palace yard and its lifeless windows, a longing for the past and those who peopled it.

The sun has disappeared and the air will soon grow cold; the elevation of Yawngwhe is nearly three thousand feet. I slip into pajamas, pile an extra quilt from the second bed over the bed nearest the window, prop two pillows against the wall, and settle down to read *The Book of Salt*, the fictional memoir I got from Maureen in Hsipaw, a story about a Vietnamese man who cooked for Gertrude Stein and Alice B. Toklas when they lived like royalty in Paris.

* * *

February 8: The guesthouse restaurant is reminiscent of a Minnesota Northwood's lodge with its wooden walls and furniture. This morning it is full and noisy: There are three Germans and one American man, all wearing hiking boots, an Austrian man, one noisy woman from Prague, a Chinese woman, and a Japanese man. They are eating scrambled eggs and white toast or thick pancakes. I have one of the heavy, honey-drenched pancakes and coffee, while listening to English spoken with German, Czech, Chinese, and Japanese accents. The Germans and the American are planning a hike; the woman from Prague prattles on about previous travels. I sit with the Chinese woman and the Japanese man, who do not talk with each other.

When I introduce myself, the Japanese fellow says he would like to travel in the U.S. but is afraid of guns. He asks if I have a gun and seems surprised when I say "No." I tell him I think he would be safe traveling in the U.S., but I can tell he does not believe me.

Few travelers worry about guns in Burma. China keeps the military heavily armed, but few civilians have guns—they are too poor and too frightened—which makes it easy as a duck shoot to drive ethnic groups like the Shan from their land. According to *Human Rights Watch*, three Shan State villagers were executed by the Burmese military when soldiers found an old rifle they used for hunting. This is where guns must be feared, but not by tourists—not if we do nothing the government might interpret as subversive, not if we do not teach English to Shan refugees who have fled the country.

* * *

Having devoured most of the pancake and sloshed it down with instant coffee, I cross the road to the palace fence, walk through the weedy, untended yard, and enter a door leading to museum offices and a reception desk, where I pay a two U.S. dollar entrance fee, stash my shoes on a wooden shelf, and climb a narrow teak stairway to the second floor.

At the top of the stairs is a large room where imperious-looking former Shan princes with turban-wrapped heads look out of photographs taken at the height of their power. Here are the princes of Mong Yai, Mong Nai, Mong Naung, Mong Pon, and Hsipaw, areas I have heard about from Shan students in Thailand, who were born in the various princedoms after they were under Burmese rule.

I wander from room to cavernous room, past ancient silk robes dating from the 1800s and worn by Shan princes who preceded Sao Shwe Thaike. Photos, robes, and thrones, but little history in this "history museum." There is no mention at all of Sao Hearn Kham, the twenty-year-old woman who came here as a reluctant bride in 1937.

Sao had dreamt of attending university, but was forced by her brother Hom Hpa, the Prince of Hsenwi, to leave school after seventh grade—she already knew enough, he said. As a young woman, she rejected several suitors before being courted by a childhood friend, whom she begged to marry, but by then Prince Shwe Thaike was courting her, too.

Shwe Thaike had one of the wealthiest princedoms in Shan State and was an adopted son of King Thibaw, the last king of Burma. Although the British deposed Thibaw, the association with him gave Shwe Thaike added status. Sao's brother insisted on their marriage. The prince brought her here, where his one living wife still occupied one of four apartments attached to the main building. In respect for Sao, or perhaps on instructions from the prince, the other wife remained sequestered during Sao's homecoming.

After the birth of her first child, Sao was called *mahadevi*, royal mother. In the villagers' eyes, she was a goddess, a Celestial Ruler, alongside the god-prince. She joined her husband in governing the princedom—but her royal status did not deter the prince from taking a schoolgirl concubine, the younger sister of his other wife. He never married her, but sent her to school and treated her as a minor wife.

Sao treated her as a younger sister, although she was embarrassed and humiliated by her presence, and frequently spoke out for a "one husband, one wife" system of marriage. Sixty-eight years later, I feel sad for the woman whose hopes and dreams were swallowed by men who felt they owned her and could direct her life.

Soon Sao was stuck in a marriage where she was forced to share her home and her husband with his lesser wives. Yawngwhe villagers had believed two of Shwe Thaike's earlier wives died because they were commoners. They thought he needed a royal wife. He chose Sao, who was a princess in her own right. I suppose she could have done worse. The prince was kind, and there was some satisfaction in ruling alongside him after the birth of her first son, Tiger.

Standing now in the Great Hall of Audience, bright with light from the south windows, I look at the raised platform along the west wall where the symbol of royalty, folded white umbrellas, gray with the grime of time, stand at either side, and I imagine Sao wrapped in stiff Burmese silk, sitting alongside the prince as villagers kneeled in front of them and touched their heads to the floor in obeisance—small comfort for the loss of her dreams.

I leave the Audience Hall and walk to a concrete patio that connects the front of the palace with rooms at the back, where Sao had a private apartment next to the prince's other wife and his concubine. Cactus-like plants with red and yellow flowers are lined up in earthen jars against the east wall. I stand with my back to the sun and wonder how the three women and their children accommodated themselves to each other and to their respective roles in the prince's life.

If I had been Sao, I might have remained indoors, burying my thoughts and longings in books as I looked out at the bright sunshine that beat down on the heads of the prince's other two women and their children. Sao's biographer, Patricia Elliott, said Sao also buried herself in books. She became an expert on English history. And she passed time by walking through the market, more fascinating than her children, whom she left to the care of others. She had seven children in all: Tiger, Tzang, Tzang On, who died in infancy, Harn, two daughters, "Ying Sita and Leun," and Hso Hom Hpa, nicknamed Myee and named for the brother who forced her to marry Shwe Thaike.

Myee ran outside when he heard shots during the 1962 military coup. Burmese General Ne Win's troops had opened fire on the family's home at Kokine Road in Rangoon. After Shwe Thaike was marched off to Insein Prison, Tzang found seventeen-year-old Myee in the yard, a bullet hole in the back of his head.

Thinking about Myee, about the horror of finding him dead on the lawn, I am grateful for my own children. For Brent, my first-born son, and Bryan, his younger brother, the sons who live far from me and whom I seldom see, but whose presence in the world is a comfort and a joy.

* * *

Back on the gravel road, I meet children in green uniforms, returning from school, hand embroidered book bags slung over their shoulders. They smile, say, "Hello. How ah you?" in English and continue on their way.

Yawngwhe is a confusing place—so peaceful. There is not a soldier nor policeman in sight, nor have I seen any since I arrived. Maybe this part of Shan State has been thoroughly pacified; the way the Japanese pacified it during World War II.

At the beginning of the war, Aung San, now revered as Burma's hero of independence and the father of Aung San Suu Kyi, fought with the Japanese to drive the British out of Burma, while Shwe Thaike fought with the British. By 1942, the Japanese were in control of the country, and Aung San joined the Allies to drive out the Japanese. British collaborators were threatened with beheading: Shwe Thaike and his family fled to nearby Inle Lake.

* * *

February 9: At 9 a.m., I see a round-faced, smiling fellow waiting for me outside the guesthouse. For five thousand kyat, a bit more than five dollars U.S., he will be my guide for an all-day trip on Inle, famous for stilt houses that surround the thirteen-mile-long lake, for floating gardens, and for fishermen who power their flat-bottomed boats by wrapping one leg around an oar and paddling, while standing stork-like on the other leg.

Behind the guide is a tall, broad-shouldered man. He introduces himself as Pierre, a name as romantic as he is handsome, and says he is from Paris, pronouncing it Pair-ee. He will make the trip with me. Ah, yes, an advantage of traveling alone: being thrown together with handsome younger men who accept me as a peer. What more could a seventy-two-year-old woman ask? Except, perhaps, a trishaw. I am not sure how far it is to the lake and wonder if my knees will take me there.

The guide leads us through the dirt streets of Yawngwhe. Still, I see no policemen, no military. We pass the market, where Shan men and women with colorful turbans wrapped around their heads and Akha women wearing silver headdresses gather in a large courtyard to buy and sell fruits, vegetables, and fish. The fishy aroma follows us down the street as we pass guesthouses, restaurants, and teashops where cheroot-smoking locals sit on low stools, chatting and assessing the foreigners in town.

* * *

At a channel to the lake, we board a flat-bottomed boat with a long-shafted motor. A mild-mannered boatman, who speaks no English, starts the engine and delivers us to an office at the water's edge. There Pierre and I each reluctantly pay four U.S. dollars to tour the lake, money that enriches the coffers of the military regime.

Our guide sits in the prow, scanning the long lake as we glide onto open water. A gentle breeze brings with it the odor of decaying water plants and fish, reminding me of my youth when we went to Big Pine Lake for picnics on Sunday afternoons. My mother would prepare potato salad, baked beans, and fried chicken, and we would drive two miles to Uncle Adolph's Resort, where my brothers and I would wade in the water—no swimming, Mama said, or we might get polio—and climb the big hill where it was rumored Indians had lived. That time has been lost to the advent of travel trailer owners, who now crowd next to the cabins at what was Uncle Adolph's Resort. But I am happy to be here, on this lake and have no time for regret.

Pierre breathes deeply and raises his face to the sky. Looking blissful, he says, "There is no pollution in this country." Yet the hills surrounding the lake are shrouded with blue smoke from slash-and-burn agriculture. I point it out but do not persist. Let him have his day in paradise.

At the entrance to a bay on the east side of the lake, men in small flat-bottomed boats paddle with one leg wrapped around an oar, the other solidly balanced on a flat projection at the stern. They stop and cast funnel-shaped nets into the water, performing feats of balance and dexterity worthy of Barnum and Bailey's. We cruise past them to a pier near the shore, where the guide jumps from the boat and ties it to a heavy post, holds a hand down to help me out, and says, "Market here. You shop." He points to a path traversed by pale-skinned tourists walking into the woods, and I wonder how far it is to the market. Seeing people who look older and feebler than I heading down the path, I decide to try it.

We follow the other tourists along a dusty trail, past scruffy trees that look like weeping willows too tired to lean over as they cry. In a few minutes, we reach a large open-air market, where over-eager vendors tend table after table of merchandise. Not wanting to disappoint anyone by appearing interested and then not buying, I look only from the corner of my eyes.

Pierre and I separate, and I wander through displays of silk scarves, hand woven cotton shirts, embroidered shoulder bags, silver and jade necklaces and earrings, imitation antique Buddhist scrolls in the Pali and Shan languages, high-collared Shan jackets, imitation antique triptychs with images of Buddha inside, and oval-shaped intricately carved boxes. Markets are intoxicating places. Sao would have loved this place. The foreign sights, smells, and sounds fascinate me, too, but the obvious poverty of the vendors fills me with fear and shame. Shame about having too much while others have so little, fear that the world and I will never change.

The urgency of the vendors makes me want to run away, to immerse myself in a book, to erase my knowledge of the real world, to become the kind of Republican who believes everyone can help themselves if they really want to. To sleep.

"Madame, Madame, Madame," the vendors call. I smile, shake my head, and walk past. I cannot carry anything extra in my small travel pack without risking more injury to my joints.

I move to the center of the market where canopies shade vendors selling tomatoes, avocadoes, tangerines, and red chili peppers. The odors of tobacco, animal dung, and urine are overcome by the fragrance of frying garlic, ginger, and chilies that might tempt me to buy a snack if I did not know the vendors have no place to wash their hands, and the chilies would trigger convulsive coughing fits.

The aisles are crowded with betel-chewing men and women who spew streams of red saliva onto the pathways, covering them with rusty red splotches. Overwhelmed by the market, I head toward the lake where there is a slight breeze, and oxen graze beside wooden carts or lie next to them lazily chewing their cud.

"Where from, Mother?" calls a vendor.

"I am from the U.S."

A juicy red smile and an exclamation, "America! America boss country. Everybody rich. Please buy something."

I hate the "boss country" image of the U.S., particularly in the midst of the Iraq War when most of the world sees us as a bully boss. "Mai Soong Ka," I say, the Shan words used for both hello and goodbye, and walk away, carrying only the hand-woven shoulder bag I bought in Mandalay and my guilt about having so much in this land of need.

I see Pierre's hat and his broad, blue-shirted back at one of the tables. He bargains fiercely and remorselessly, buys a Buddha-image triptych for five U.S. dollars, one-quarter of the asking price. He is excited by the atmosphere and proud of his purchase. I tell him to take his time—I am returning to the boat. He catches up with me along the dusty path, and soon we are back on the water, gliding past woven-bamboo houses on stilts.

Shirtless brown-chested children in shorts stand in doorways, waving and yelling, "Hello, hello. Goodbye!" They have no solid ground to walk upon, and I wonder at the task of raising children in such a watery wasteland but realize "wasteland" is not a proper name for this fertile lake where pink and yellow flowers and tomatoes float in earthen gardens atop islands of reeds.

The boat weaves through the houses to a channel and a long dock. "Silk factory here. You see," says the smiley, round-faced guide. He jumps onto the dock, ties up the boat, and reaches a hand to me. I step up with my stronger leg, the right one, and follow a board walkway to the factory.

Women of all ages, all with thanaka-powdered yellow faces, sit next to each other at hand-operated, wooden looms, weaving fine silk threads into works of art. I linger over a long shawl in two iridescent shades of green. It costs ten dollars U.S., more than it would cost in Thailand, and it is stiffer than Thai silk. I think about Sao, wrapped in the elegant fabric as she performed her official duties at Yawngwhe Palace, and decide it would be a fitting memento of my travels here. Besides, it will fit into my backpack, and maybe the sale will benefit the women at the looms.

* * *

Back in the boat, the midday sun beats down on the conical peasant's hat I bought in Hsipaw. The relative wind created by the boat's movement blows it off my head and I cling to it, as we progress from channel to channel, where long-horned buffalo stand in water up to their thick necks, some with their owners beside them, lovingly dribbling water over the buffaloes' heads or stroking their backs.

Next, we visit a Buddhist pagoda that glitters with gold leaf and has an altar with a sign below: "No ladies allowed." Men and boys stand on the altar, gilding thick gold balls with additional layers of gold leaf. I stand below, watching them and feeling angry about the blatant discrimination. A nasty thought about men and balls occurs to me, and I wonder how Sao coped with it.

This is probably the pagoda Patricia Elliott wrote about in *The White Umbrella*, the one Prince Shwe Thaike, Sao, and their family used when they exiled themselves to an island during the Japanese invasion. Two weeks into their stay, they received word it would be safe for them to return to Yawngwhe. The business about beheading British collaborators had been forgotten, and Shwe Thaike, his wives, and children moved back to the palace where they managed to accommodate themselves to sharing their home with the Japanese troops who quartered themselves there. I am jolted from my reverie when I see Pierre heading down the marble stairs. He buys gold leaf from a vendor at the bottom, and we return to the boat.

We cruise through a labyrinth of watery channels and stilt houses, stopping for a lunch of fried rice on a channel with restaurants on either side. Next, we visit a pagoda, where, with the patience born of boredom, monks have trained cats to jump through hoops, and then a boat factory, a cheroot factory, a silver factory, and a blacksmith shop, as primitive and hot as the one my father took his ploughshares to for sharpening when I was a child. Finally, we stop at the ruins of ancient pagodas, reminiscent of Angkor Watt.

It is past 5 p.m., and I am weary, when the boatman turns back toward Yawngwhe at the other end of the lake. The sun will soon slide below the Shan hills, and the air is cool again. I pull out my silk shawl and wrap it around my shoulders.

Looking at the water and hills surrounding us, I wonder who remains to remember the Japanese occupation and the weeks that Sao Hearn Kham and the royal family lived on an island in this lake. I think about Sao's death in 2003, take on the burden of those who do not remember, and mourn her passing.

* * *

The sweet-faced guide inches back from the prow of the boat and sits cross-legged at my feet, reading a book. I see some English words and ask to see the book. It is a Burmese-English dictionary of phrases. He has found what he wants. Looking up at me, he says, "How ohl ah you?"

"Seventy-two," I say.

He smiles and says, "Ah, that is good. Very good."

He is twenty-three, he says, then points to a phrase in the book. "How you say?"

"May you have good luck," I say, reading the phrase.

"You say that when go away someone?" he asks.

"You can," I say. "Or you can say, 'Goodbye. Good luck.'"

When we reach Yawngwhe, the guide hands me out of the boat with great care—Southeast Asia is a wonderful place for an older woman to travel. I want to kiss his sweet, round cheek but know he would be shocked.

"May you have good luck," he says.

As Pierre and I walk away from the boat, he calls: "Goodbye! Good luck."

The effects of the Extra-Strength Tylenol I took before leaving the Inn have worn off. My left knee throbs with pain as I walk toward the guest-house with Pierre at my side. I wonder if I will be able to make it, but keep trudging with a smile on my face. The day has seemed like a waking dream, one that could include lying back in Pierre's arms as he carries me the last few blocks to the Remember Inn.

REFLECTIONS IN RANGOON

Some people think that if they change the names of things, the things them-selves will have changed, too. —David McKay

February 11, 2005: Rangoon: I say it in my head, and a thrill courses through my body in the taxi from Yangon Airport. I know the dirty se-crets of this city, and they add to my excitement at being here, the per-verse excitement of being in an exotic place where evil has been done.

Throughout my time in Burma, I have had to remind myself I am here because Shan refugees have asked me to visit their country, not because I am lured by the names of exotic places, not because I want to empty myself and be absorbed by foreignness, though both are true. I am here because they wanted me to see Burma's beauty and understand its horror, the horror I have seen in refugees' photos of villages burned out of exis-tence and men and women lying dead upon the ground. But I have seen nothing of it. It exists in small villages and in the jungle; it exists where travel is not allowed. I wonder about the quirk in my psyche that allows me to know such dreadfulness exists and still feel happy to be here.

My excitement grows as the taxi drives along palm-tree-shaded streets, past fences vined with red, pink, and yellow bougainvillea. There is a large lake on our left. "Inya," says the driver, who speaks little English.

Never sure of what I am hearing, I say, "Inya?"

At my last medical exam the doctor said I had some hearing loss in my right ear, but assured me it was not enough to necessitate a hearing aid—just enough to irritate others with my constant need for repetition.

"INYA LAKE," the driver says loudly, and I shudder.

In 1988, there was a massacre near Inya. After twenty-six years of in-creasingly repressive military rule, students from Rangoon University protested here. I met two of them in Minnesota, refugees who did not want to talk about the demonstrations or about their fellow students who were killed.

The students were joined by thousands of ordinary citizens, and the military slaughtered them indiscriminately, many of them on Tade Phyu Bridge, the "White Bridge."

Burman poet, Nyein Chan, writes:

> [The White Bridge was a place for]
> . . . Couples in love to meet and dream . . .
> A place designed for the rest of the soul.
>
> Now blood has turned it red . . .
> The laughter has turned into screams of fear,
> Dreams have sunk to the bottom of the lake.

I know the White Bridge is near Inya Lake, but there are no bridges in sight. Only later do I learn the bridge was destroyed by the military, as though its physical destruction could erase it from memory. The lake shimmers through heavy, humid air; lime green, manicured grass covers the slopes next to it.

It was shortly after the slaughter that Burma became Myanmar and Rangoon became Yangon, names with no student demonstrations or bloody massacres to tarnish their image. The generals also repressed the history that should have been taught in public schools.

Recent Shan refugees in my English classes knew about Aung San, the hero of Burmese independence from the British; they knew he had been assassinated in Rangoon in 1947 and that the assassination was attributed to General Ne Win, who instigated the 1962 coup. Most had never heard of Aung San Suu Kyi, who was born in Rangoon, and was two years old when her father was assassinated.

I like to think about Suu Kyi, to know there are women like her who are willing to give their lives for what they believe. And I would like to think that in some small way she is like me. Suu Kyi loved her mother dearly, and although she had been educated at Oxford and married an English scholar, in 1988 she left him and her two sons behind in England to return to Rangoon and care for her ailing mother who had suffered a stroke. I, too, cared for my mother after a stroke. I know the devastation of losing the first and most important love of my life. That devastation bound me to the Shan refugees with whom I had found a different but most profound love, the Buddhist love of students for their teachers, a love that became reciprocal. Suu Kyi rose above the sadness of her mother's death to work for her people.

Two weeks after the White Bridge slaughter, Suu Kyi addressed a half-million people, asking for democratic reforms. That fall the National League for Democracy was formed, with Suu Kyi as general secretary.

As her popularity grew, the military felt increasingly threatened by the slim, eloquent woman with fragrant, white frangipani and jasmine blossoms wound round her black hair, and in 1989 Suu Kyi was placed under house arrest. When I tell her story to Minnesotans and explain why she was arrested—because she became so popular the military regime felt threatened by her and feared losing power—people cannot seem to comprehend what I have said. "Why?" they say. "Why was she arrested?"

It is hard for Minnesotans to believe that although Suu Kyi's National League of Democracy party won the 1990 political elections, the military regime refused to recognize the results, and kept her locked up. She has had brief bouts of freedom since then, but is once again under house arrest, living in her father Aung San's now decrepit villa on Inya Lake.

I know it is unwise to show interest in Aung San Suu Kyi, but she is my hero. I take a chance and ask the driver if we might see her home. He says nothing, keeps driving.

Traffic proceeds in an orderly, unhurried fashion on wide, well-kept streets toward the city center, where I anticipate seeing what the *Lonely Planet* calls "one of the most exotic and striking cities in Southeast Asia," with an eclectic mix of ancient Buddhist temples and colonnaded colonial buildings, for Rangoon was the capital of Burma under British rule.

A large pagoda glistening with gold leaf reflects the fiery afternoon sun on a hilltop at our left. Its golden spire a symbol of Rangoon, Shwedagon Pagoda was once used as a fortress by Japanese soldiers.

In 1942, shortly after Pearl Harbor was bombed, the Japanese invaded Burma. In '44, Shwedagon became their last stronghold against Allied troops fighting to free the country for the British. At war's end, the bodies of tens of thousands of Japanese soldiers were collected from the pagoda grounds and cremated. Their ashes were loaded onto a boat on Rangoon River and carried out to sea.

The driver nods his head at the distance, where the western sun glints off another golden spire that reaches toward the sky. "Sule Pagoda," he says, and soon we are at the May Shan Hotel. Sule, the two-thousand-year-old pagoda believed to enshrine a hair of the Buddha, is in the next block. It is considered the center of Rangoon "from which all distances in Burma are measured," according to Monique Skidmore. An anthropologist, Skidmore studied the Burmese people in Rangoon and wrote *Karaoke Fascism, Burma and the Politics of Fear.* Traditionally, no building in the city was supposed to be higher than Sule, Skidmore wrote, but "narcoarchitecture" has changed the skyline, and concrete skyscrapers paid for with laundered money from the generals' heroin profits now tower above the pagoda.

I give the driver four thousand kyat, a bit more than four U.S. dollars, and step out of the taxi. The humid Rangoon air descends on me like a wet sheet. Within seconds, my travel-worn clothing droops damply against my body. I hoist my pack onto my shoulders and enter the air-conditioned lobby of the May Shan, which is decorated with garish imitation jade ornaments hung from braided red macramé ropes.

I picked this hotel because of its name, hoping for Shan owners and staff, relatives of my refugee friends in Thailand, perhaps. The disinterested desk clerk might be Shan—she says she is from Inle Lake—but the owners who stare at me from heavy, red upholstered chairs appear to be Chinese. The clerk calls a young woman wearing a short, tight black skirt and stiletto heels and asks her to show me a fifteen-dollar room, the highest price I have paid in Burma, the cheapest price in this hotel.

A small elevator lifts us slowly to the second floor. The eyes of the woman with me are thickly outlined in black. Unlike the interested, courteous young women who have greeted me throughout Burma, this one examines her long fingernails until the elevator jolts to a stop.

Through an open hall window I see a large yellow building with long, many-paned windows: city hall. In 1947, Aung San and his colleagues were assassinated in a government building near here. I shiver, wondering if they were killed in this graceful yellow structure; later a taxi driver will tell me they were killed in a red stone building, blood red. Now there is little time for speculation—my guide is tip tapping down the hall. I follow her.

She stops at the end and opens the door to a room on the left. It has one tiny window over the bathroom sink, the only natural light in the elegant room, an air-conditioned teak and ceramic-tile, closet-like space. A mirrored closet door gives the illusion of a second window and quells my claustrophobia. I can manage for two nights.

I shower, dig *The Book of Salt* out of my backpack, and pull back a blue brocade bedcover, exposing coarse white sheets with patches growing out of patches, some three layers thick. Like Burma, I think, where a veneer of normality gilds a troubled base, where you cannot know what is going on unless you expose what lies below the surface.

I ask myself what I have learned, if my travels here have added to my understanding of the Shan, and know that they have not. The oppression they endure is hidden in places I could not visit, where small men like those I have come to think of as "my boys" lie dead and rot into the vegetation, while I sit reading my book in a teak and ceramic tile room.

REFLECTIONS IN RANGOON, PART TWO: LUCKY

Paranoia is the belief in a hidden order behind the visible. —Unknown

February 12, 2005: The hotel clerk looks up in annoyance. She would be a perfect character in a film noir movie: A stereotype of disinterest, she is filing her fingernails. I look at my own, as neat as a nail clipper can make them without an emery board to smooth the edges, and I sigh.

The clerk knows I am from the United States: She examined my passport when I checked in. That had been a cause for celebration throughout most of Burma. I remember trishaw drivers giving me thumbs up when I said I was from America. "America good," they said. It must be something about Rangoon, I decide, or maybe about this particular hotel—maybe it hires only women with well-manicured fingernails, maybe they only like to help such women.

"What should I do today?" I ask. "I have only one day in Rangoon." She looks puzzled. "Is there a city tour?" I prod.

She laughs, says, "No tour. Take the train. Two and one-half hours. Circle ride around the city."

"What will I see?" I ask.

She laughs again. "Common people you will see." I wonder what the laugh is about. More prodding brings the small woman out from behind her desk to wave an arm in the direction of the train station.

I am wearing my coolest cotton blouse and slacks. They flap loosely around my body for a few minutes, then cling to my clammy skin. It is six long, hot, knee-jarring blocks to the station, which is slightly below street level, off Sule Paya Road.

There are many entrances to the long brick building, all of them guarded by soldiers. Only the front door is open. As soon as I enter, a soldier escorts me past rows of benches in the waiting room to an inside office where I am marched past a line of people to a small desk. There another soldier checks my passport and for two thousand kyat, about two U.S. dollars, gives me an all-day ticket that will allow me to circle the city by train.

This seems to be an office for questionable passengers—those who need military clearance. Most people standing here wear Western clothes; a few wear *longyis*. I look at them, marveling at how quickly I have become accustomed to seeing men in skirts, usually plaids or checks, but otherwise identical to their female counterparts who wear plain colors or floral prints.

With ticket in hand, I look around questioningly. "Where?" I say. And a small man, a full head shorter than my five-feet-one, says, "I will take you."

He hikes his *longyi* to his knees and leads me to steep marble stairs. I follow him to a landing where garlicky smells announce an open living area. We walk past rows of sleeping mats where military men in khaki trousers and white tee-shirts lie sleeping. Others sit, lacing their boots, while still others eat noodles from metal bowls. I am dismayed by their lack of privacy, almost feel sorry for them, until I remember the way the military has been systematically slaughtering the Shan.

At the end of the improvised barracks, I follow the small man down another flight of stairs. Wheels clang against steel tracks, and an ancient train grinds to a stop in front of me. Passengers lift their *longyis* and step into the train. I follow.

The cars have long wooden benches positioned on either side below glassless windows. I enter a car that has only one other passenger, a thin man in a red and green checked *longyi* and large, dark-rimmed eyeglasses. His face might have inspired Spielberg's E.T. An E.T. with ears, that is. Big ears. He has a longish neck, a round face with big, wide-set eyes, and thin lips fixed in a grin. "England?" he says.

"America," I say, and his smile broadens. His name is Ye U Myint Maung, he says, and he is an English headmaster. When I say I, too, teach English, he chuckles in delight, seems even more delighted to find out I am alone.

"Oh!" he says. "I will spend the day with you. It is Union Day. I will take you to a Union Day celebration." So there are friendly people in Rangoon. Only later do I remind myself there is no union in Burma, only the Burmese military united in driving the ethnic people from their land.

Myint reaches into a red shoulder bag with white embroidered letters that say "Vision and Views" in English. He pulls out several long, rectangular cards printed in Burmese. I am surprised to see that both of his hands are adorned with rings—one ruby and one sapphire.

A schoolteacher with jewels is an anomaly in this country where teachers make barely enough to buy rice. I think of Ying Tzarm's Shan schoolteacher parents who fled to Thailand because they could no longer afford to feed their two daughters, remembering their work-worn, unadorned hands. And I remember Shan students telling me that Burmese teachers refuse to teach all that is necessary to pass exams so they can extort money from students for private tutoring. I ask myself if I should spend the day with this Burmese teacher, wonder if he is a government spy, but reason that a spy would not be sitting on the train, waiting for foreigners to arrive.

Myint holds two cards in his bejeweled hands and says, "My poem." He reads it aloud, translating it into English line by line. Either it suffers from the translation or it is an atrocious poem: In English, every other line starts with the word "therefore." The gist of it is okay, though: "Riches are never as satisfying in reality as in anticipation; only a quiet mind brings happiness."

"You like? You like?" he asks, childlike.

"Yes, I like. It is true," I say, telling myself I am not being hypocritical, since I do like the message.

A military man in a khaki-colored shirt and a checked khaki and blue *longyi* boards the train and sits opposite us. He ties a frayed green rope across the width of the car so no one can enter the space in which we sit, roping off a large plastic garbage can, himself, Myint, and me; then he rests a thonged foot on the wooden bench. His officious manner indicates he is in charge here.

The train starts with a lurch. Myint leans toward me and looks significantly at the green rope. "What is that for?" I ask.

"Very important people," he says. "Only policemen and military men can sit behind the rope," and I wonder who this man is who has glommed onto me. "You like?" he asks.

"No," I say. "As your poem says, it cannot make us happy."

He beams. "You remember!"

Like an untamed horse, the train bucks and rolls along the tracks, past floating islands of discarded plastic bags and skinny dogs rummaging in heaps of garbage. The exotic city described in the *Lonely Planet* cannot be seen from this train. No wonder the desk clerk laughed when she recommended this ride: a good joke to pull on an unsuspecting foreigner.

In time with the train's clanking rhythm we are thrown from side to side on the hard wooden bench. For ten minutes we rock along the tracks before stopping for more passengers.

A small *longyi*-clad woman climbs gracefully aboard, balancing a huge, fabric-covered basket on her head. She stands at a railing near the door and lifts her hands to either side of the basket, carefully lowering it to the floor. Her faded and worn *longyi* and blouse are matching shades of teal blue. She is obviously poor, but manages to look more like a ballerina than a vendor. Even the rolled fabric circle on her head, designed to hold the basket in place, is a coordinating color.

Other passengers, oblivious to her beauty, press past her and stand in the aisles, looking longingly at the uncrowded benches behind the nylon rope. I wonder if I would be arrested if I lifted the rope to let others enter but decide not to find out.

Wind from the open windows sears our faces as we sway with the train past miles of brown grass backyards littered with plastic bags. One half hour after boarding, Myint says, "We must get off here for the Union Day celebration. It is in a museum."

Feeling as though I am still rocking with the train's movement, I walk with Myint through the station, and emerge in an alleyway where a dog with ribs showing through his skin digs in a huge garbage heap. He snarls viciously when smaller dogs approach. I hold my breath against the stench until we come to a main street. Myint guides me through traffic, holding my hand. He keeps holding it when we are safely at the other side, squeezing it occasionally, a smile creasing his E.T. face. I question the squeezes until I see his joy: He looks like a child with a new friend.

He flags a taxi, speaks Burmese to the driver, and ten minutes later we arrive at a fenced compound with a long white building at the center. Red and blue Burmese flags flutter in the wind. Male and female soldiers sit at a table inside the gate. "Security," says Myint.

The soldiers search my shoulder bag: a notebook and pen, a packet of tissues, a bottle of water, and a comb. Then they search my waist pack: a Pentax camera wrapped in a handkerchief, lipstick, money. Handing bag and pack back to me, a uniformed woman says, "How ohl ah you?"

"I am seventy-two," I say.

She looks at her companions; they speak Burmese among themselves and I hear the echo, "Seventy-two, seventy-two, seventy-two." "Beautiful, Madame," says the woman.

Myint looks at me. "Seventy-two! I don't believe. I don't believe."

I open my sun-reflecting umbrella and walk toward the bright white building. Only then do I see the big, black letters inscribed across the top: TATMADAW. The Burmese word for the military. I feel fearful, anxious, and wonder whether I should turn and run. Whether the compliments were a ruse to get me here without a fuss, whether the government has discovered I teach English to Shan refugees and is going to imprison me.

I remember Blanche Dubois in *The Streetcar Named Desire* and the words she spoke to the doctor she believed would help her: "I have always depended on the kindness of strangers." Depending on the strange doctor may not have been the thing to do, but she had no choice; the orderlies accompanying him would have hauled her away anyway. I have no choice either. Even if I ran the other way, I could not escape the gauntlet of military personnel at the gate. I look sideways at Myint, and my panic subsides. His face is suffused with innocent joy—he cannot be leading me to disaster.

We enter the building, and across from the doorway see a huge portrait of the man in charge of the Burmese Army, General Than Shwe, staring sternly at us from an altar-like area roped off in red velvet. Looking away from the General, I see photographic displays lining the walls. A few artifacts are displayed below and beside the photos. A military exhibition hall— that is what this is.

Near the entryway, a group of middle-school students, wearing headphones and green and white uniforms, sit at a cluster of desks with a sign overhead that says "Language Lab" in Burmese and English. Myint points proudly. "Like our schools," he says. But Burmese schools are renowned for being poorly equipped places that have to abide by military-approved curricula.

I am incredulous. "Your schools have *that* equipment?" I ask. Myint nods, smiling broadly. "*Everyone* can use it? *All* of your schools?"

The smile fades from his face. "Maybe the rich," he says, which makes me feel better about him. He leads me to the exhibits.

Photographic displays purport to honor Burma's ethnic groups, variously reported as being between forty and one hundred thirty. Photos show handsome people in the colorful tribal costumes of the Kachin, Chin, Karenni, Karen, and Akha. There is also an exhibit for the Shan. I try not to linger or look overly interested. I comment on a leather drum, as long as I am tall, displayed in front of the photos. I have heard such drums played by Shan exiles in Thailand, but do not tell Myint. He looks pleased at my interest, perhaps because there is such an obvious lack of interest by the Burmese people.

Aside from the guards and the rich schoolchildren at the language lab, there are few people in the hall. Only someone who feels safe from censure, I think, only a supporter of the murderous regime would dare to enter, and again I wonder about the real identity of this bejeweled English teacher whose heavily accented English I can barely understand.

He stops in front of plaster figures of soldiers arm in arm with civilians. In front of them is a broken plaster stick. Myint translates the Burmese sign below the figures, "United we stand. Divided we fall," and points to the broken stick. But the Burmese people know as well as I do that this is a façade, a fraud. If they believed in the masquerade of unity, they would be here celebrating it with Myint and me.

As we leave the hall, Myint says, "You are lucky you met me. Very lucky. You were able to celebrate Union Day!"

I choke back a groan and smile. If I had thought this E.T. look-alike was leading me to a military exhibit, I would not have followed him. Yet he got me in and out without event, without threat from the khaki-uniformed guards at the gate, so I suppose he is right. I am lucky.

* * *

Back in the clammy heat of Rangoon, we walk a few blocks to a teashop with low tables and stools in a leafy courtyard. Myint orders in Burmese, grins, and takes one of the poetry cards from his shoulder bag. Again he reads to me: His poetic persona owns many cars, which do not make him happy.

A young boy brings us two bowls of soup, stinky with a smell I do not recognize, and thick with noodles, parsley, and two kinds of meat, one black and the other liver-like. Myint takes two metal spoons from a plastic container, wipes them clean with sheets of toilet paper torn from a roll on the table, and hands one to me. "You are very lucky," he says. "Me, too."

The soup tastes better than it looks—I eat a few mouthfuls, then say, "I am sorry. I cannot eat much." Myint does not object. He is slender as a bamboo wand and probably does not eat much himself.

On the chance he is who he says he is, simply a schoolteacher who wants to show me Rangoon, I insist on paying for the soup, four hundred kyat, about forty U.S. cents. As I hand the waiter the money, Myint tells me he is retired and gets a small pension: Four thousand kyat per month. Four thousand kyat! A bit over four U.S. dollars per month. He cannot possibly live on that, yet he paid the two thousand kyat fare for the taxi ride to the Tatmadaw exhibit. My suspicions about his alliance with the military subside when he says, "I am very lucky. My wife is also an English teacher. She is very busy. Make money every day."

He leads me back to the street, where the sun beats down with vengeance on our heads. "Now we will take a bus," Myint says. "You must experience."

We join a crowd waiting at a street corner, and when a rickety red bus appears, Myint takes my hand and pushes and pulls me into the throng of people standing inside. I feel as though I will faint in the crush of bodies crammed into the small, airless space. Windows stand open on either side, but the air reaches only those sitting next to them. Someone vacates a single seat next to a window and shoves through the crowd to reach the door. Myint pushes me into the empty seat. "You are very lucky," he says. I agree.

A breeze from the open window cools my perspiring face as we pass a brilliant gold pagoda.

"Shwedagon?" I ask.

"Yes," says Myint. "You want to see?"

Tired from the heat, the swarms of people, and the Union Day tour, I say, "No," and the bus takes us back to the train.

We board at a different station, one where we do not have to run a gauntlet of starving dogs. It is mid-afternoon, and the train is crowded; there is no roped-off VIP area reserved for us. I am relieved—this might mean Myint is an ordinary citizen, not a spy.

A woman turns her hip, looks at me, and pats three inches of space she has vacated. The woman on the other side accommodatingly turns her hip away from me, too, and I press onto the crowded bench. Myint stands next to the wall of the coach, balancing elegantly in his long red and green checked skirt, his red "Vision and Views" bag swaying from his shoulder.

The train lurches forward, and steamy air streams through the windows. We pass acres of littered yards and rubbish-clogged canals where white flowers bloom. In the train, betel nut vendors spread their legs wide for balance and roll white paste into lime leaves. Men grab the green packets as soon as they are complete, and I worry about the cascades of spit that will splatter at my feet, relax in relief when they tuck them into shirt pockets for later use.

The woman on my right leaves at the next stop, and two drunken men crowd into the space she vacated. With sloppy red mouths and maroon-stained teeth, they carry on a yelling argument in Burmese with a woman on the bench across from us. Myint has found a space next to her, and looks from the men to me, as if apologizing. I am grateful when they leave at the next stop.

A couple dressed in formal Western clothes, she in a fifties-style big-skirted nylon dress and he in a suit, board together with a son and daughter in similar clothing. They stand teetering in the aisles next to a young woman balancing a baby on her hip. I motion to the girl in fancy dress to sit on my lap and discover she is not easy to hold. She sprawls her legs into the aisle, and the wide-skirted nylon dress she is wearing wants to follow. I curse myself for inviting her onto my lap but manage to hold onto her till they leave ten minutes later.

Looking after the departing family, I see a sign reading "Insein." It sends a shock through me. Insein is the name of a Rangoon suburb, but it is also the name of the infamous prison where Sao Shwe Thaike of Yawngwhe died, where countless others believed to be a threat to the government have died of torture and neglect. The name fills me with horror and a ridiculous sort of fear. Insein is still filled with political prisoners, victims of military paranoia, the same feelings of suspicion and fear that have pervaded me all day.

* * *

Forty-five sweaty minutes later, we arrive at the station near Sule Paya Road where I boarded. Myint takes my hand and leads me to the street, asks me to accompany him to his home to meet his wife. "Is very near to here," he says. I wonder whether I should once again follow this bejeweled schoolteacher, decide there is nothing to fear, and allow him to lead me through three or four filthy blocks to an alleyway where children kick a ball back and forth and men in *longyis* stand chatting.

"Here," Myint says, pointing to a four-story building with a stairway that opens onto the street. "My home is here."

We climb narrow stairs that are caked with dirt and look as if they have never been washed. Garbage has drifted to the sides of the stairs. At the top of the third flight of stairs, Myint turns toward a door covered with heavy metal grating, inserts a key into the grate and another into the door, and steps inside a room where dark brown, glass-faced cabinets are filled with books, photos, and lots of dolls, all with fair skin. The place is immaculate. He slips out of his thongs, holds a hand to me, and asks me to sit on a sofa near the door. "I will take off my shoes," I say, leaning to untie the laces. "No, no. Not here," he says. "Shoes fine."

He leads me through a narrow, crowded bedroom, filled with two beds and stacks and stacks of books—the entire place is as small and compact as an old-fashioned mobile home. The bedroom opens onto the kitchen where his wife sits at a small table, an array of dishes in front of her: noodles, soggy green vegetables, and a meat and rice dish, fragrant with ginger and garlic. A round-faced, chubby woman, she is eating, but stands to greet me, and though I urge her to continue her meal, she insists we go back to the living room. Myint talks with her in Burmese, explaining my presence, and we walk back through the crowded bedroom to the room with the doll collection, where I am urged once again to sit on the sofa.

Myint brings me a glass of cold water, and says, "I tell my wife we meet on train." Her English is better than Myint's, more precise, more clearly enunciated. We chat, and she says she has tutored two students today. Glancing at the bookcase over her head, I see a photo of Myint receiving an award from a man in a khaki uniform. If he is not a spy for the military, he is obviously in a state of grace with them. Having suspected some such thing, I have revealed little of myself, certainly not my connection to the Shan. I feel duplicitous and am embarrassed when he goes into the bedroom, returns with the red "Visions and Views" bag neatly folded, bows, and hands it to me. "My wife and I give you this," he says.

A wave of shame washes over me. I have questioned this man's motives all day, and all I have gotten from him is kindness. I want to refuse the bag, but fear he will be offended. Can one be a friend of the military regime and still be a good person, I wonder, and decide he may simply be unthinking and unknowledgeable—not bad. Then I remember that Hitler was kind to German children, but had no qualms about murdering the children of Jews. I set my moral quandary aside, thank him, and tuck the Visions and Views bag into the hand-woven shoulder bag I bought in Mandalay.

Later, outside the May Shan Hotel, Myint asks if the taxi driver can use my camera to take our photo; then he grabs my hand. I look at the digital image and see two people who might have been friends, a tall, slim Burmese man with an E.T. face and a small American woman whose face does not reveal her suspicion and distrust, two teachers who were lucky to find each other in Rangoon.

* * *

February 13: Today I am returning to Chiang Mai. In the taxi to Yangon International Airport, I take a chance on the same risky question I asked on the way into Rangoon. "Aung San Suu Kyi lives on the way to the airport, doesn't she?"

This driver is friendlier and speaks more English. "Yes, lives on Inya Lake," he says. "But we cannot see her home."

"I will go close," he says, and we detour from Pyay Road to circle closer to Inya Lake. We drive a few blocks, and he turns back. "No more," he says. "Very dangerous to pass her house. Military zone. Many soldiers." I wonder if the soldiers ever chuckle at their assignment: battalions of men with guns to guard a small woman who won the Nobel Peace Prize for her pacifistic approach to democratic change. Probably not.

In Burma, the paranoia of the military is so catching it clung to me all yesterday, as I listened to Myint's poem, toured the Union Day Exhibit with him, and saw the sign for Insein as we traveled on the train around Rangoon. Paranoia: a contagious disease that can tinge a lucky meeting with distrust.

PART FOUR:

Caring for Others

If you find it in your heart to care for somebody else,
you will have succeeded. —Maya Angelou

IN CHIANG MAI WITH SHANG PHUN

I urge you to celebrate the extraordinary courage and contributions of refugees past and present. —Kofi Annan, UN Secretary-General

<u>December 13, 2004:</u> Chiang Mai, Thailand: This evening Shang Phun visits me at my hotel. He had tried to get refugee status for a year, calling the International Refugee Center in Bangkok every Friday, when they would tell him to call back the following Friday. He gave up and is again working with a backpack team, traversing the mountainous jungle and fording the rivers of Shan State, bringing medicine and money for rice to those who are hiding from the Burmese military.

Backpacking across the nine-thousand-foot-high mountains of southeastern Shan State requires a hardy disposition. One team member did not have sufficient endurance; they left him in a village along the way. The work agrees with Shang Phun. He looks healthier than he did last winter while working ten-hour days, twenty-eight days a month in a Bangkok garment factory. The fresh air, exercise, and the knowledge that he is helping his people have made him stronger.

He feels safe, he says. Soldiers from the Shan State Army (SSA) accompany the backpack team. The SSA is one of the few groups still resisting the Burmese takeover. The Shan soldiers precede the backpackers into villages to make sure there are no Burmese soldiers around, take shifts watching over them at night, try to keep them safe from landmines, an impossible task. During the last trip, an eighteen-year-old SSA soldier stepped on a mine and was killed.

Shang Phun has photos. The Shan who escaped relocation camps when Burmese soldiers burned their homes and took their rice fields, have built shanties in the wilderness. The thatched roofs of their shacks are barely visible above high grasses. They have no plumbing or electricity, no access to medical help; the children cannot attend school and are often hungry.

They line up for photos, looking remarkably neat and clean, but most cannot read or write; they press inked thumbs onto paper, acknowledging receipt of medicine or of money to buy rice. Shang Phun estimates that only forty percent of the Shan within Burma are literate.

He points to fields of flowers and says, "Very pretty, Teacher." Acres and acres of pink and white poppies cover the mountainsides. Poppies are a never-fail crop in this region. Their opium-producing potential means they bring more money than most crops, and there is no shortage of buyers. Khun Sa, former leader of the Shan State Army, which he betrayed, now has the blessing of the military junta with whom he shares drug profits. With their implicit permission, he commissions traders to travel long distances on horseback, exchanging food for drugs. But farmers are at the mercy of the traders, who never give them enough money to cover their needs. Worse, some become addicted to the drug.

Shang Phun says the SSA has started a program to help such addicts, giving them small amounts of money to abstain from opium. If they regress and start using, they lose the stipend.

"The Burmese don't care if they use opium, Teacher," Shang Phun says. "They want the Shan to destroy themselves."

I remember traveling in Kengtung, remember the truckloads of soldiers who swooped through the streets. This evening, Shang Phun has shown me why they are there, to subjugate the people of Shan State in areas that are off limits and invisible to tourists.

I worry that in that invisible Shan State, Shang Phun, too, might be destroyed while helping others. One misstep and his young body and wonderful spirit could be blown to bits by a landmine and I might never know.

WHEN YOU ARE OLD

Teacher: The child's third parent. —Hyman Berston

February 15, 2005: There are no thermometers in this Thai village, so I tell the temperature by my degree of discomfort. Today my body says it is one hundred degrees with high humidity. Today I look forward to returning in a few weeks to Minnesota's cold March winds.

I turn the fan on high, get a glass of cold water from the small refrigerator in the corner of my room, and sit on my bed propped against pillows, listening to birdsong and looking through a ragged green and yellow notebook. Yellow: the color of my youthful persona, a woman who believed one way and acted another. Yellow, the color of cowardice. But this book is mostly green, the color of spring, the color of hope. It is filled with notes I took while traveling through Burma, some of them in shorthand, a skill I learned in the 1940s, used here to confound the Burmese military if they happened to see it.

In my fancy, the notebook cover, more green than yellow, represents a change in my character. I am growing up, becoming the integrated person I always wanted to be.

A rapping at the door, and Sai Soe bursts in, gathering me exuberantly into outstretched arms. He stands aside as Sai Hseng enters behind him and folds me into a gentler hug. They seem unfazed by the heat; it is only in the cooler months that they suffer. I motion them to a cushioned bench and return to my seat on the bed.

Although they are both twenty-three years old now, they look and sound like enthusiastic boys, like my sons might have sounded when they returned from an amusement park. They are taking advanced English classes that I paid for with the help of friends before leaving for Burma, and they immediately start talking about them.

"The school, it is very good, Teacher—only the teachers they have British accents. Sometimes we cannot understand." I remind them that before they met me all of their English teachers had British accents, the legacy of British colonialism in Burma. In 2002, they had a hard time understanding my American accent. "You will get used to them," I say.

"In my class we learn the word 'scramble,' Teacher. Mean like run quickly to catch a taxi," says Sai Hseng, who is the editor of the Shan language newsletter they produce for migrants, and who loves learning new words.

"It can also mean to mix eggs or other food with a fork," I say.

"Mix eggs!" he says, as though he has been let in on a wonderful secret.

Sai Soe, who is in a more advanced class, is not to be outdone. "My class have new words, too, Teacher. Today we learn 'hassles.'"

When I ask what the word means, he says, "Our Shan people they are hassled by the government."

Hassled. In Burma they are hassled for simply existing, hassled because the military wants the wealthy Shan land. In Thailand they could be hassled for any misstep: A minor motorbike accident could mean they would have to show identification that says they are temporary workers from Burma, and they would face large fines and possible deportation. Their impossible situation of being caught between two countries is, in part, what binds me to them. Persecuted in Burma, illegal in Thailand, they remain determined to help themselves and their country people.

I think about these two men, culling news about Burma from international sources and word-of-mouth accounts from recent refugees, researching health issues such as HIV and AIDS and writing about them in their newsletter for Shan migrants. I think about them teaching English and Shan language classes to migrants, Thai citizens, and monks in barren monastery classrooms, lively and loving as they write on the blackboard with dust-spewing chalk. I see them standing at the head of the classroom, smiling and nodding as students respectfully chorus answers to their questions.

Looking at them sitting bright-eyed and excited on the bench, I remember when I tried to introduce them to birth control and venereal disease prevention—sex education is not taught in Burmese schools—remember how they blushed when I tried to give them a packet of material from Planned Parenthood and some condoms. "No. No, Teacher," they chorused, avoiding my eyes. I remember sealing the information and the condoms into an envelope and telling them to open it when they got home.

Those images are juxtaposed with photos taken since they started working for an NGO organized to fight HIV and AIDS in migrants: Sai Soe sits on the floor of a jungle home lit by candles stuck into tin cans. The circle of men, women, and children around him watch intently as he stretches a condom onto his thumb, demonstrating its proper use. In another photo, children blow the condoms into balloons. "To make them comfortable, Teacher. Our people they are very shy."

Another knock at the door. Shang Phun. He puts an arm around my shoulder; then he sees Sai Soe and Sai Hseng sitting on the cushioned bench, and his face falls. These three men had been the first to call when I returned to Thailand this year, the first to visit me. Maybe the presence of Sai Soe and Sai Hseng reminds him he is late. "Sorry I am late, Teacher," he says.

"It's okay," I say, and gesture toward the bench. He looks at it, and then sits beside me on the bed.

Shang Phun lives and works far from here and survives on minimal amounts of money from his organization: Fifty cents here, fifty cents there. Fifty cents to take a pickup truck to see me, a long trek, with one transfer along the way.

I tell him how healthy he looks, contrast his robust appearance with the thin, coughing man he was when he worked in the garment factory. "I am helping my people, Teacher."

Helping their people: that has been the primary concern of most Shan refugees I have met. In *Twilight Over Burma*, Inge Sargent wrote about her husband, the Prince of Hsipaw, who studied mining engineering at Colorado School of Mines so he could return to Shan State and "help his people benefit from the wealth buried under their soil."

His intentions were never realized. He was murdered by the Burmese military, and the government manned Shan State's ruby, diamond, and jade mines with Shan workers who toiled from sunrise to sundown, picking at the reluctant stone and inhaling its dust for wages that did not allow them to feed their families.

Thinking about Hsipaw, I remember the German tourist I met there. For no apparent reason and with little preliminary conversation, he had asked me if I knew any Shan dissidents. It seemed an odd question, and I gave him a quick "No," but thought about it afterwards. Dissident: dissent, disagree with policies of the existing government.

Of course I know dissidents. The three young men in this room are dissidents. They hate the way the government has treated their people, are concerned with righting the wrongs inflicted on them. All twenty-five students in my first English class for Shan refugees were dissidents; all twenty-eight students in the second class were dissidents. That is why they were refugees.

I think the German man meant rebels—had I met any Shan rebels who actively worked against the government. The answer to that, if I had been inclined to give it, would have also been "Yes." In hidden places and secret ways, the parents, uncles, aunts, and cousins of many Shan students had actively opposed the Burmese military regime and were still opposing it.

Five former students had been soldiers in rebel armies. They were older than the other students, quiet men, concerned with helping others. At the school, four of them selected and nurtured younger male students, assuming the role of older brother to lonely, bewildered young men. The fifth soldier became attached to a staff person's baby. During recesses and after class, he carried the child in his arms and lifted it to smell the fragrance of frangipani blossoms.

Dissidents. Rebels. I had been surrounded by them for four years and had never known gentler people.

"Teacher, did you go to Inle?" Shang Phun asks.

"The boats, Teacher," says Sai Soe. "The men who row with one leg, did you see them?" All of them had told me about the fishermen who rowed their boats with one leg, a sight they had never seen and probably never would see.

"Yes. They look wonderful," I say. "Like herons, birds that stand on one leg and catch fish in their beaks."

They grow quiet when I tell them about Inle Lake and Yawngwhe Palace, how peaceful they were, and how I did not see any soldiers.

"Teacher," says Sai Hseng. "Something bad happen when you were in Burma. Ten of our Shan leaders are arrested." Ten leaders of the Shan Nationalities League of Democracy political party. Sai Hseng's face grows pale with the telling.

"They are in prison," says Sai Soe quietly. "Insein."

"Our leaders are arrested," Sai Hseng repeats, as if he cannot believe it. "Now we cannot know what to do."

"How did they find them?"

"They invite to a meeting, Teacher. And then they arrest. That is how they do it."

"When?"

"First part February, Teacher," says Shang Phun, looking at the floor. During the first part of February I was in the peaceful villages of Hsipaw and Yawngwhe.

I remember the suspicion that tinged my meetings with Burmese people: the soldier who befriended me on the train to Hsipaw and the E.T. look alike, Myint, in Rangoon. I know now it was wise to be suspicious, to keep my stories to myself.

Most of the leaders arrested were affiliated with Aung San Suu Kyi's National League of Democracy Party. "Maybe now they will give Aung San Suu Kyi a rest," says Sai Hseng. "Because they put our leaders in jail." He is joking, of course—does not expect her to be released.

I marvel that I was in the country when the arrests were made, marvel that not a word seeped out through Burma's tightly controlled state media, and with a jolt of fear I remember the Mandalay trishaw driver for whom I bought a radio. "Now I can know what is happening in my country," he had said. I hoped not, hoped he had not heard about the arrests, hoped the radio had been broken and discarded, for yesterday I saw Internet news about political prisoners in Burma, one of whom had been arrested several years ago for listening to Voice of America. I had bought the cheaper radio, the one without short wave capability, but what if by some fluke he got the forbidden station?

"Now there is more fighting in Shan State, Teacher," says Shang Phun. "More villages are burning." He talks about Burma's "Four Cuts" program, about how Burmese soldiers are once again rampaging against the ethnic people, burning villages and sending villagers to encampments to be used as unpaid laborers. The four things they cut, he says, are food, money, intelligence information, and recruitment between civilians and opposition groups like the Shan State Army.

I stand, pull my sweaty clothing away from my body, go to the refrigerator and fill two glasses and a cup with pomelo juice and bring them to the young men.

"I am sorry," I say. "I wish I could help."

"No, Teacher. No," says Sai Hseng. "You help too much." Two scholarships, a small food stipend, a bit of spending money for Shang Phun. A drop of rain in a drought. But they are enormously grateful. Their gratitude shames me, for I know I have not done enough. And I worry about the time when I can no longer return to Thailand to give them even this small amount of help, worry that they will never get well-paying jobs.

With these three young men I feel as comfortable as I do with my two sons who returned to Minneapolis recently to celebrate my seventy-second birthday. We ate thin-crust vegetarian pizza, drank beer, and listened to folk music. These three men are drinking pomelo juice and telling horror stories about Burma, but the feeling of warmth and love that suffused the evening with my sons is replicated in this room.

In Minnesota, people have wondered aloud why I am helping Burmese refugees when there is so much to be done at home. They got me thinking.

I did not come to Thailand to help others. It just happened. I fell in love with a group of young people, not only those in this room, but an entire classroom of men and women who reminded me of my sons and my granddaughters and who seemed to love me as they do.

Sitting with these men I think of as "my boys," I recall a summer day when I was three years old and the smell of new mown hay filled the air. Looking for my mother, I wandered into the barnyard and found her standing behind the barn wrapped in my father's embrace. He saw me first. "Well, if it isn't little honey," he said pulling me into the middle of their hug. That is how I feel right now, surrounded by all this love.

Looking at Sai Soe, Shang Phun, and Sai Hseng, I remember my sons at the ages these young men are now, how idealistic they were, how they attended concerts to raise money for the poor and worried about the condition of the world. Now in their forties, they support children in poverty-stricken areas. Like the young men in this room, they are concerned with helping their people and are wise enough to know that all the people of the world are their people.

I remember a Shakti Gawain type of New Age saying about "When love happens, follow it"—or maybe I made it up. At any rate, that is what I have done.

Shang Phun puts his arm around my shoulder, and his voice breaks as he says, "If I have a good job sometime . . ."

I know what he is going to say; he has said it before, and it always makes me cry. I turn my head away as he finishes, "I want to take care of Teacher when Teacher is old."

I love Shang Phun's way of speaking, never addressing me as "you," but always as "Teacher," his way of showing respect. I smile through my tears.

"No," says Sai Hseng. He is the quietest of the three, but his voice is assertive as he says, "Three months with me, three months with Sai Soe, and three months with you."

"Yes, Teacher," says Sai Soe. "When you are old, Teacher."

The words send a wave of pleasure through my body. "When I am old," they say, but I have already lived longer than most Thai or Burmese people do. Maybe to them being old means not being able to take care of yourself. When that time comes, they probably could not afford to take care of me, but I know that they would try. That keeps me coming back.

ENDINGS AND BEGINNINGS

October 2008

I wanted a perfect ending. Now I've learned, the hard way, that some poems
don't rhyme, and some stories don't have a clear beginning, middle and end . . .
—Gilda Radner

Each man must look to himself to teach him the meaning of life. It is not something discovered it is something molded. —Antoine de Saint Exupéry

Seven years have passed since I first traveled to Thailand to teach English
to Shan refugees. I have returned every year, except for the year I had knee
surgery. In 2002, 2003, and 2004, I taught English to the same group of
refugees I met in 2002. Then they got busy with jobs, one of which was
starting schools for Shan refugee children in migrant camps, a project
friends helped me support.

The schools have been enthusiastically accepted and continue to grow.
I visit once a year to see the schools and meet with teachers, a heartwarm-
ing task. Students' admiration and respect for their young refugee teachers is apparent in their behavior and in their performance. A Shan youth
in our tuition program recently won top honors in a class of forty-five
students, most of whom were Thai.

After that first year, when I lived in the village near the school where
unlit streets and bands of dogs kept me housebound after dark, I have
stayed in Chiang Mai. There I have friends from Canada, Israel, Den-
mark, and France, winter sojourners like me. Former students who travel
to the city to visit me are shocked by the luxury of my one-hundred-dol-
lar per month room. I am embarrassed, knowing that by U.S. standards
I live humbly.

Most speak English fluently now; some offer to find me a cheaper room;
some come to discuss their studies, their work, and their future plans.
Most of them have had a modicum of success; a few have excelled.

* * *

Ying Tzarm and **Nang Kyi** are among those who have excelled. Nang Kyi, the girl with cheeks the color of ripe mangoes, who would stroke my hands and feet as I sat on the school patio, graduated from Foreign Affairs Training and works for a women's group in another village. It is four years since I have seen her. Ying Tzarm graduated from Journalism School.

Both women have responsible jobs. Ying works for the Women's League of Burma, an activist group to which Nang Kyi also belongs, and which espouses the belief that *"the contribution of women in the struggle to bring about human rights, democracy and equal rights for all nationalities in Burma will have a great impact, and their participation in the national reconciliation and peace-building process is essential."* To that end, the organization promotes the education and advancement of its members. In 2007 Ying and Nang Kyi traveled to Denver as representatives of Shan State at a worldwide peace conference.

I saw Ying at a 2007 Chiang Mai celebration commemorating the 60th anniversary of the Panglong Agreement, an agreement formulated in 1947 when Shan State and Burma became independent of Great Britain, an agreement that resulted in freedom for Burma and garrisons of Burmese soldiers for Shan State.

On this anniversary, refugees from Burma—Shan, Kachin, Karen, and Burmese—came together to speak and to sing songs of lament. Ying was among them. Elegant in a long, hand-woven gray skirt and matching blouse, she came to me. Kneeling at my feet, she said, "You enjoy, Teacher?" I kissed her forehead, remembering the 14-year-old girl who had assigned herself extra homework, spending her evenings looking up English language words in the dictionary and writing sentences using them.

A group of Ying's former classmates gathered on the stage and she rose to join them as they sang about oppression, betrayal, and exile, a plaint for justice.

* * *

Nang Lwin, who used to dance toward me, her long braid swishing from side to side, attended midwife training at Mae Sot Clinic, run by Doctor Cynthia Maung, a Karen refugee who trekked through the jungle for ten days to escape from Burma. In 2003, I visited Nang Lwin at the clinic. She loved her studies, she said, but not her living space.

She took my hand, led me through a windowless hallway permeated with the stench of a communal toilet, and took me to her room, a bamboo and plastic-sheeted hovel she shared with seven other young women, each of them with a narrow rectangular space to spread their sleeping mats. Dr. Maung will turn no one away. The medical complex is crowded with refugees suffering from diarrhea and malaria contracted while fleeing through the jungle to Thailand. There is little space left for students like Nang Lwin. We sat cross-legged on the floor while she rummaged through the few possessions stacked at the head of her allotted space and found a lacy white scarf she had knitted. I was teary eyed when she handed it to me saying, "I make for you, Teacher. Is very cold in your state."

In 2005, having completed midwife training, she returned to Shan State, planning to attend university. I did not see her again, and she has not used the government-monitored e-mail system in Burma—she might let slip a reference to Thailand and get herself and her former classmates into trouble.

* * *

Nang Yot, the only student who had attended university in Burma, is one of the few who returned to the same job she had before attending the School for Shan. She lives in Bangkok and works as a nanny and maid. Sometimes I see her when I stop in the city on the way to northern Thailand, for she attends the Baptist Church next to my hotel. She brings me gifts of potato chips and dried fruit and at every meeting asks me how she can get a better job.

* * *

Nang Myo, the regal-looking beauty the boys called their "queen," worked with prostitutes in Thailand for a while, exchanging English language lessons for Thai. Then she returned to Burma. I have received only a two-line message from her, the standard, "How are you? I am fine." And I hoped she truly was fine, no longer bitter about the former boyfriend who had married another.

* * *

Nang May, the girl who suffered from severe anxiety, returned to her recently reopened school near the Thai-Burma border. In 2006 she graduated from tenth standard. I visited her that winter and found a self-composed, attractive, young woman, quite different from the fearful girl who had refused to speak when I met her at the School for Shan. Her anxiety, it seems, had been caused by skirmishes between the Burmese military and Shan who had escaped into Thailand, a barrage of cross-border bullets so severe and extended that her beloved school was closed for two years.

In 2007, Nang May started attending a branch of Chiang Mai University. Juggling her classes with a full-time job at a human rights organization, she managed to do justice to both. When the job fizzled out in 2008, she left the university and returned to the village where she was raised, near the border with Burma. There, she teaches English and math to novices in a Buddhist monastery.

* * *

Sai Leng, the talented young man who wrote "Refugees without a Camp," returned to Burma. He has sent several e-mail messages. In the first, he said, "We can do our work here if we are careful." He is married and has two children, and I wonder if he reunited with the girl who smelled like jasmine.

* * *

Kham La, the guitar strumming, cane-ball player, who attended Teachers' Training but was not allowed to teach, has also returned to Burma. I have heard nothing from him since he crossed the border, but one of his classmates said he is attending university. In my mind, I see his agile body contorting itself into backward kicks to get the cane ball over the net. In reverie, I hear his sweet voice singing, "I'm leaving on a jet plane." I had listened with tears streaming down my cheeks, thinking then that it was I who was leaving, not he.

* * *

Sai Khin, who had monitored school snacks, making sure each student got the same portion, and who sang *You Are My Sunshine* with gusto, visited me in Chiang Mai during the winter of 2007. He is working as a driver for a large hotel in northern Thailand, he said. "Very expensive, Teacher. Two thousand baht one night." That's the equivalent of more than fifty dollars U.S.

"Good tips?" I asked.

"No, they are very stingy, Teacher," and ignorant, I thought, wondering if tourists would be more generous if they knew he was a refugee.

Then with a look that hovered between embarrassment and pride, he said, "I am married now, Teacher." He paused and said, "One baby."

* * *

Sai Nok, the former monk, who wrote, "I must learn English," while others studied, is also married. After graduating from the School for Shan, he worked ten-hour days, six days per week, carrying heavy cartons of fruit to vendors, a job more suited to an ox than to a man. He took one day off to attend a 2003 party for me, and I was horrified to learn he had lost his job as a result. Now I know it was a good thing, for he is working at an artisans' market, selling wooden carvings to tourists. He likes the work, he says, because he can "speak English." He is married and has one child.

* * *

Khun Ohn, the shy fellow who once said he wanted to be a politician, seems to have resigned himself to life as a janitor. I have tried to encourage him to attend advanced trainings so he could get a better job, but the uncle he lived with asked him to stay nearby, a request that has relegated him to washing floors and cleaning toilets.

* * *

But most students have success stories. After graduation, six students banded together to share living expenses and formed a group dedicated to helping other refugees: former monk, Sai Sam; love-crazed Murng Zuen; Sai Ping, the youngest male student; Sai Soe, the dreamy-eyed fellow who had been given away three times before he was three years old; and Sai Seng, memorable for his kindness.

Sai Seng was the first group member to earn money. He used it to buy rice for the group and to pay rent on an old farmhouse, where they slept on the floor.

The lives of the six former classmates have diverged slightly since then, but their organization is intact and now has more than twenty members, all of whom attended Charm Tong's school. Most of them have work permits and are legal though temporary residents of Thailand.

* * *

Sai Sam slipped back into Shan State in 2005 and returned indignant because Burmese soldiers had confiscated the few cassette tapes he had carried with him. The loss could not dim his happiness—he had returned with a 19-year-old bride, whom he adored.

The previous year Sai Sam had sent me an e-mail, asking for a scholarship for advanced computer training. He completed the course and became an instructor in a computer class for refugees, a class administered by the group of six former classmates.

In November 2006, Sai Sam took me to an International Migrants' Day party. It was a chilly evening and we huddled together on thin, woven mats placed on the ground. Paper plates held small candles that flickered as if exchanging Morse code chitchat with the stars. Migrants sang and danced on a stage in front of us, while young people brought us dishes of peanuts and spicy vegetable salad, and then quietly sat on the mats surrounding us; they were Sai Sam's students from the computer class. Watching the way they hung on his words, I was proud of him, knowing he had worked hard to earn that popularity.

* * *

Sai Ping was Sai Sam's workmate. At fifteen, Sai Ping had had two passions: the environment and computers. After applying unsuccessfully for environmental training classes, he immersed himself in computers and became a self-taught expert. With the help of friends, I provided scholarships for advanced computer classes, and he is now known throughout the Shan community for his expertise.

* * *

Murng Zuen, the academically gifted and love-crazed young man who danced the Boogy with me on Valentine's Day was also fascinated by computers. After completing various training programs, he, too, became a computer instructor, working with Sai Ping.

Murng Zuen returned to Shan State when contacted by the group that had funded his attendance at the School for Shan. They did not make use of his quick mind but relegated him to washing dishes. He returned to Thailand but not to his job. Sai Sam had replaced him. Murng Zuen got a job working with a company that produces books and videos about Burma.

In 2006, working independently and without the other's knowledge, both Murng Zuen and Sai Ping developed fonts for the Shan language. In Shan State, the Burmese military regime has outlawed teaching Shan in schools, but Murng Zuen and Sai Ping have posted the font on the Internet to share with as many Shan writers as the Internet can reach.

* * *

Sai Hseng still works for the NGO that helps Burmese migrants in Thailand. His primary job is holding educational seminars that teach migrants about HIV and AIDS, and he remains a key member of the group that banded together for six months to live on his meager stipend.

As a group, they administer and work in a computer school for refugees from Shan State. They also administer and teach in schools for Shan migrant children funded by friends who heard the children's story, a story of deprivation and poverty, of uneducated children living in shacks of bamboo and plastic sheeting at the foot of the luxurious homes their parents built for middle class Thais.

I visited the schools in the spring of 2007 and was surprised to find that, inspired by their teachers' example, most of the children now attended Thai schools. The daily treks to school had not damped their ardor for the night classes held in a bamboo shack and taught by my young Shan friends. The teachers represented hope, the hope that one day they, too, might become teachers.

* * *

Sai Soe now has a full-time job in the Health and Safety Department of an NGO that serves migrants. He investigates building sites, where Shan workers endure cruelly difficult work, carrying huge loads of bricks and concrete blocks on their skinny backs, balancing on flimsy bamboo scaffolding to reach the buildings' upper stories.

Many are injured in falls; others get serious electrical burns from faulty wiring. In the summer of 2006, Sai Soe wrote telling me about a worker who was electrocuted on the job. "Is very sad, Teacher," he wrote. "Now there is just the mother, two small children, and an old man who cannot work much," and I imagined him pressing his hand to his heart, the way he had the year I brought along a cane, in case my arthritic knees acted up. "I feel it here, Teacher," he had said.

Sai Soe counsels the workers, and he holds classes, warning them of the dangers inherent in their jobs, suggesting safety measures. I saw him several times in 2007 and was impressed with his ideas to help others: a self-financed health care fund for migrants, education incentives for their children. Sitting on a bench in my room, he rested his forearms on his knees and looked up at me. "What do you think, Teacher?" he said. "Should we try to start a school for mountain children? Their parents work on farms—they are very poor."

Sai Soe and Sai Hseng worked without pay to register the children for school. Their tuition and was paid by generous friends who heard me tell their story. Despite being in a foreign country where classes are taught in a foreign language, all of the Shan migrant children have passed their classes in the Thai schools they have now attended for two years.

In 2007, we started a weekend school for parents and children at this mountain site. The parents, many of them formerly illiterate, learn the Thai language so they can communicate with their employers; the children study the Thai, English, and Shan languages as well as basic mathematics.

* * *

Sai Sai, who wrote about holding his father's hand and running from Burmese soldiers who had torched their family home, overcame the fear that kept him from completing advanced training. After interning with an environmental group, he studied advanced English, got the equivalent of a U.S. General Education Degree, and is now studying Law at a Bangkok university. Occasionally he sends e-mail messages to his former classmates. Sounding both proud and encouraging, he advises them to follow their dreams, as he has. He still has trouble sleeping.

* * *

When I met these young people in 2002, they were frightened and discouraged. Accustomed to hunger and deprivation, they had little hope for a future they could not imagine. Thinking about them now, I wonder if ever young people have accomplished so much under such difficult circumstances. True, schooling is a fraction of U.S. costs, and friends who trusted my judgment have helped many of them on their way. They have also been helped by NGOs, which offer free training programs to deserving refugees. But it is they, my former students themselves, who accepted each tiny seed of opportunity and germinated it with desire and compassion, until they had created abundant gardens of possibility.

Not only do they help other migrants, but they delight in their work, always planning how to do more for them. I find that deeply gratifying, as though I were the impetus for their success, which I am not. My feelings are akin to those of a grandmother who looks at her grandchildren with pride, hoping their make-up includes a little bit of her. But there is more to report.

* * *

In 2006, I returned to Burma and visited **Ohn Win**. She was teaching English in a Mormon school for children of the poor, those who comb the streets of Mandalay, picking up plastic bags, taking them to recycling plants, and earning a few kyat to help their parents buy food. When I visited the school, they gathered round Ohn Win in ragged clothes, pajama bottoms and hand-me-down shirts, pajama tops and ragged slacks, and at a cue from her they sang *You Are my Sunshine.*

She and her mother lived in a decent house, the rent paid by her foster father Gregg, and she had a boyfriend. All seemed well. Then the boyfriend got a job in Singapore and ended their relationship. Heart-broken for a few months, Ohn Win soon learned to be content with studying and teaching English.

In 2007, she hopped on a motorbike rented by an elderly American tourist and ferried him from place to place, showing him the Puppet School and Mandalay Hill, where tourists gathered to watch the sunset. The man was known to the military regime; he worked for an organization that promoted human rights for Burmese citizens.

Ohn Win soon noticed two men following her wherever she went. One day, when Ohn Win was out, Burmese policemen went to her house and asked her mother where she was. When her mother said she did not know, they hauled her off to jail. She was detained for two days before Ohn Win found her.

I know this because the American who got Ohn Win into trouble took her to Rangoon, helped her get a Thai visa, and paid her transportation to a town in northern Thailand, where I met her in February 2007.

Walking toward a prearranged meeting place, I saw Ohn Win, dressed in blue jeans and a red tee-shirt, running toward me. She hugged me the way she might have hugged her mother the day she got out of jail. She told me the rest of that story over a plate of *Pad Thai*, fried noodles sprinkled with bamboo shoots and crushed peanuts.

"I went to the jail," she said, puffing out her small chest, as though she were a big and angry person. "And I said, 'Give me back my mother. I didn't do anything wrong.'" They released her mother, but continued to follow Ohn Win until she escaped to Thailand. There she has become one of thousands of migrants, trying to find a way to survive.

Ohn Win has an advantage over most refugees who are doomed to lives of hard labor in foreign countries: She meets people easily and turns new acquaintances into fast friends. A prominent Thai citizen of Burmese origin is trying to get her into school; an American man who owns a restaurant is trying to get her a work permit and a job.

The irony of Ohn Win's forced exile is that she was extremely loyal to the Burmese military government, never wanting or daring to say a word against them. "They are our father," she had said. So loyal had she been that when she lived in Mandalay she had identified herself only as Burmese. In exile, she said she was part Shan.

* * *

I also saw **Maung San** in 2006. He pedaled me through Mandalay in his trishaw, his left eye still blurry from using acid in a paper factory job. In 2005, I had given him some money to help pay for eye surgery, so when we stopped at a tea shop and were sipping weak Chinese tea, I said, "Your eye?"

"Too much money," he said. "I went to doctor, have not enough money."

I told Maung San I was going to visit Pagan, a plain dotted with thousands of ancient golden-spired pagodas near the Irrawaddy River, the former home of kings. "I would like to go with you," he said.

Two days later, we boarded a ferry on the placid Irrawaddy River. Now it seems like a dream—twelve hours moving slowly up river, gliding past farmers in thatched roof huts, past oxen pulling hay-laden carts, past a large, moored boat where brown-skinned women held out hand-woven wall hangings.

In Pagan, Maung San called me "mother" and took care of me like a son, carrying my backpack, pointing out the most important sights. Everything delighted him: inhaling incense as he knelt barefoot in front of a Buddha statue gleaming with gold leaf, sitting at low tables sipping tea, eating stir-fried vegetables with rice.

The night before he boarded a train for Mandalay, Maung San knocked at my door. He stood on the porch outside, fresh from a cold-water shower. There was hot water in the showers, but Maung San was accustomed to bathing in the Irrawaddy River. He had said the warm water hurt his eyes. "I come to say I love Mother," he said, and his sweet words reverberate through my memories.

I could not return to Burma in the winter of 2007, so I gave one hundred dollars to friend Laurie, who was traveling there. (Maung San had said the eye surgery would cost eighty dollars.) Laurie sent me a thank-you note he had dictated to her. In it, he said, "Dear Mother, Thank you for the gift. I remember you. Now my business is not so good. Can you give me advice?" There was a lump of sadness in my chest as I read the message, knowing Maung San would use the money to buy food for his family rather than for eye surgery.

* * *

Henry, the broad-shouldered young man who took me to the top of Mandalay Hill on his motorbike, is no more. He died of Hepatitis C, according to Ohn Win. That knowledge infuriates me. Hepatitis C is a treatable disease, but not in Burma, where the generals in charge of the country spend tax monies to drive the ethnic people off their land, rather than providing treatment centers for the ill.

* * *

Now back to Shan refugees: **Shang Phun**, who spent years in a sweat-shop, his body naked to the waist as he pushed a gigantic loom from side to side in strength-draining rhythm, and then left the factory to deliver food and medicine to displaced persons in the Burmese jungle, completed a year-long training program that prepares refugees from Burma to be-come advocates for their people.

He is married to a woman whose dedication to the Shan equals his. They study English together during their free time, and Shang Phun has become eloquent. They visited me several times in 2007. Then, as many times in the past, he said, "Teacher is very good to our Shan. I never for-get," but it has been an honor to be good to people like Shang Phun.

When I think about the future, I see him standing at a podium, speak-ing to human rights groups worldwide, exposing the genocide of Shan by a Burmese military regime that claims its actions are self-defense, defense against people they have driven from their homes to hide in the jungles, a proud but skeletal people who have been robbed of the physical and emo-tional strength to fight back. I see Shang Phun, his intense eyes reflecting the pain of a persecuted people as he tells their stories. Honest, sincere. The perfect advocate.

* * *

The Shan have another outstanding advocate: **Charm Tong**, the direc-tor of the School for Shan, who has accumulated an impressive array of awards in recent years. Remembering the twenty-year-old girl in blue jeans whom I met in 2002, I chuckle. It's the kind of chuckle I might emit in front of a Burmese military general, if I were bold enough, the kind of chuckle that means, "Ha, ha, this young woman whose parents feared for her safety under your murderous regime, this young woman who grew up in an orphanage, has achieved more than you have!"

In 2004, she was one of ten women honored as "Women of the World" by Marie Claire Magazine. That was just the beginning.

In 2005, she was one of four young people worldwide to receive the Reebok Human Rights Award, was designated an "Asian Hero" by *Time* magazine, and was nominated for the Nobel Peace Prize. That was the year I went "home" with her for Christmas, home to the orphanage where she grew up in northern Thailand.

Christmas weekend was cold and rainy in northern Thailand. I huddled into a sweater and jacket and played games with the orphanage children, while Charm Tong assumed a traditional daughter's role with sixty-seven-year-old Teacher Mary, the orphanage director who raised her.

Lady-like in a long skirt and a pink sweater that her mother in Shan State had knitted for her, Charm Tong bustled through the orphanage kitchen and grounds, joining first one group of Shan women and then another as she helped them chop vegetables and wash dishes, preparing for a celebration which would include the entire Buddhist Shan community, paying homage to Teacher Mary and her Buddhist/Christian values, values instilled in her by the nuns who raised her at a Catholic orphanage. In a quiet moment with Teacher Mary, I said, "You must be very proud of Charm Tong." Her answer was simply "Yes," but her eyes gleamed with the depth of her pride.

Charm Tong received more recognition in 2007. In Norway, students honored her with their Student Peace Prize. In Burma, the military regime designated her as a "terrorist." The label worried me, as I thought about Nobel laureate Aung San Suu Kyi confined by the military to her heavily guarded home in Rangoon. Charm Tong was amused. "They are crazy," she said, and went about her preparations for the next school term.

EPILOGUE: SHAN STATE AND BURMA REVISITED

February 2009

Courage doesn't always roar. Sometimes courage is the quiet voice at the end of the day saying, "I will try again tomorrow." —Mary Anne Radmacher

In the summer of 2007, Burma's military regime announced huge increases in the prices of gasoline, diesel, and natural gas. These changes were more than impoverished Burmans could bear. On August 19, Rangoon citizens took to the streets in peaceful protest. Buddhist monks joined them. By September, the number of protestors had swelled to twenty thousand, and soldiers with guns at the ready walked beside them.

A group of monks, intoning chants of peace, marched from Shwedagon Pagoda, where Aung San Suu Kyi once spoke to political supporters, to the crumbling lakeside home where she had been detained for twelve of the eighteen years since her arrest in 1989. A soldier lowered street barricades and allowed monks to approach her fenced garden wall. Thin and pale from years of confinement, Suu Kyi walked to the fence and prayed with the monks, the last peaceful moment of the growing protests.

The demonstrations grew larger until, at the end of September, the atmosphere had changed and soldiers were aiming to kill. A photo smuggled to the foreign press shows a Japanese journalist lying on the pavement, holding his camera overhead, while a soldier trains a gun on him. Seconds later the journalist was shot and killed. Another photo shows one of Burma's revered monks lying face down in a pool of bloody water.

In October, *The Irrawaddy* Magazine, published in Thailand, reported, *"The territory is held for now by the military forces who won the first engagement by killing their own people and the monks who called for freedom from four decades of oppression."*

Demonstrations stopped after hundreds of Burmese citizens were killed, thousands imprisoned. Monasteries were surrounded by the military; some were occupied by soldiers; a monastery in Arakan State was burned to the ground.

* * *

In the early part of May 2008, nature conspired with the military to deliver more death and destruction to the Burmese people: Cyclone Nargis was building up in the Irrawaddy Delta, but those who lived in the affected area received no warning. Nargis swept ashore, devastating the region, including Rangoon, with heavy rain, high winds, and storm surge.

Photos smuggled out of the country showed cyclone survivors huddling on the dirt floors of bamboo homes with nothing but the corner posts remaining, while hundreds of bloated, dead bodies floated in nearby flood waters. The military made no effort to bury the dead.

United States naval ships sped to the Irrawaddy Delta loaded with relief supplies: tents, tarpaulins, water purification equipment. By June, the U.S. started withdrawing the fully loaded ships. The generals refused help—they did not want aid workers going ashore.

The generals accepted monetary aid from the United Nations but devised a special exchange rate for such donations. On August 19, an article in the *Asia Times* reported that the military junta had *"used a dual exchange rate to divert funds away from the humanitarian efforts overseen by the United Nations . . ."*

They valued the kyat, the local currency, *"at 20% to 25% less than the prevailing market rate . . . The UN has suffered losses of at least U.S. $1.56 million* [due] *to the distorted exchange rate."*

Reports of the dead and missing vary. In October 2008, the online journal, *Burma Rescue* reported that *"Cyclone Nargis left 200,000 dead and 2.5 million people homeless."* Orphans roam the streets of Rangoon.

In the aftermath of the cyclone, some local Burmese who helped those suffering from lack of food and medical supplies, have been given lengthy prison terms. Zarganar, a popular Burmese comedian, who organized hundreds of entertainers to bring relief to Nargis victims, was vocal about his disdain for the Burmese military regime. In an interview with *Irrawaddy Magazine*, he said the regime's pledge of 5 billion kyat, approximately four and one half million US dollars, was "extraordinarily mean-spirited" considering they have "around $4 billion in foreign exchange reserves," which, he added, "is the people's money," dangerous words in Burma, where there is no freedom of speech. He was sentenced to fifty-nine years in prison, later reduced to thirty-five years.

* * *

The generals who rule Burma were seldom visible during Cyclone Nargis relief efforts. They remained secluded in Naypyidaw, the new capital they are building on hundreds of square miles of land three hundred miles north of Rangoon. In Naypyidaw, Burma's makeshift road system gives way to eight-lane highways.

In September 2008, the British newspaper, *The Independent,* described the new capital as a bizarre place "populated only by government employees forced to relocate." It came into being because General Than Shwe, head of the military junta, got a disturbing prediction from his astrologer that there would be trouble in the country. The regime, reported the *Independent*, "selected a site in the remote badlands of central Burma and set about turning their mad vision into bricks and mortar."

Most parts of Burma get electricity for only a few hours each day. In Naypyidaw, three golf courses and a zoo will be lit twenty-four hours a day; the cost is apt to be supplemented by money skimmed from donations to Cyclone Nargis victims.

* * *

Completion of the fortress-like new capital was not the only issue to divert the generals from Nargis relief efforts. While thousands of newly homeless people wondered how to rebuild their lives, the government held a referendum to approve a new constitution. Written without the input of Aung San Suu Kyi, whose party won the 1990 elections, the document will permanently bar her from taking public office.

There were numerous reports of the regime's threatening citizens with the loss of their jobs or businesses if they did not vote to approve the new constitution, which gives the military a permanent role in the Burmese government as well as the right to take total control in emergencies.

In Shan State, entire villages were threatened. If a village voted "no" to the referendum, it would be considered a "rebel village," which could result in the burning of homes and confiscation of rice fields. Those who did not escape could be forced into unpaid labor as porters, carrying supplies into military zones.

The constitution was approved, guaranteeing "free elections" in 2010.

* * *

Throughout the beatings, murders, and imprisonment of those who demonstrated for reform, throughout the devastation of citizens and countryside during Cyclone Nargis, Nobel Peace Prize laureate Aung San Suu Kyi remained confined to her home.

Although Burmese law states that a political prisoner can be held for only five years without reprieve, in June of 2008, Suu Kyi spent her sixty-third birthday under house arrest, and was in her sixth straight year of confinement, a condition she has been subjected to for thirteen of the last nineteen years.

That summer she started refusing food deliveries to her home. The regime, afraid she would die under their watch and the world would turn against them, allowed her request to see her attorney. He filed a lawsuit on Suu Kyi's behalf, appealing for her release.

Despite a comment by a regime officer that Suu Kyi "should be flogged," supporters throughout the world are hopeful she will be released. She remains an icon of democracy for the Burmese people.

* * *

Persecution of the Shan persisted, with severe restrictions imposed by the Thai government upon those who fled to its borders for protection, restrictions that turned policemen into bounty hunters.

It started in June 2007, when the *Sanloitai* online newspaper reported that *"Police in Chiangmai province have been ordered to arrest at least 10 illegal migrant workers from Burma and collect 1,000 baht per arrested migrant worker.... In addition to that reward, they will also get a commission on the total number of arrested migrants each month."* Detained migrants are fined, imprisoned, or sent back to Burma.

Shan who escape the police traps are subject to restrictions. A curfew was set up restraining migrants to their homes between 8 p.m. and 5 a.m.; gatherings of five or more migrants are banned. They are forbidden to use cell phones.

In Shan State, more farmers were forced to leave their homes and abandon their rice fields. They joined thousands of Shan, hiding in the jungle, without medical care, schooling, or sufficient food.

A Shan relief team based in Chiang Mai Province brought medical supplies and rice to the displaced. In a journal kept by an aid worker inside Shan State during February 2008, he reported that they had planned to give relief to the poor *". . . but we heard that the patrolling Burmese troops were on the way . . . We could not go there and slept in the forest . . ."*

Two days later, the aid worker reported that they had *"called the villagers to come into the forest not very far from the village to receive relief."*

Attached to the report were photos of those receiving aid, signing receipts with their inked thumbs. The aid worker estimated that the literacy rate of Shan living within Burma is only thirty percent.

* * *

In August 2008, a former student sent me a report on the situation in Shan State: Fourteen additional villages and at least twenty-two thousand people had been displaced from their homes during the past year. Some of them had lived on the "152 acres of farmland" confiscated by the military for a new coal mining project.

Some displaced Shan fled to the jungle; some were ". . . forced to construct military camps" or become soldiers. Some will escape to Thailand and make their way to the School for Shan Refugees where I first met and taught English to those I have written about in these pages.

The less fortunate, who fled to migrant camps and worked in construction, carrying back-breaking loads of bricks and other supplies for Thai employers, as well as those who worked on farms, exposing themselves to cancerous levels of insecticides in order to make enough money to feed their children, have recently experienced more indignities from the Thai people among whom they live and work.

On February 8, 2009, a 22-year-old accounting student at Mae Jo University in Chiang Mai, was found dead. She had been raped and murdered. The online newsletter, *Stateless Person*, reported the arrests of two Shan workers, who lived in a nearby construction camp.

The arrests did not satisfy university students at Mae Jo, a group of whom gathered at the construction camp, demanding it be dismantled. They also petitioned the police and the governor of Chiang Mai, asking them to get rid of all migrants near the school.

According to the article, "... groups of students have accompanied police on raids and pitched in, chasing down migrants trying to evade arrest. [At times] they are said to have taken matters into their own hands, and mobs of students have attacked and beaten suspected migrants." All Chiang Mai police stations have been instructed to crack down on migrants.

The foreign press reported none of the events, not the rape and murder of the university student, not the subsequent arrest of Shan migrant workers, not the punitive reaction of the Thai community. Only Thai and Shan news media followed the ensuing pogrom against the Shan, who now fled from Thai persecution as they fled from Burmese military persecution in Shan State.

On February 11, 2009, the online newsletter, *The Shan Herald Agency for News,* quoted a migrant worker as saying the current raids were different from the past. "Before, there was no physical abuse and threat to the migrant workers. Yesterday, the authorities beat and fired at workers who tried to escape."

In a February 18 update, the news agency reported that, frightened for their lives and livelihoods, "at least 40 to 50 people" were arriving in a Thai border town every day, preparatory to crossing over into Burma, where they would face the ongoing persecution of the Burmese military regime.

Those migrants who remain in the Chiang Mai area exercise great care to avoid Thai authorities. My former students, who oversee schools for Shan migrant children, have stayed away from the camps, as have the teachers. During the height of the rampage against the Shan, some teachers hid in the jungle with their students.

* * *

In Chiang Mai Province, day after day, former Shan students quietly wait out the virulent xenophobia that has seized university students and Thai police; in Shan State, they brave the Burmese military to bring food and medicine to displaced families hiding in the jungle; and they make an unvoiced vow. It is the same vow their brothers and sisters make; the same vow Cyclone Nargis survivors make, as they rebuild their huts next to the watery graveyard of the Irrawaddy Delta; the same vow comedian Zarganar makes, as he contemplates a prison sentence that will send him back to the world an old man; the same vow the suppressed Buddhist monks and Aung San Suu Kyi make: They vow, all of them, to "try again tomorrow."

BIBLIOGRAPHY:

Aung San Suu Kyi. *Freedom from Fear*. London: Penguin Books, 1991.

Collis, Maurice. *Lords of the Sunset*. New York: Dodd Mead & Company, 1938.

Elliott, Patricia. *The White Umbrella*. Bangkok: Post Books, 1999.

Fink, Christina. *Living Silence: Burma under Military Rule*. London and New York: Zed Books, 2001.

Koetsawang, Pim. *In Search of Sunlight: Burmese Migrant Workers in Thailand*. Bangkok: Orchid Press, 2001.

Larkin, Emma. *Secret Histories: Finding George Orwell in a Burmese Teashop*. London: John Murray (Publishers), 2004.

Lintner, Bertil. *Burma in Revolt: Opium and Insurgency since 1948*. Chiang Mai: Silkworm Books, 1994.

MacLean, Rory. *Under the Dragon: Travels in a Betrayed Land*. London: Flamingo, 1999.

Marshall, Andrew: *The Trouser People: A Story of Burma in the Shadow of the Empire*. London: Penguin Books, 2002.

Maugham, W. Somerset. *The Gentleman in the Parlor*. London, 1930. Reprint Bangkok: White Orchid Press, 1995.

Milne, Leslie. *Shans at Home*. London: 1910. Reprint Bangkok: White Lotus Co. Ltd., 2001.

Mirante, Edith, *Down the Rat Hole: Adventures Underground on Burma's Frontier*. Bangkok: Orchid Press, 2005.

Orwell, George. *Burmese Days*. New York: First published Harper & Brothers, 1934. Published Great Britain, Victor Gollanez, 1935. Reprint England: Penguin Books, 1986.

Pascal Khoo Thwe. *From the Land of Green Ghosts: A Burmese Odyssey*. United Kingdom: Harper Collins Publishers, 2002.

Sargent, Inge. *Twilight over Burma: My Life as a Shan Princess*. University of Hawaii Press, 1994. Reprints, Chiang Mai, Thailand: Silkworm Books, 1994, 1996, 1998, and 2001.

Schulz, William F. *In Our Own Best Interest: How Defending Human Rights Benefits Us All*, Boston: Beacon Press, 2001.

Seagrave, Gordon. *Burma Surgeon*. New York: W. W. Norton & Company, Inc., 1943.

Seagrave, Gordon. *Burma Surgeon Returns*. New York: W. W. Norton & Company, Inc., 1946.

Seagrave, Sterling. *Lords of the Rim: The Invisible Empire of the Overseas Chinese*. New York: G. P. Putnam's Sons, 1995.

Sell, Julie. *Whispers at the Pagoda: Portraits of Modern Burma*. Bangkok: Orchid Press, 1999.

Skidmore, Monique. *Karaoke Fascism: Burma and the Politics of Fear.* Pennsylvania: University of Pennsylvania Press, 2004.

Webster, Donovan. *The Burma Road: The Epic Story of One of World War II's Most Remarkable Endeavors.* New York: Farrar, Straus and Giroux, 2003. Reprint, London: Pan Books, 2005.

Wintle Justin. *Perfect Hostage: A Life of Aung San Suu Kyi, Burma's Prisoner of Conscience.* Great Britain: Hutchinson, 2007. New York: Skyhorse Publishing, 2007.

HOW TO HELP SHAN REFUGEES

What do we live for, if it is not to make life less difficult for each other?
—George Elliott

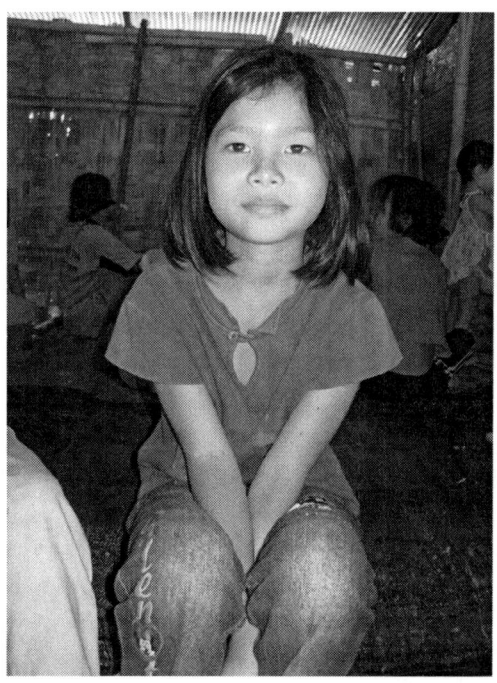

Through the years, I have kept returning to the Shan refugees in Thailand, sometimes without planning or willing my return, as though my body knew what I should be doing when my mind was unsure. Fear of responsibility, fear of failure, fear of attachments. All of those fears had been overcome the first morning I met my former students and they rose in unison with clasped hands to chant, "GOOD MORNING, TEACHER." But my conscious mind did not know it.

It was with initial reluctance that I decided to find deeper ways to help the Shan. Now I write about those ways with joy, for the people we are helping have given life a new meaning.

The group that gathered together for emotional and material support after graduating from the School for Refugees from Shan State started with what they called "Bernice's Rice Pot," a small monthly stipend that continued for three years, just enough to ensure they were not hungry. During that time they developed into a community of young people who work in the migrant camps, teaching Basic Mathematics and the English, Shan, and Thai languages to the children of refugees, activities supported by donations from friends who heard and were moved by their stories.

We also helped individual refugees: a monthly stipend for the refugee who worked without pay to help displaced persons escaping Burmese military persecution by hiding in the jungle, another for the boy who studied the Thai language, tuition for those refugees who took advanced classes in English and Computers.

Those who took advanced English language classes now have good jobs that require the use of their English language skills. All three of those we sent to computer classes have become instructors, passing on their knowledge to others, the Shan way. One of them writes articles for a dissident Burmese newsletter and manages their website.

In 2008, the "Rice Pot" group added another activity in the migrant schools we support. Having become fluent in the Thai language, they now teach the language to Shan adults, most of whom are illiterate, teaching which should enable refugees to better negotiate with their Thai employers. They also manage a tuition program for Shan children whose parents cannot afford to send them to Thai schools.

To continue our work with the refugees, three young American men have joined me in starting a charitable organization, Schools for Shan Refugees Inc. With young people in the organization, Schools for Shan Refugees will continue when I no longer can.

To make donations to our programs, you may write a check to Schools for Shan Refugees, and send it to:

Bernice Johnson
Schools for Shan Refugees
2928 Dean Parkway
Minneapolis, MN 55416

We pay all administrative and personal expenses, so every dollar donated goes to the refugees.

Website: www.ShanRefugeeSchools.org

THANKS

Many thanks to the Shan and Burmese friends who shared their stories with me. Special thanks, also, to Pippa Curwen, friend and advisor to Shan refugees, and to Kuehnsai, the wise and learned Shan elder, both of whom suggested changes to my manuscript before approving it. Closer to home, I want to thank Minneapolis writers for their pithy criticisms; my Aunt Marie, who taught me how to read; my sons Brent and Bryan whose interest in me, in my travels, and in my refugee friends, has encouraged me to keep writing; Rose Marie Khub and Inge Sargent, who encouraged me by liking my stories; friend Nancy, whose keen eye has helped me avoid grammatical disasters; friends Penny Lyn and Pat Olin who read drafts of the manuscript and pointed out typographical errors; and the select group of friends I call Clever Companions, who have been generous with praise and encouragement. Many thanks, also, to my publisher, Samuel Maung Stone, who is intimately acquainted with the heartbreak of refugee life.

Printed in the United States
150689LV00003B/47/P